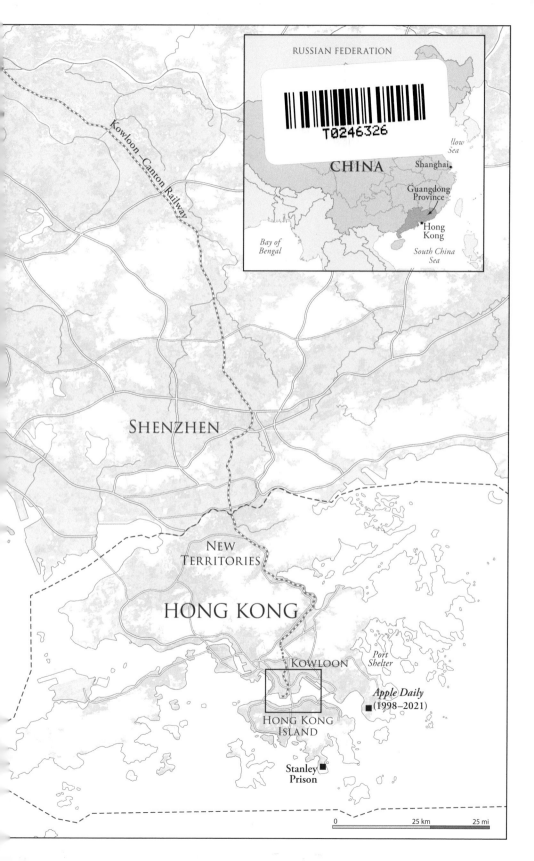

RUSSIAN FEDERATION

T0246326

CHINA

Shanghai

Guangdong
Province

Hong
Kong

llow
Sea

Bay of
Bengal

South China
Sea

Kowloon – Canton Railway

SHENZHEN

NEW
TERRITORIES

HONG KONG

KOWLOON

Port
Shelter

Apple Daily
(1998–2021)

HONG KONG
ISLAND

Stanley
Prison

0   25 km   25 mi

*f*P

ALSO BY MARK L. CLIFFORD

Today Hong Kong, Tomorrow the World
Let There Be Light
The Greening of Asia
Troubled Tiger

THE TROUBLE MAKER

How Jimmy Lai Became a Billionaire,
Hong Kong's Greatest Dissident, and China's Most Feared Critic

MARK L. CLIFFORD

FREE PRESS

New York   Toronto   London   Sydney   New Delhi

Free Press
An Imprint of Simon & Schuster, LLC
1230 Avenue of the Americas
New York, NY 10020

First Free Press hardcover edition December 2024

FREE PRESS and colophon are trademarks of Simon & Schuster, LLC

Simon & Schuster: Celebrating 100 Years of Publishing in 2024

For information about special discounts for bulk purchases, please contact Simon & Schuster Special Sales at 1-866-506-1949 or business@simonandschuster.com.

The Simon & Schuster Speakers Bureau can bring authors to your live event. For more information or to book an event, contact the Simon & Schuster Speakers Bureau at 1-866-248-3049 or visit our website at www.simonspeakers.com.

Interior design by Wendy Blum

Manufactured in the United States of America

10 9 8 7 6 5 4 3 2 1

Library of Congress Cataloging-in-Publication Data is available.

ISBN 978-1-6680-2769-1
ISBN 978-1-6680-2771-4 (ebook)

To the people of Hong Kong, in the belief that they will one day win the freedom that is rightfully theirs.

Do not get lost in a sea of despair. Be hopeful, be optimistic. Our struggle is not the struggle of a day, a week, a month, or a year, it is the struggle of a lifetime. Never, ever be afraid to make some noise and get in good trouble, necessary trouble.

—John Lewis

CONTENTS

FOREWORD

My Dear Friend and Comrade in Arms, Jimmy Lai

I had the good luck and very special experience of having three extended discussions with Jimmy Lai in the last weeks before his arrest. These were one-hour-long conversations via Zoom. A man of seventy-two, surrounded by his beloved family, Jimmy was preparing himself to be arrested and probably spend the rest of his life in the prisons of one of the most merciless regimes in the world. He had a lot of questions about my nine years in the Soviet Gulag and asked how to cope with isolation, uncertainty, and fear when the heavy doors closed behind you. This brave man hardly needed any advice. What I learned from hard experience, he grasped instinctively. He already understood that jail can't humiliate you; you can only humiliate yourself. And while your body may be shackled in prison, your spirit can be free.

Jimmy already knew that he stood at the center of a historic struggle. I asked him, "Why won't you try to escape? You are a rich man. You certainly have airplanes and whatever you need to escape. You have British citizenship and no doubt many countries in the free world will be glad to host you." "I can't do it," he answered. "I called my people to fight. They look at me. I can't let them down."

It is so simple. So clear. But it is often difficult for people to understand. When Alexei Navalny, the Russian dissident leader, decided to

xiii

go back to Russia, many journalists asked me: Is he crazy? Is he stupid? Doesn't he understand that he will be arrested at the airport? My answer to them: It's you who don't understand. He is not fighting for his survival; he is fighting for the future of his people. And his message to his people is: I'm not afraid of Putin and you also shouldn't be. In the end, Putin killed Navalny in prison, but his life and his message inspire millions in Russia.

Another political prisoner in Russia whose actions some people might fail to understand is Vladimir Kara-Murza. He had survived two attempts of poisoning by Putin's regime and was living a comfortable life as a historian of the dissident movement and a political journalist in Washington. But when Putin invaded Ukraine, he felt that, in order for his articles and films to have a real meaning, he had to be in Russia. He was sentenced to a twenty-five-year term in a Russian prison and was jailed for twenty-eight months before being released as part of a prisoner swap between Russia and the West.

I had my own experience with this refusal to understand. In 1977, I was arrested "for anti-Soviet activity and high treason." The free world fought for my release, and after six years, American diplomats felt they had found a good compromise. Soviet leaders agreed that if I wrote and asked them to release me for humanitarian reasons because of my poor health, they would do it. The American diplomats were astonished and bewildered that I was unwilling to do this. They refused to understand what was so obvious to me and my wife. After the hard years of the struggle against the Empire of Evil, I could not recognize their "moral authority" to punish and pardon.

It is an almost unique feeling when your every word and step is important for a political struggle. Jimmy is now seventy-six years old and to survive even one more day in prison is a challenge. But he decided long ago that physical survival cannot be the ultimate aim. Because if it is, you don't start such a struggle in the first place. How long you survive physically in prison doesn't depend on you. But there is one thing that does depend on you: to remain a free person to the last day of your life. This is what makes Jimmy and people like him so dangerous to a totalitarian regime. They keep the spark of freedom alive, and the authorities are afraid that this spark can turn into a fire spreading to millions. This is what should make him feel victorious.

My conversations with Jimmy ended on an optimistic note. Of course, he said, the struggle for democracy is a very, very heavy burden. But it is also uplifting. I'm in a position to do such a wonderful thing. How can I miss it? And then, comparing our experiences on a purely personal note, he finished our conversation with the words: "Like you, I have a great wife. Like you, I'm a religious person, and I believe in the victory of Good. I hope to see you soon."

We all in the free world have to pray to see him soon and work very hard to make it happen.

—Natan Sharansky
Jerusalem

CHRONOLOGY

1948   Jimmy Lai and his twin sister, Si-wai, are born; their birthday is celebrated December 8.

1949   Communists take power in China; Mao Zedong declares People's Republic of China.

1958–62   Great Leap Forward; the worst politically induced famine in history kills as many as 45 million Chinese.

1950s   Lai works as a porter in the Guangdong railroad station; mother sent to forced labor site, leaving Lai, his twin sister, and an older sibling alone.

1961   Lai enters Hong Kong as an illegal immigrant; works as a child laborer; lives in the factory where he works.

1966–76   Cultural Revolution convulses China.

1975   Lai and partner found knitwear manufacturer Comitex.

Chronology

1976   Mao Zedong dies; hard-line associates known as the Gang of Four, including his wife, arrested.

1978   Deng Xiaoping emerges as Chinese leader and launches economic reforms; Shenzhen, bordering Hong Kong, soon picked as a Special Economic Zone where capitalism is permitted.

1981   Lai founds fast-fashion retail chain Giordano.

Comitex ranks one of Hong Kong's largest sweater manufacturers.

1982   Deng Xiaoping warns Prime Minister Margaret Thatcher that China will take control of Hong Kong no later than 1997.

1984   Sino-British Joint Declaration sets out terms of the colony's handover to China in 1997.

1989   Following weeks of pro-democracy protests, a massacre on June 4 sees hundreds, perhaps thousands, killed by the military in Beijing and around the country; support for protesters is strong in Hong Kong.

1990   Lai founds *Next* magazine.

1991   First popular elections held for Hong Kong's Legislative Council, after 150 years of colonial British rule; pro-democracy candidates are victorious.

Giordano lists on the Hong Kong stock exchange.

1992   Deng Xiaoping's "Southern Tour" jump-starts economic reform.

Giordano opens in mainland China.

The last governor of Hong Kong, Chris Patten, arrives and pushes democratic electoral reforms against opposition from Beijing and the local business community.

Lai takes British citizenship. Passport states date of birth is November 8, 1948; birthplace is Canton.

1994   Lai attacks Chinese premier Li Peng (popularly known as the "butcher of Beijing" for his role in the Tiananmen massacre) in *Next*, calling him a "turtle egg" ("bastard").

Chinese authorities close Giordano store in Beijing in retaliation.

Lai resigns as chairman of Giordano.

1995   *Apple Daily* founded. Paper quickly becomes a leading newspaper in the colony's competitive market.

1996   Lai sells his 27 percent stake in Giordano following pressure from Chinese authorities unhappy about his pro-democracy activities, netting $185 million.

1997   People's Republic of China takes over Hong Kong after 156 years of British colonial rule; the handover was done without consulting the people of Hong Kong.

The Basic Law, a mini-constitution, enshrines a wide variety of freedoms, and China promises fifty years of "Hong Kong people ruling Hong Kong."

Lai converts to Catholicism.

2000   Chen Shui-bian is elected as president in Taiwan, ending authoritarian Kuomintang's (KMT) dominance.

Lai moves to Taiwan; later starts Taiwan editions of *Next* (2001) and *Apple Daily* (2003).

2001   China enters the World Trade Organization.

2003   *Apple Daily* and *Next* support protests against Hong Kong's proposed national security law; 500,000 people join the crowd.

2010   Chinese dissident writer Liu Xiaobo awarded Nobel Peace Prize in absentia; Lai attends Oslo ceremony.

2014   September–December, Umbrella Movement led by students stages seventy-nine-day Hong Kong protest; Lai joins the occupation with a tent by government headquarters; he is teargassed; assailants dump pig offal over him.

2019   June–November, protests against a law that would allow suspects to be extradited to mainland China prompt repeated million-plus demonstrations in Hong Kong as well as unprecedented police and protester violence.

November district council elections see pro-democrat sweep amid record voter turnout.

2020   March, Covid restrictions put in place prohibit gathering of more than four people; used to prohibit June 4 Tiananmen commemoration.

June 30, National Security Law introduced.

August 10, *Apple Daily* is raided by 250 police.

December 31, Jimmy Lai is jailed.

Chronology

2021   April, Lai is convicted and sentenced to fourteen months in prison for civil disobedience charges stemming from 2019 rallies and marches.

May, authorities freeze Lai's 71 percent shareholding in his publicly listed media company, Next Digital, publisher of *Apple Daily*.

May, Lai is sentenced to another fourteen-month term for a 2019 rally.

June 17, *Apple Daily* is raided by five hundred police.

June 24, *Apple Daily* prints its final edition after its bank accounts are frozen, without a court order, under the National Security Law.

June–July, six *Apple Daily* staff, in addition to Lai, are jailed indefinitely without bail.

December, Lai receives a thirteen-month sentence for lighting a candle at the June 4, 2020, Tiananmen commemoration.

2022   October, Xi Jinping is confirmed for his third five-year term as Chinese Communist Party general secretary, cementing his role as the most powerful leader at least since Mao Zedong.

December, Lai is sentenced to five years and nine months in prison after being convicted of illegally subletting part of the company's office.

2023   May, Lai is denied his choice of lawyer in upcoming National Security Law trial.

December, Lai's National Security Law trial begins.

Prologue

THE TROUBLEMAKER

A deep harbor separates Hong Kong Island from the city's Kowloon district. Three tunnels link the island with the mainland. They only close in extreme circumstances. In July 2022, the eastern tunnel was shut during a visit to the city by Chinese Communist Party General Secretary Xi Jinping. Another tunnel was shut again in December 2023 for a different kind of dignitary. Authorities organized a special motorcade for Jimmy Lai, the businessman and democracy activist, to transport him in chains from the maximum-security prison where he is kept in solitary confinement to a special trial that could see him sent to prison for life.

The strip searches required before he leaves prison don't faze Lai, for he knows that he will see loved ones during court appearances. "Tomorrow, I need to go to court and have to go through a body search, taking off all my clothing in front of the guards," he wrote before a 2021 court date. "Humiliating, but I don't care, for I get to see my family members, friends, and supporters. Seeing them puts me back into the reality of the world outside and the emotional exchange is so uplifting."

Streets were closed to traffic on that December morning as a convoy of police cars and motorcycle outriders accompanied an oversized armored car carrying the prisoner, who sat shackled inside a cage. The lumbering vehicle wound along the narrow oceanfront road from Stanley Prison on Hong Kong Island's southern coast before turning north and entering the Aberdeen Tunnel and then the Cross-Harbour Tunnel on its way to the West Kowloon Courts.

Outside the court, dogs and one thousand police guarded against any potential disruption. They provided the sort of security one would expect for a president or a high-profile terrorist rather than a seventy-five-year-old devout Catholic who had long professed a commitment to nonviolence. The show of force accompanied the trial of Hong Kong's most committed dissident and China's best-known political prisoner.

Inside the court, Lai sat in a glass box, listening to the proceedings with the help of hearing aids. He had eye surgery not long before the trial and, even with the help of glasses, struggled to read material projected onto the courtroom screen. He was thinner than he was before he entered prison. He survived Covid in jail and has aged during the three years he spent behind bars before his trial began. At six feet one, he has a commanding presence; the tens of pounds of weight he has lost during his time in prison imbue him with a newly ascetic appearance.

Lai swapped his brown convict's uniform for a blue oxford shirt and a light-colored Loro Piana blazer. It was a show trial and authorities had let the main character dress as he wished.

Defendants in Hong Kong often wear nice clothes in hopes of conveying respectability to a jury. That wasn't the case with this trial. Contrary to promises made by China for continued jury trials, authorities denied Lai this right, trying him instead before a panel of handpicked judges. He wore his clothes for his own dignity.

Lai built his fortune on sweaters and polo shirts but outside of jail had built his wardrobe around jeans and button-down cotton shirts or loose-fitting linen ones. He favored clip-on suspenders and for a time even sported overalls—a style unique among Hong Kong's tycoons.

It wasn't just clothes that set Jimmy Lai apart. For more than three decades, he had fought for freedom and democracy as a vocal and effective critic of Hong Kong's and China's leaders. Like millions of others among Hong Kong's seven million people, he distrusted communist China and wanted the city to enjoy the rights and freedoms it had been promised when Beijing took control of the British colony in 1997.

He had money—a fortune estimated at $1.2 billion before the government came after him, his wealth earned after he arrived in Hong Kong as a twelve-year-old with less than five dollars in his pocket. He spent well over $100 million of his own money to fund Hong Kong's pro-democracy movement.

His enormously popular *Apple Daily* newspaper and *Next* magazine set the political agenda in Hong Kong, ultimately becoming an opposition force in a city that has never known democracy. "The Chinese Communist Party hates Jimmy so much because they are afraid of his media empire," says veteran journalist Ching Cheong, who had been sympathetic enough to Beijing that he had earlier held a senior position at the communist mouthpiece *Wen Wei Po* in Hong Kong. "His media is very important for the democratization of Hong Kong. The CCP treat propaganda as one of their lifelines. Jimmy's media empire succeeded in refuting many of their lies."

He is fearless. In 2020, when the government banned commemoration of the Tiananmen massacre, Lai defiantly knelt alone in Hong Kong's Victoria Park, the traditional remembrance site. He lit a candle. "If commemorating those who died because of injustice is a crime, then . . . let me suffer the punishment," he told the court before being sentenced to fourteen months in prison for this act of "inciting" an "illegal assembly."

Hong Kong has scores of billionaires, but not one of them dared to stand up to China while the city's freedoms were whittled away. And Hong Kong has spawned many brave democracy campaigners, but none could nurture the movement with a mass-media spotlight, let alone bankroll it. Lai played a significant role in mounting the biggest democratic challenge to the Chinese Communist Party since the 1989 Tiananmen Square student movement. He is literally one in a billion. In a conversation in 2020, as the charges against him multiplied, Lai mused: "It is just natural they nail me. I have the newspaper, which is an opposition newspaper supporting the movement. I am very vocal opposing the Communists. I participate in every resistance [that is, demonstration and protest march]. For them, I am a troublemaker. It is hard for them not to clamp down on me and silence me."

Lai defies easy characterization. His success as a pragmatic businessman meant that he approached human rights activism in a results-oriented way. He's interested in freedom, but you won't hear him talk much about social justice. His philosophy verges on libertarian, contending that government should play a limited role beyond providing order and a strong rule of law. A Catholic, he is a militant anticommunist in the mold of John Paul II, the Polish pope who encouraged the democratic uprisings in Eastern Europe and the Soviet Union in the 1980s and 1990s.

Jimmy Lai is one of the most important political prisoners of our age, yet he has many more champions on the right wings of the American and British political spectrums than on the left. He's a voracious reader and a prolific columnist who aspires to the role of a public intellectual, but he is too action-oriented to fit into the intellectual tradition of China's Liu Xiaobo, the Soviet Union's Aleksandr Solzhenitsyn, or Poland's Adam Michnik.

Unlike many prisoners of conscience, he isn't affiliated with a political party. He doesn't seek political power, unlike long-detained activists such as South Africa's Nelson Mandela, Poland's Lech Walesa, or Russia's Alexei Navalny, who was murdered in a Russian prison as I was finishing this manuscript and whose death makes Lai's case all the more pressing. A businessman, he has faith in markets and believes in the importance of economic growth in promoting freedom. Policy-making bores him. He has an entrepreneur's certainty and bluntness. His solutions are simple, bordering on simplistic—they revolve around more freedom, more democracy, and less government regulation. He talks less about universal human rights than about "values," especially what he calls "Western values," by which he means freedom and tolerance and the use of law to give people a sense of security.

"He is very different," notes Notre Dame political scientist and Hong Kong native Victoria Tin-bor Hui. "A lot of freedom fighters tend to be lawyers—activists who raise their arms or intellectuals. He is a businessman who just basically really cares about his home, Hong Kong, and the cause of democracy." In late 2019, when he gave a talk with Martin Lee at the Council on Foreign Relations in New York, observers found themselves surprised that "he didn't say anything too provocative" and was "so mild and so shy," she remembers.

There are many courageous people in Hong Kong. Lai's wealth and international stature set him apart. So, too, does the role that *Apple Daily* and *Next* magazine played in developing the pro-democracy movement. "Without *Apple Daily* there would be no Hong Kong pro-democracy movement," says attorney Kevin Yam, a prominent overseas activist who is wanted by the Hong Kong authorities. "It's as simple as that."

The publications, under Lai's leadership, did more than just push a democracy agenda. They helped the people of Hong Kong believe in themselves and shake off the sense of being second-class citizens that often characterizes people in colonies. Lai and his team nurtured a sense of political and civic engagement in a city that its residents had often treated as a transient stopping-off place.

The combination of his wealth and stubborn defense of individual liberty makes Lai a dangerous opponent to Chinese authorities. So afraid is Beijing of this septuagenarian that he faces the very real possibility of spending the rest of his life behind bars for the crime of "colluding" with foreigners—notably by meeting with the likes of Vice President Mike Pence and Secretary of State Mike Pompeo and calling for sanctions against human rights abusers in Hong Kong.

Totalitarian governments cannot tolerate dissent. Everyone who fights against the lies and propaganda in Xi's China must be treated as a threat. One person opposing the government today could be one hundred tomorrow, one thousand next week, and one million a month from now. Indeed, Lai and his journalists showed that they could generate that sort of opposition to the Hong Kong government, since his newspaper and magazine helped bring hundreds of thousands and then millions of protesters into the city's streets in 2003, 2014, and 2019.

For more than two decades after Hong Kong's handover to China, Lai pushed for democracy. A British citizen since 1992, he traveled abroad frequently, especially to the United States, often with the prominent lawyer and fellow democracy activist Martin Lee. Lai was well-known in Washington.

China reacted with fury to his meetings with Pence and Pompeo in 2019. "The U.S. is well aware of who Lai Chee-ying is, what his stance is and what role he plays in the Hong Kong society," fumed a spokesperson from the Ministry of Foreign Affairs, using his full Chinese name. "At the current sensitive period in Hong Kong, top U.S. officials lining up to meet with such a person have ulterior motives and sends a serious wrong signal."

Pence doesn't see it that way. He met Lai in the White House at Pompeo's request, in order to host "a great courageous champion of democracy in Hong Kong to encourage him." For Pence, Lai ranks with heroic Soviet-era dissidents like Andrei Sakharov and Natan Sharansky. Pence is impressed that Lai has been "willing to take a stand and ultimately to be walked out in handcuffs when he could have been anywhere else. He didn't have to stay, but he stayed. It was incredibly inspiring to me."

Lai had every chance to leave Hong Kong before his arrest and imprisonment in 2020. He owns houses and apartments in Kyoto, London, Paris, and Taipei, and he knew that the Chinese Communist Party would target him if he stayed in Hong Kong after it imposed a sweeping national security law on the city in mid-2020. Instead of fleeing, he doubled down. In his last five months of freedom, he livestreamed weekly video programs featuring politicians, diplomats, journalists, and religious figures. He preferred to go to jail for freedom and democracy rather than abandon the city that, he says, "gave me everything."

Lai has received a slew of media freedom awards since going to prison. Groups honoring him range from the Committee to Protect Journalists to the Catholic University of America to the libertarian Cato Institute. The city of Lyon bestowed honorary citizenship on him in recognition both of his love of freedom and his love of French food.

For Lai is no ascetic. He is knowledgeable and deeply invested in fine food and wine. He entertains generously—many a foreign correspondent has been a guest in his home, as have countless business associates, foreign politicians, religous figures, and other dignitaries. As a young entrepreneur in the fast-fashion trade, Lai lived a bawdy, even lascivious lifestyle. All that is past. He's now embraced a monkish existence inside Stanley Prison, reading exclusively Catholic philosophy, and painting and drawing Jesus Christ and the Virgin Mary. He doesn't complain. He has chosen his path.

I met Jimmy Lai in 1993 when I interviewed him for a profile for the *Far Eastern Economic Review* and saw him several times a year over the next three decades. He is generous and, as a result, I enjoyed dozens of excursions to Hong Kong's outlying islands on his boats, the first a modest junk (*Free China*) and the next an Azimut luxury yacht bearing his wife Teresa's middle name, *Lisa*. On scores of other occasions, I joined lunches and dinners with journalists, professors, missionaries, economists, and political leaders. Lai and Teresa were renowned for their hospitality, good food, and the warmth with which they welcomed visitors into their homes and onto their boats.

In May 2017, I took part in a weeklong bus tour of America with Lai and more than a dozen others; human rights campaigner Ellen Bork, who for a time had worked in Hong Kong for pro-democracy legislator Martin Lee, suggested at a November 2016 dinner at Lai's house that we should travel around the country to better understand newly elected Donald Trump's appeal. Lai had supported Trump in that election, and he jumped at the idea. The trip started in New York City and traveled via Harrisburg, Pittsburgh, and Cleveland to Chicago. From there we headed south, through Des Moines, Topeka, and Dallas to Houston before jogging east to New Orleans. Meetings with senior leaders at three universities—Carnegie Mellon, Notre Dame, and Northwestern—to discuss subjects ranging from artificial intelligence and machine learning to the changing media world constituted the intellectual highlights of the trip. We also met prominent Republican figures, including Kansas governor Sam Brownback and former Louisiana governor Bobby Jindal. We got a little closer to ordinary concerns when we ate at a restaurant in

Cleveland staffed by formerly incarcerated people and, the following morning, met with a woman on the front lines of the opioid crisis.

I served on the board of directors of Lai's media company, Next Digital, from 2018 until authorities forced it to close in 2021. Lai had founded the Hong Kong stock exchange–listed company, known first as Next Media and later as Next Digital, and owned 71 percent of it. I also moderated most of the approximately twenty weekly livestream shows that he did from July 2020 until he was imprisoned in December. As such, I participated in some of the events at *Apple Daily* and elsewhere that are at the heart of the government's case against Jimmy Lai. What amazed me the most is the courage and dignity with which he has embraced his fate.

I have the privilege of being free—following Lai's imprisonment, six *Apple Daily* colleagues were jailed, including one of my fellow Next Digital directors. The company's bank accounts were frozen and the newspaper forced to close. The government launched four separate investigations into the company's collapse, looking into what responsibility that the directors—including me—might have; this Kafkaesque turn of events in blaming the victim would be laughable were my colleagues not in jail. I am outside of Hong Kong and have no business or family ties there, making retaliation less likely. I now head the Committee for Freedom in Hong Kong Foundation, which seeks to free all of Hong Kong's political prisoners, including Lai.

I never expected to write a book about Lai, but the extraordinary circumstances in which he finds himself demand it. If Jimmy Lai is guilty, he is guilty of excessive optimism, guilty of believing that China would keep its promises to leave Hong Kong alone for fifty years.

History is littered with examples of single individuals posing earthshaking threats to totalitarian regimes. Oddly, it is precisely at those moments when dictatorships are wielding their most repressive power—when all others have receded into terrified silence—that these stubborn personalities prove most vexatious. As Xi's grip on power tightens, and as China's democracy movement reaches at its lowest ebb in decades, Jimmy Lai refuses to yield. That is why the Chinese Communist Party fears him. His courage matters.

Chapter One

"FOOD IS FREEDOM"

Jimmy Lai was three or four years old when his father said goodbye. A successful businessman, Lai Sim-lam decided in about 1952 to leave his family in southern China for the safety of the nearby British Crown Colony of Hong Kong. In 1949, the Chinese Communist Party had declared the founding of the People's Republic of China. "The Chinese people," intoned party head Mao Zedong, "have now stood up." Hundreds of thousands of Chinese were fleeing the hunger and political persecution in Mao's China for the uncertainty of life in the British colony.

Lai's parents both received permission to go, a backhanded reward for their support of the anti-Japanese resistance and the Chinese Communist Party itself in the 1940s (as well as a payoff to a local cadre), but only on condition that they leave their children behind. Lai's mother, Liang Shaoxia, chose to stay. His crying father picked the young boy up as he was leaving and said, "You are going to do great things." The scene would haunt Lai for decades, fueling his belief that he was somehow a chosen person even as he hunted for the father who had abandoned him.

Jimmy Lai's current British passport states that he was born on November 4, 1947, thirteen months before what he believes is his actual birth date. Lai and his twin sister, Si-wai, celebrate their birthday on December

8. But no one really knows the date of their birth. There's even confusion about the year; Lai eventually predated his birth to November 1947 so that he could more easily work as a youngster in Hong Kong and most official documents use that year. His mother dated their birth to the year of the rat in Chinese cosmology: 1948. Tradition holds that those born in rat years are, in a typical characterization, "smart, quick-witted, flexible, adaptable, and outgoing," an apt description of Lai. Indeed, his first British passport, issued in 1992, states that he was born November 8, 1948.

What's certain is that they were the last two of their mother's birth children. Shaoxia was in her midthirties when she gave birth to the twins. Her oldest son had died as a child and a daughter died when she was in her twenties. Regarded by her family as something of a Florence Nightingale figure, Shaoxia for a time fostered another girl. For much of his childhood, though, the family consisted of Lai, Si-wai, and the next-youngest sister, Huanying, two years older.

His older half-siblings had gone to private schools in Guangzhou in the precommunist Republican period. Lai literally lived in a different country, growing up in the People's Republic at a time when it was consumed by political struggles. He lived in poverty and had the most rudimentary formal education, yet held on to the idea that he was destined for greatness. "Jimmy always thought he was born in the old world and fantasized about how good it was in the past," says his wife Teresa. "He always thought, 'I am privileged, don't look down on me.' He felt that he was chosen. He didn't mind if people looked down on him. He knew he was different." Lai's attitude, she says, was "I don't mind even if I kneel down to tie your shoelace because when I stand up I will be much taller than you."

The country had been at war since Japan invaded in 1937, with troops over the next two years sweeping south along the country's east coast and into Guangdong province. Hundreds of thousands of refugees fled China and sheltered in neighboring Hong Kong, which Japanese troops captured in 1941. Britain recovered Hong Kong after Japan's defeat in 1945 as the Chinese Communist Party (CCP) and the anticommunist Kuomintang (KMT) renewed their conflict on the mainland with increased ferocity. Lai's family was just one of the tens of millions whose lives were torn apart by invasion, civil war, revolution, and their brutal aftermath.

Lai's father had married into a prosperous shipping family and joined the family business. As his first wife battled ill health, Lai's mother was recruited into the family as a second wife, a common practice among China's wealthy. Shaoxia came from a peasant family and was chosen for her strong constitution. Her husband's family wanted her both to take care of his existing children and give birth to more. As the first wife fought for her last breaths, her mother humiliatingly forced Shaoxia to put her mouth against that of the dying woman in a sort of reverse artificial resuscitation. This practice reflected a superstition that the spirit of the dying woman could inhabit her successor.

"Mother Number Two." That's what Lai had to call his own mother throughout childhood. Although the first wife was dead before Lai's birth, his mother could not oppose the demands of her prosperous in-laws. She would be forever known even by her own children by this demeaning appellation.

The extended family lived in a substantial house in Shunde, on the southern outskirts of the provincial capital of Guangzhou. Family lore has it that Lai's grandfather owned the first Rolls-Royce in Guangdong province. Shunde, like much of the Pearl River Delta, is a marshy, low-lying area crisscrossed by waterways. Birthplace of the martial artist Bruce Lee, Shunde was insular yet had easy access to Guangzhou and other cities along the Pearl River Delta estuary—notably the Portuguese colony of Macau and the British colony of Hong Kong.

After the Chinese Communist Party took power in 1949, authorities ordered the family's single-family home subdivided into apartments. China's new rulers assigned outside families to live in the house; bathrooms and a kitchen became communal. Lai's father had allowed the communists to hold secret meetings upstairs in his house as the civil war raged; his reward was persecution. He lost his business, and he lost his home. The experience shattered him.

Sometime in the early 1950s, as the young twins Chee-ying and Si-wai rested while their mother was out on an errand, Simlam tried to commit suicide by hanging himself in the same room. Shaoxia returned in time to save his life but was furious at the thought that the family would be further persecuted if he succeeded in what would be treated as a counterrevolutionary act. He largely broke off contact after leaving for Hong Kong, where he started a new family. Lai, his mother, Si-wai, and Huanying (whom Lai refers to as "my slightly mentally retarded sister") were left behind. Lai himself didn't speak until he was three and a half; his family worried that he was a mute.

Lai was the youngest son from this second marriage. He had a brother, Lai Choi-ying, who was seven years older, as well as another older sister, Biying. With their father gone, Lai's older siblings scattered, and he only saw them irregularly.

He shared a bond with them that Si-wai didn't—the *ying* ("hero") character in his given name. In traditional Chinese naming convention, the surname is typically followed by two characters—one is unique to the individual (*chee* in Lai's case, meaning wisdom or knowledge), and one is shared among the siblings in the same generation. Lai shared the *ying* character with his older brother and three sisters but not with Si-wai; this reflected the hopes that his father and his parents had for his youngest son.

A peasant until she married, his mother now had wealthy in-laws and a businessman husband who had fled to Hong Kong. Communist authorities deemed her a class enemy. "We were unfortunate because our family was rich, so naturally when you are rich you become the enemy of the people," Lai remembered. He saw his mother forced to kneel on shards of broken glass, wear a dunce's cap, and bow her apologies as Communist Party officials vilified her and paraded her in front of crowds.

Lai's mother was pronounced guilty as the wife of a runaway business-man. She was periodically sent to what Lai called a labor camp—though usually able to return on the weekends. Four-year-old Lai and his two siblings were left to fend for themselves for most of the week. Though she was a good cook, she would deliberately burn rice in the kitchen at the forced labor site to be able to bring the charred grain home to feed her children.

Lai's childhood in revolutionary China haunted him for years. For three decades, he suffered nightmares from seeing prisoners executed. "Adults were very busy being cursed or being sent to labor camps," he later said. "I didn't know what was going on. We had to struggle. But we were kids. We didn't know any better." Lai isn't one to dwell on the difficulties of his past. In a telling understatement, Lai remembered it as "a very confused time. We just had to survive, struggle."

He scraped through five years of schooling, repeating at least one grade. The ease with which his sister Si-wai breezed through lessons, able to look at a passage and memorize it, underscored Lai's difficulties. His mind wasn't on academics, and his attendance appears to have been irregular at best. At the age of six, he started hustling on the street. He'd scrounge tobacco from half-smoked cigarettes and reroll the leftovers for sale. He stole food. He carried luggage for train passengers. As his mother cycled in and out of forced labor, he became the fractured family's main breadwinner.

Lai had repeated run-ins with the police. Because of his age, he avoided serious punishment. Some of the local police even developed an avuncular attitude. Once, he opened the door to find a policeman standing there. "I didn't do it!" he shouted. The police officer and his colleagues just wanted to treat the hungry youngster to a meal. Lai developed handwriting skills as a way to avoid serious punishment. Using his handsome calligraphy, he wrote propaganda posters for the authorities in an era before copying machines. He appears to have been fascinated with words from a young age. Although he didn't like school, Lai always loved reading thick books to impress people.

When Lai was seven, he went with someone he describes as a cousin to a place near Guangzhou with the aim of buying lighters and flints to sell on the black market. (From other of Lai's writings, it's likely that the older man was a black-market trader who was not related to him. Lai also worked as a street hawker at the time. He experimented with cutting prices in order to increase volume; he was beaten up by rivals for undercutting the going rates.)

His "cousin" brought the young boy along as cover because traveling with a young child generally brought less hassle from the police. The black-market contact hadn't arrived, and the cousin decided to wait. But Lai didn't want to stay overnight, fearing his mother would be worried and angry.

Lai went back to Guangzhou on his own. He later wrote about his harrowing train ride. All the passengers wore oil-stained blue Maoist clothes. In a car filled with "stern faces and blank eyes," coughing and spitting were the only sounds.

> I don't know if they were tired or sad, but the atmosphere in the car was sad and depressing. Crowded in the carriage, I was oppressed by the tense atmosphere. Looking out the window, I saw tall chimneys blowing thick black smoke everywhere. The black smoke dyed the evening glow miserably and gloomily, which was terrifying, and made me even more frightened, worrying that these people would take me hostage somewhere.

He was a child on his own, not daring to look at the other passengers, afraid to ask directions, straining to hear the station announcements. Finally, he heard "Guangzhou" and charged off the train, only to find that he had gotten off several stops too early—far from his destination. He ran back to the train but it was already rumbling away. "I was so frightened that my legs became weak, and I couldn't stand up anymore. I fell to the ground and cried."

When he got up, everyone had left the station. The place was deserted. Lai describes the terror of an abandoned child:

> I seemed to be forgotten by the whole world, like the people buried in the cemetery. When I stood up again, the feeling of loneliness and emptiness was as if my whole heart had been taken away. My whole body was exhausted and weak, as if haunted by a ghost, and I couldn't lift my feet at all.

Somehow he got home safely. Looking back, Lai felt that his return constituted a miracle, one that fit both with the Catholicism he adopted later in life and the sense his father had earlier instilled in him as someone chosen. Writing on Christmas Day more than a half-century later, Lai recounted his salvation that day. He encountered a young girl—he literally believed that she was an angel—who helped him buy food from a sesame seed cake vendor and gave him directions for a bus to get home. Though it was after midnight when he returned to Shunde, his relieved mother stroked his head and told him how lucky he was.

Around the age of eight, Lai became a porter at the Guangzhou train station, the northern terminus for the Kowloon–Canton Railway. The railroad had opened in October 1911, just five days before a revolt began that brought about the overthrow of the Qing dynasty and the end of more than two thousand years of dynastic rule in China. The railway represented a transparently imperial attempt to keep British Hong Kong as a key trade center that pulled in goods from Canton and southern China when a competing French railroad threatened to siphon away commerce.

Soon after the communist takeover, direct rail service to Hong Kong stopped. Exports from Guangzhou collapsed. The Korean War, which started in June 1950, further isolated the new People's Republic. Embargoes imposed by the United States and the United Nations to punish China for supporting North Korea curtailed trade and travel. The number of international air flights plummeted, as did the frequency of shipping services.

The Kowloon–Canton Railway provided one of the few links, however tenuous, to the outside world. In the mid-1950s, the railway's limited service represented one of the only ways outsiders could get into the People's Republic. It was a memorable crossing. Passengers had to disembark at the Hong Kong border town of Lo Wu and walk across a bridge spanning the Shenzhen River into China, where they boarded another train to complete their journey to Guangzhou. Jimmy Lai was among the porters, jostling to carry their bags.

Lai considered himself lucky to have found work at the station. "I became one of the privileged people, so to speak," having at the age of eight or nine ingratiated himself with the gang bosses who controlled work at the station. The money he earned fed his sisters and mother, but he acquired something more. "Working in a railway station gave me the privilege of accessing those who came from outside," he remembered five decades later. "When you live in a communist country surrounded by all the lies, you are scared of the outside world, because you hear how terrible the outside world is."

The Chinese Communist Party, like all totalitarian regimes, draws much of its power from the stories it tells about its foes. China's revolution, the party warned, needed to be protected from enemies within—people like Jimmy Lai's mother, a peasant woman sentenced to forced labor, the frightened teachers and doctors paraded through the streets in their dunce caps with accusatory signs hung from their necks, people like those whom Lai saw executed at the killing grounds in Guangzhou. Visitors from Hong Kong represented particular danger, with their freethinking, free-spending ways. Outsiders might threaten the revolution by bringing in the disease of capitalism.

As a porter at a train station that welcomed more foreigners than any other entry point in China, most of them Hong Kong Chinese, Lai quickly became conscious of the gap between the official story and reality. He began to understand the communist lies for what they were. "The bags I carried for foreign visitors had such a great aroma," he marveled. "I could see how well people dress, how well they speak, how well they treat us. I was never treated that well in China by Chinese. It was an experience that was very educational to me. It changed my view of the world. I said to myself, 'I want to live in this place. I want to go to Hong Kong. I want to go to the outside world.'"

A bar of chocolate marked a turning point. One day, after carrying baggage for a disembarking passenger, the man reached into his pocket and gave Lai a half-eaten Bar Six chocolate. Wrapped in foil with a bold orange paper wrapping, the Cadbury's candy was unlike anything produced in China. Lai, feeling shy, turned away from the man to take a bite. "I was so hungry. It was so tasty. It was amazing. I turned and asked him 'What is this?' He said, 'Chocolate.' I said, 'Where are you from?' He said, 'Hong Kong.' I said, 'Hong Kong must be heaven because I never tasted anything like that.' That triggered my determination to go to Hong Kong."

That taste of chocolate probably occurred in 1960, a year of famine in China. So desperate was the food shortage that Lai remembers grilled field mice as a delicacy he savored in those lean years. His childhood was marked by hunger and sadness. "The wound is deep and the scar is deeper," he later wrote of his childhood. After he tasted the promise of another world, Lai begged his mother for permission to go to Hong Kong. "It took me a year to convince her."

Hong Kong wasn't just the land of chocolate. It was also his father's new home. A year or so before he left, the eleven- or twelve-year-old Lai wrote a poem in which he poured out his yearning to see his father: "who has been separated from us for nine years. . . . Who will take care of my father in his misery? / Only my soul is by his side." His mother worried that "going to Hong Kong is like going to the moon 'because I will never see you again.'" She finally relented, though she didn't send him to his father. Shaoxia's sister lived in Hong Kong, and she would be more trustworthy as a first stop for the young boy.

Lai says he left when he was twelve and a half, in the first half of 1961. His flight took place in the midst of the Great Leap Forward, perhaps the greatest human disaster in history. In 1958, Mao Zedong, determined to develop the country economically, launched a crash industrialization and agricultural development program. The Chinese Communist Party abolished private farming and collectivized agriculture. Crop production plummeted, but no one dared tell Mao. Officials seized every bit of grain they could find. Mao wanted to impress other leaders with his revolutionary success, so he exported grain to the USSR while the Chinese starved. In China, relentless functionaries accused famished peasants of hoarding grain.

Mao's industrialization program envisioned backyard steel mills. This crackpot scheme added to the country's problems. People melted down perfectly good tools and cookware to produce substandard steel. The young Lai tried to take part in the campaign by contributing household metal but his mother forbade it. (He did eventually sell a variety of the household's metal on the black market; when he had exhausted supplies at home, he began stealing from his neighbors.) Not everyone proved equally wise. Zealous cadres destroyed an estimated 30 to 40 percent of the housing stock in a misguided search for smelting fuel and material. Mao ordered people to kill all the country's sparrows, believing them to be nothing more than crop-stealing pests. The "successful" campaign spawned a plague of locusts, their numbers unchecked by sparrows, their natural predators.

The Great Leap Forward led to the greatest famine in human history. Between 1958 and 1961, an estimated thirty to forty-five million people died or were driven to kill themselves, mostly because of hunger. Overwork, torture, and political persecution added to the death toll. People ate anything they could—dirt, bark, roots, and leather. At least a few desperate villagers resorted to cannibalism. Lai's childhood was inevitably marked by hunger. His mother knew he might die if he stayed.

Neither the Chinese Communist Party nor the government of the People's Republic of China has ever given an accounting of the disaster that constituted the Great Leap Forward, let alone held those guilty of these crimes to account. China's subsequent success, during which hundreds of millions of people emerged from poverty, should not obscure the needless deaths of tens of millions. This was the China that Lai wanted to escape.

China didn't let its citizens leave freely, and Hong Kong certainly didn't welcome them. Even if Lai did manage to get out of China, he needed to cross Hong Kong's armed border. British troops manned frontier posts protected by barbed wire along the short land border that linked Hong Kong with mainland China. The Royal Navy patrolled coastal waters. The colony, swollen with more than a million refugees during the 1950s, didn't want more people competing for scarce housing.

Lai managed to get a permit to go to the nearby Portuguese colony of Macau thanks to an unscrupulous official. In return for reporting on rival suitors for the man's girlfriend, who lived in one of the apartments carved out of Lai's family house, the officer rewarded the boy with a permit to visit Macau. Lai's duty to the official done, he left the same night, traveling sixty miles to Zhuhai's Gongbei border crossing.

As he lined up to exit China at the Macanese border, Lai saw a commotion ahead of him in the line. Officials had arrested someone trying to take gold out of the country. Lai's mother had sewn a gold coin into his underpants so that he would have some money in Hong Kong. Terrified at being discovered, figuring that it was better to arrive penniless in Hong Kong than remain stuck in China, Lai got out of the line and hid the coin. He entered Macau without incident.

From Macau, Lai still had to make the forty-mile passage to Hong Kong, on the eastern side of the Pearl River Delta. Many people drowned trying to make the crossing. The British military sent those it caught back to China.

Lai later made the risky voyage sound like catching an ordinary ferry: "I was lucky enough with connections" in Macau and quickly got on a fishing boat bound for Hong Kong. The crew secreted scores of people in the bottom of the vessel. Lai isn't sure how many but at least forty, perhaps eighty would-be Hong Kong immigrants crammed into the hold. After a few hours, when "everyone was vomiting because it was very bumpy," the captain briefly allowed passengers to come up for fresh air. They then had to go back below to hide from British navy patrol boats. They landed on a remote stretch of the New Territories, on the western edge of Hong Kong.

Five decades later, Lai reflected back on his first moments in Hong Kong as he stood with the people-smuggler, known as a snakehead, who had guided him from Macau. Even allowing for the gauzy backward look by someone who has thrived, the account gives a good sense of what Hong Kong meant to Lai:

> I didn't look back at the vast ocean behind me. . . . It is a new place to me, the people, their values are all new to me, even their clean beaches are new to me.
>
> I come from a very dirty place. Not only the streets, the air, the politics, but also the way that people think are all dirty. It's not the kind of filth you would find in garbage or dirt, it's the ugliness in those people's hearts. Only having seen this kind of ugliness can you then know what filth is.
>
> When I looked at the new world ahead of me, I know I have arrived; I have arrived at a world where life is worth living. I was a twelve-year-old boy. I just had a close brush with hell. But once I set foot on the beach I have grown into a man.

The captain deposited the immigrants in small batches along the coast to avoid attracting attention. The snakehead piled the twelve-year-old and four others into the back of a waiting vehicle. He invited a woman to sit with him in the front seat and promptly started to fondle her. Lai was aghast. "Sitting in the back, I couldn't see her anymore, but my heart trembled. This is not heaven after all. I saw the ugliness of people. Is being poor ugly? No, the world of the rich is uglier."

The snakehead took Lai to his aunt's place in Kowloon and collected his forty-seven-dollar fee. "I was shocked! This is their home?" They had constructed a tiny hut of iron sheets and boards set on bare earth. A mosquito net covered the single bed. A pot and a small wok perched on a stove in front of the bed. A small wooden bucket that served as a chamber pot completed the furnishings.

Hong Kong might have been the land of chocolate, but Lai's aunt and uncle lived more poorly than Lai had back in Shunde. Their squatter village was just one of scores clinging precariously to Hong Kong's steep hillsides. The subtropical colony's typhoons and torrential rainstorms often washed these shacks away. Periodic fires burned out thousands of people. A fire on the evening of Christmas Day in 1953 in Shek Kip Mei, not far from Lai's aunt's flat, drove out more than fifty-three thousand people in a single night. The photos of that roaring Shek Kip Mei fire looked like the firebombing of Tokyo during World War II.

Overcrowded flats and shantytowns like the one Lai's aunt lived in provided a dismal showcase for Hong Kong's supposed abundance. They were no deterrent to refugees who fled the People's Republic for the sanctuary of the British colony. Most families in Hong Kong lucky enough to be in a proper building shared cooking and bathroom facilities. An ambitious government housing program started after the Shek Kip Mei fire to build large apartment blocks simply aimed to provide a single 125-square-foot room for each family, with communal toilets and kitchens. Even these rooms, smaller than the average American kitchen today, represented a big step up for those families lucky enough to get one of the units. There were long waiting lists for these bare-bones dwellings.

Lai had arrived with nothing more than the clothes on his back and a couple of dollars in his pocket. His aunt took him to buy necessities—clothes, a quilt, towel, toothpaste, and a toothbrush. They met his uncle for a celebratory meal of simple Hakka food in Kowloon's bustling Sham Shui Po district. With no room for Lai at their shack, the couple needed to find a place for him to sleep that night.

After dinner, his aunt took him to a nearby factory, the Zhiqi Glove Factory on Fuk Wing Street. The factory manager hired him as an odd-job worker. Lai remembers him as a middle-aged man named Uncle Ren, "not tall, fat, with a pair of big eyes and a small smile." He gave Lai $1.30 "and asked another worker ["Ah Xian"] to take care of me . . . find a place [for me] to sleep, and do the math [about payment] tomorrow, and then he left." After being introduced to some other workers who also slept in the factory, Lai bedded down. "I found a packing table to sleep on and slept soundly."

He woke at six the next morning to the smell of food. It was just rice cooking, but for Lai it was also the smell of freedom. Ah Xian took him to one of Hong Kong's ubiquitous outdoor food stalls, *dai pai dong*, where he ate "white porridge, rice rolls, and deep-fried ghosts," a kind of fried dough stick. This is happiness, Lai remembered thinking. "It's not just food. The people here are poor, but the open-minded atmosphere is full of opportunities and hope."

Six decades later, Lai elaborated on that first breakfast in Hong Kong for listeners of the *New York Times* podcast *The Daily*:

It was the first time I saw so much food. It was the first time I realized, food is actually freedom. When you have the choice of food. I was so emotional about food that when the food was served, and I ate the first bite, I stood up to eat it. I don't know why. It's like paying respect to food. And I was poor, but I never felt I was poor. Because I was so hopeful that, you know, one day I will be rich.

For all his bravado about having "become a man" when he set foot on Hong Kong's shore, he was still a twelve-year-old boy who had fled his country and would have to make his way alone in a new city. But he was smart, with an easy and engaging personality, and willing to work at anything. His aunt helped as much as she could. About this time, he took the name Jimmy; like many Hong Kongers he liked the cachet of having a foreign name. Lai lived in the factory and worked long hours for eight dollars a month. "We had to wake up before 7, we had to sweep the floor, open everything . . . we had to work until ten o'clock." At bedtime, "you just put a few chairs together and slept. You were so tired and my back was aching but you wake up and you were okay. It was a very happy time." He earned thirty-five cents a day.

He had a simple aim—to prosper. "I knew I had a future," he later said. "I knew I was chosen," repeating a theme that he embraced after his father's parting words of encouragement. Lai always minimized the difficulties he faced. He sometimes had so little to eat that other workers would each put aside a little of their food so that he wouldn't go hungry. He lost a fingertip in an accident at the glove factory when the end of his right ring finger was sliced off. He suffered permanent hearing loss in one ear from working too close to heavy machinery without sound protection. Yet he rarely talks about losing his finger or his hearing or the dirty and dangerous work he did in his first years in Hong Kong.

Lai had hustled from his early childhood days in China. Now he lived in a city that celebrated a get-up-and-go attitude, that rewarded hard work with cold cash. The opportunities in Hong Kong fanned the quick, hard-working, and eager-to-please teenager's desire to get ahead.

He quickly learned that speaking a foreign language guaranteed advancement in colonial Hong Kong. He worked for a West German company and initially studied German at the Goethe Institute, a government-funded cultural center that promoted the country's culture and language. Then he figured English would be more valuable. "I noticed that everybody who made it spoke English." He met a man who had retired from his factory but came in to help with the English-language correspondence. "He took a liking to me and in his spare time he taught me English." This may have been the first in a series of older men who helped him and served as teachers or mentors.

When Lai wasn't working late, he would read the dictionary to improve his vocabulary. He used a language primer that, he remembered, revolved around simple words and repetitive phrases like "a man and a pen, a pen and a man." He read English-language newspapers and went to evening classes. Lai improved his comprehension by listening to the Voice of America, a U.S.-government-funded radio station. Although it enjoyed editorial independence, it was part of the U.S. government and explicitly served its foreign policy interests, particularly during the Cold War.

Lai took a big gamble in leaving China as a twelve-year-old, but staying may have been the more dangerous choice. "I learned risk without knowing it was risk. Life in China was so bad that taking risks was fashioned into hope." By taking bold steps like fleeing China, "you [were] not taking a risk but cashing [in on] the future," investing in another possibility. "I focused on [the hope] there is a better world, a better life—so risk was not in my consciousness."

He landed in Hong Kong at the right moment. The population had dwindled to about 600,000 people during the Japanese wartime occupation. By the 1949 communist victory in China, the British colony's population had surpassed its prewar level of 1.5 million, with more than 1.8 million. By 1960, just before Lai's arrival, it had almost doubled, to three million people.

Colonial officials worried about what they called "the problem of people" and the disease, crime, and poverty that accompanied the influx of refugees from China. In doubling the population in little over a decade, the new immigrants put almost unimaginable pressure on Hong Kong. Shantytowns blanketed hillsides. The British military dished out rice at emergency food stations. Cholera and tuberculosis were just two of the many infectious diseases that threatened the colony. The KMT and CCP struggled for refugees' loyalties, sparking riots in 1956 that killed more than sixty people.

The Chinese revolution had destroyed Shanghai as a business center and then the country's economy was walled off from the free world by the

Korean War embargoes. Hong Kong took over China's role in the international economy. Many of China's most prominent entrepreneurs, notably from Shanghainese textile families, moved to Hong Kong and reopened their businesses. China's loss proved Hong Kong's gain. Lai was living in a city buzzing with energy and opportunity.

Lai would eventually find his father in Hong Kong, though the relationship was never an easy one. Lai rarely talked to others about his father, who died in the late 1960s when the nineteen-year-old Lai was on a business trip to Japan. Years later, Lai wrote, "I seldom mention my father, so I save these few words for last. I had an estranged relationship with him and saw him very little."

Still, he continued, "even now I wonder what he would think of me."

Since I was conscious, I have taken my father as my goal. I have been hiding this matter in my heart, and my family members do not know. Whenever I encounter difficulties, I would ask myself, what would he do? . . . Even today, I still think about it that way. I have always lived in his shadow.

I've actually been looking for someone all these years. I have been to the places he has been, sat on the chairs and stools he sat on, stood on the cliffs he stood on, wandered on the road he walked, put myself in his place and thought about what he thought about. I have read the books he has read, experienced his love, savored his favorite food. . . . I have been looking for him, but I don't know where he is. I lost his address a long time ago. Dad, where are you?

Whatever psychological toll the unresolved relationship with his father took on Lai, it had unanticipated benefits. Again and again, Lai found himself drawn to older men as mentors. They would prove pivotal to his development, intellectually and spiritually as well as in business. His charisma, his openness, and his passionate energy drew others to him. He made the most of their willingness to help.

Chapter Two

"WHAT'S YOUR MAGIC?"

Early on in his time in Hong Kong, Lai was out with some friends and picked up a *lo mai gai*, an everyday Cantonese dish made of sticky rice mixed with chicken, mushrooms, and Chinese sausage wrapped in a lotus leaf. Holding it out, he proclaimed his ambition: "I just want to be rich enough to have one of these every day."

It's a goal that made sense for someone who often lived on rice, oil, and soy sauce that he bought on credit and cooked himself. But he always had higher ambitions.

By 1975, Lai had been in Hong Kong factories for almost fifteen years. He had worked in factories. He had lived in factories. He had managed factories. Now he wanted to own one. He was twenty-six.

Before the age of twenty-one, Lai had risen to manage production at the Tak On Weaving Factory, a sweater manufacturer that employed three hundred people. "I was able to perform and make [a] profit, that they hadn't made in a couple of years." Beginning in his late teens, he had toggled between production management jobs and sales. As a salesman, he entertained foreign buyers when they visited Hong Kong. If they wanted a wild time in the "Far East," Lai would provide it. Women, whiskey, or weed: Lai could help with any or all.

Hard work, good luck, and hustle could lead to wealth. Hong Kong boasted a feverish start-up culture in the late 1960s. It wasn't posh and it wasn't high-tech, but it became the foundation for many fortunes. Li Ka-shing, now Hong Kong's richest man, with a net worth of more than $30 billion, started out making plastic flowers. "You came into Hong Kong in those days and you didn't have to have an education, you didn't have to have a background, you didn't have to have connections," remembers Sandrina Caruso, a clothing designer and buyer from Montreal who met Lai during her trips to Hong Kong in the 1970s. "All you had to have was guts, ambition, and ideas and you could make it. It was the land of opportunity."

Bob Aschkenasy, a clothing buyer from Los Angeles, first met Lai in 1975. He had checked into the Peninsula hotel a few hours earlier after a flight from the United States. The grand hotel stood on the Tsim Sha Tsui waterfront, facing Hong Kong Island but within easy distance of the textile factories in Kowloon and the New Territories. Claiming the world's largest hotel fleet of Rolls-Royces, the spot was a favorite destination for foreign executives.

After Lai and his boss came to his room, Aschkenasy showed them a design for a new sweater he wanted made in Hong Kong. Lai said he could do the job and bid the clothing buyer goodbye. Then he went to work. Aschkenasy still marvels at what Lai did overnight. "At ten p.m. he went to the factory, found some similar yarns and colors, fooled around with the punch cards [used for manufacturing] and at ten a.m. he was back with a sample sweater." Lai's capacity for work stood out even in Hong Kong.

And he wanted more, his appetite whetted by the wealth he saw around him in Hong Kong. Lai began playing the stock market. He started with a stake of $900 and borrowed another $385 from a colleague named Liang Jurong. Lai set up a margin trading account and promised to share the profits with Liang. The margin account would allow him to buy more stock, turbocharging any gains but also amplifying any losses. "I am not someone who has the patience to save money," he reflected later. "I said, 'Let's try my luck.' I speculated in the stock market." The economy was booming on the strength of surging exports, powered by the sorts of clothing factories where Lai worked. All those export earnings meant lots of money sloshing around Hong Kong's small economy, fueling a sizzling stock and property market. The market more than doubled in 1972, soaring 147 percent.

Always a reader, Lai in the 1970s often had a get-rich-quick book in hand, hoping to learn the secrets of investing successfully. *Reminiscences of a Stock Operator*, a fictionalized autobiography of renowned speculator Jesse Livermore, was a favorite. Lai's reading proved profitable. "Before I knew it, I made a quarter million," parlaying that initial $2,000 stake into almost $50,000.

Notwithstanding his success, Lai decided that stock trading wasn't for him. He found playing the market too nerve-racking. "When I made money, I was so excited I couldn't sleep. When I lost money, I was so depressed I couldn't sleep. I asked myself when I was going to sleep." And the get-rich books? "Reading these books is like eating instant noodles," rued Lai. "There is no real nutrition and it is not very helpful to increase knowledge."

He went from stocks back to the garment business. His colleague at the Tak On Weaving Factory, Liang Jurong, agreed to go into business with Lai. Although Lai admitted to being "domineering and arrogant," Liang could put up with him. Liang would specialize in technical production details while Lai concentrated on sales. But first they needed a factory. The bull market that had made Lai's fortune soured in 1973. The market fell 49 percent. Matters worsened with the October 1973 Yom Kippur War and ensuing Arab oil embargo. Oil prices quadrupled as OPEC cut exports. Hong Kong's export-oriented economy suffered. The Hang Seng Index plummeted 61 percent in 1974. The colony went from boom to bust. Lai had cashed out of stocks before the market plunged but he saw many friends wiped out. Three decades later he still talked about how the experience had seared him.

The global economic downturn drove many Hong Kong exporters out of business. That meant bankrupt factories were suddenly for sale. A 4,000-square-foot sweater factory in the bustling San Po Kong industrial district came on the market. The factory had been seized by a bank after the failure of the previous owner. Lai knew that a used plant like this one, with existing machinery, would keep his company's costs low and minimize the time needed to get the business up and running.

San Po Kong was a compact factory area just north of Kai Tak Airport, nestled at the bottom of the steep hills that led up to the colony's iconic Lion Rock, a prominent natural outcrop. A popular television series from this period, *Below the Lion Rock*, debuted in 1972. It celebrates the hardworking bosses and factory hands in San Po Kong and neighboring areas who were pulling Hong Kong out of poverty. The show broke new ground in looking at tough issues in Hong Kong, from the fires that burned shantytowns to the challenges of mainland immigrants. *Below the Lion Rock* was Lai's world.

A more established businessman also had his eye on the San Po Kong facility. Boss Ma, as Lai called him, owned a wool-dyeing factory. He was "a nice gentleman" and worked with Lai's existing employer. Although Lai and his partner had been looking at other factories, "once we knew that Boss Ma was also interested in this factory, we became very anxious and determined to win it."

Lai went to the bank and tried to preempt Ma by offering to immediately buy the factory. The bank official in charge was "very disturbed" by Lai's pushiness. Ma was a long-standing customer. He had a track record. Lai didn't. The bank said it would give Ma the right to decide whether or not he wanted the factory before considering Lai's offer.

Lai could have backed off. After all, plenty of other factories were up for sale. He liked this factory precisely because Ma wanted it. He and Liang Jurong arranged to have dinner with Boss Ma at the Celebrating Encounter restaurant on Waterloo Road in Kowloon. Ma knew that Lai and Liang planned to start a business, and he hoped to get some of their dyeing orders. He told Lai what the young would-be entrepreneur already knew: Ma, too, wanted to buy a sweater factory. But, said Ma, his family worried about his age and poor health. They thought that taking on another factory might exact too high a toll.

Ma told Lai that he planned to consult a fortune-teller to help divine the way forward. Fortune-telling was—and is—common in Hong Kong. Successful business owners regularly consult feng shui masters for design and building advice so that their offices, factories, and homes are aligned with geomancy principles. Fortune-tellers at temples are also popular. Lai told Ma about a Taoist priest who told fortunes and had correctly advised a factory owner friend to move a factory; heeding the priest's advice, Lai's friend saw his business boom. Ma asked Lai the priest's name; Lai promised to find out.

There was no friend and no famous fortune-teller, but Lai pushed ahead with the ruse. He went to the Wong Tai Sin temple the next morning determined to find the most famous Taoist priest. The temple, located underneath Lion Rock and within sight of many squatter settlements, was a relatively new temple and popular with refugees. An old lady selling candles told Lai that a Mr. Li was the best-known soothsayer and had the most clients. He occupied the third stall on the right inside the temple gate. Lai found Li, waited his turn, and, with some embarrassment, explained the situation. In talking to the fortune-teller, however, Lai turned Boss Ma into his own uncle.

Lai told the priest that his Uncle Ma would visit tomorrow and ask about buying a sweater factory in San Po Kong. His family worried about his uncle's health, Lai said, "but he is stubborn and will not listen." Li asked what Ma looked like as well more details about the sweater factory. The fortune-teller was happy to further the deception: "No problem, it's a good thing anyway, and of course I'm happy to help." Lai gave the priest $128—a lot of money at a time when the priest charged just 26 cents for reading a fortune.

All went as Lai had planned. Boss Ma went to the Taoist priest at Wong Tai Sin, who told him not to buy the factory. Ma believed the priest. After returning from Wong Tai Sin, Boss Ma called Lai to suggest that he and Liang buy the factory. Lai's partner, knowing nothing of the deception, was surprised by Boss Ma's sudden decision. They quickly completed the purchase. Maybe Boss Ma would have decided not to buy the factory anyway.

Perhaps the decision preserved his health. Ma's existing company later became Lai's largest clothing dyer, so he benefited from the young man's success. Nonetheless, the story was "a hateful lie," Lai later wrote. "I knew that I was able to buy this factory because I was cheating, so I always felt uneasy."

Reflecting on this incident, Lai concluded that "young people have many ideals but few scruples . . . they have more than enough drive, but they often ignore reality; they are lax in ethics and integrity when doing business; they only see immediate benefits and ignore long-term effects and they think that others don't know how to do things as well as they do." Summing up, Lai wrote: "At least this is the portrayal of me when I was young."

Lai named the company Comitex, later explaining that he wanted to get across the idea of an up-and-coming (Com-) entrepreneur in the textile (-tex) business; he registered the company in April 1975. At last he had a company to run. He loved the challenge. Most mornings, he went to work around 6 a.m., so early that he was almost alone on the street. He bought a sausage roll or a bowl of congee with peanuts or bonito flakes from the only open food stall, trading greetings with the elderly owner as he ordered breakfast. "Going out early in the morning to make money, what a smile," she would greet him. Yes, Lai thought, "every morning when I start work, I feel excited—when I meet people, I can't help but smile."

Lai had big plans. All he needed was orders. In keeping with Hong Kong start-up practice—and perhaps his general approach at the time to business—he had counted on poaching clients from his previous employers. The business plan collapsed as prospective customers took a wait-and-see attitude, wanting proof of Comitex's quality and reliability.

Lai adapted. Since Comitex couldn't get export orders, it did piecework for other companies. It became, in his words, "a copycat factory." Comitex scraped by; crucial financial help came from Stephen Cheong, the scion of a wealthy Hong Kong family and later a legislator. Lai and Liang cut costs and simplified the company's structure. They started every morning by personally moving the fabrics, thread, buttons, zippers, and other materials needed for the day's production to each workstation so that a laborer could start work immediately and not waste time getting supplies. The labor-intensive work gave Lai an opportunity to study the production process "to continuously simplify and revise."

They tied strips of different-colored paper to clothing to help workers identify and count the garments. They made sure each worker knew what her or his task was that day. If a process was too time-consuming, they would raise the product's price. Lai's intuitive approach of making ongoing incremental changes paralleled the Japanese concept of *kaizen*, which focused on continuous improvement and helped make Japanese companies so successful internationally in the 1970s.

Lai later said he wouldn't have resigned his job at Tak On to start Comitex if he had known that the new company would be forced to rely on low-value-added piecework assembly. The early difficulties nonetheless helped build a stronger foundation for the business by forcing Lai to become intimately involved with all aspects of production. He focused on workers, learning that "close communication and cooperation with workers is the most effective way to solve problems and speed up production." In production problems, "we realized that the workers' difficulties are our difficulties and solving their difficulties would also overcome production difficulties, which made production faster." Lai had been in charge of production when he was at Tak On, but he wasn't involved on the factory floor. With characteristic intensity and enthusiasm, he threw himself into the challenge. Learning new things, solving problems, and developing new abilities, "how can I not be excited every day?"

After eight long months of barely profitable subcontract work, Lai finally won his first export order. The business came from the giant U.S. department store JCPenney. In the 1970s, retailers like JCPenney, Kmart, Montgomery Ward, and Sears were the most powerful buyers in the world's largest consumer market. Their giant department stores anchored many of the nearly 20,000 new shopping malls that developers constructed in the 1960s and 1970s to serve an increasingly suburban America. Buyers from these big chains were tough and exacting. But they bought in large volumes. Selling directly to them would put Lai on the map. It would guarantee high-volume sales and instant credibility for Comitex.

Eddie Lo, the manager of JCPenney's Hong Kong operation, tipped Lai off that one of the company's New York–based buyers would soon be in town. Joe Papa bought sweaters for the company's women's clothing department. Unhappy with JCPenney's existing factory suppliers, he wanted to find a new one. Lo said he would bring Papa back to his hotel around 7:30 p.m. Lai waited there for three and a half hours.

After 11 p.m. Lo and an inebriated Joe Papa returned. Lai and Lo accompanied Papa to his room. Papa was straightforward: "You are a new factory," he told Lai, and asked why JCPenney should take a risk that Comitex would deliver shoddy goods—or not deliver at all. "Please," begged Lai, "give me a chance."

The JCPenney buyer showed Lai more than a dozen sweater styles. Lai quoted prices and delivery dates; in the end Papa gave him an order to make five kinds of sweaters, 300 to 600 dozen of each style, for a total of 2,300 dozen. The order, totaling a staggering 27,600 women's sweaters, would be due in seventy-five days. Each of the sweaters would have to be perfect.

It was after one o'clock in the morning when Lai returned home. "I didn't feel sleepy at all. I just studied those few sweater samples over and over again, thinking in my mind, 'How can I make them better than in the samples?'" In the morning, having barely slept, he walked to the factory, meditating all the way and refreshed by an early-morning winter wind blowing on his face. The old woman running the rice noodle and congee stand asked, "Why do you look so serious today?" Lai burst into a smile. "Grandma, I hit it big." Lai later reflected that he's excited when he's chasing an opportunity but somber once he wins an order—with opportunity comes responsibility. Now he needed to deliver the goods.

Lai knew that this was his chance. JCPenney was a large company and Papa was a big buyer, with his department alone purchasing more than $100 million of goods a year from suppliers. If JCPenney paid Comitex a typical $45 price for a dozen mass-market sweaters, the initial order would be worth $103,500. "It wasn't enough to do this batch of goods well," thought Lai. "We must make it a blockbuster." In the future, "I don't want to ask him to do business." Instead, vowed Lai, "I want him to need *us*."

Lai aimed to underpromise and overdeliver. Back at the factory, Liang agreed. Each dozen sweaters made by competing factories weighed between seven and eight pounds. For the price JCPenney was paying, Lai considered the quality good. But he concluded that the feel of the sweater in the hands was too light. With a heavier material "the hand feel will be much richer." He decided to use a half-pound more material per dozen. The cost would be much higher, of course. The goal wasn't an immediate profit but the opportunity to win a steady stream of orders in the future.

Comitex produced the sweater sample in a few days. Eddie Lo professed himself happy with the product but he didn't have authority to give the go-ahead to start production. Lai needed Joe Papa's approval. He decided to fly to New York the next day and show Papa the sample in person. "If there's a problem, I will solve it with him on the spot." Lo arranged for Lai to meet Papa two days later in New York.

The first meeting went well—so well that Papa invited him to dinner at his home in New Jersey with his wife, daughter, and parents. Lai hit it off with the family. Before the end of the two-and-a-half-day trip, Papa had doubled the size of the initial order, requesting another 2,300 dozen of the same sweaters. Papa introduced Lai to other JCPenney buyers. The retailer immediately became Comitex's largest customer. Lai reflected on the combination of luck and hard work needed to win the JCPenney order.

> We are really lucky. But if you ask me which is more important, luck or hard work? Then there is no doubt that I will tell you that hard work is more important, because only hard work can make people really lucky. Would we impress JCPenney with business if we didn't see it as an opportunity to win the confidence of the customers and deliver the best quality no matter the cost? If I hadn't taken the

trouble to show Joe Papa a sample in New York, would he and his co-workers have given us a steady stream of business later on? Our hard work and optimistic orientation have brought us into a virtuous cycle; hard work makes us lucky and the luckier we are the harder we work and therefore the luckier we get. Luck is earned by hard work.

Sandrina Caruso chose Lai as her first supplier for a clothing line sold by Canada's Chateau of Clothing retailers in 1975. Canada had established diplomatic relations with the People's Republic of China in 1970 and Caruso's boss wanted to see if the company could start buying clothes there. She attended the Canton Trade Fair in 1974 but all she could buy were Mao suits. So she went to Hong Kong, where her parents were long-term residents at the Peninsula hotel, to find manufacturers. Caruso remembers that Lai stood out from other producers in the colony. She liked his "vibe." She remembers that "he had a burning ambition. He wanted to be successful, no matter what he was doing."

A year after he founded Comitex, Lai went for a swim at the Mariners Club one hot summer day. Located on Middle Road in Tsim Sha Tsui, the club wasn't far from Lai's factory by car and just a few minutes' walk from the Peninsula hotel, where Lai met Bob Aschkenasy and other buyers. Hanging out poolside with some Cathay Pacific cabin crew, he spotted a young Thai-Chinese woman on the other side of the pool. Pilunya Assapimonwait, known as Judy to her friends, had moved to the colony a year earlier to work as a stewardess for Cathay, Hong Kong's hometown airline.

With his characteristic enthusiasm bordering on impatience, Lai pursued Judy. Within a few months, he was pushing her to marry. He wanted to be with her so much that he persuaded her to quit her job immediately. She agreed, paying the airline a month's pay as compensation for not serving out the thirty days' notice Cathay required from departing staff. "Everything was so fast," she remembers. "He's like that. He knows what he wants." Judy found Lai's optimism and his belief that every problem could be solved a welcome change from her strict upbringing. "His philosophy in life is very good," she says. "Living with Jimmy, he always said, 'Why worry about things that [might] happen?' He just let go and learned from all the problems in life."

They wed in the autumn of 1976 in a simple civil ceremony at a government office in the colony's New Territories. There was no party. Lai was twenty-seven. Judy was twenty-three. They moved into the apartment he had been renting in a house on 121 Waterloo Road, near the entrance to the Lion Rock Tunnel. Their apartment was across the street from the Harilelas, a storied clan of ethnic Indians. More than one hundred family members inhabited a sprawling complex that was more like a palace than a house.

As soon as they were married, Lai wanted children. After three months with no result, he worried about fertility problems. "He complained I had something wrong with me because I didn't [immediately] get pregnant," Judy says. Lai's fear proved unfounded. His oldest child, Tim, was born in October 1977. Judy gave birth to two more children, Jade in 1979 and Ian in 1981.

Around the time of Ian's birth, the family of five rented a detached house, a testament to Lai's growing wealth. The new place was less than a half-mile away, at the corner of Nga Tsin Wai Road and La Salle Road, across the street from La Salle College, a prestigious boys' high school. They also bought a junk, a broad-beamed and slow-moving craft modeled on a traditional wooden fishing boat. Repurposed for leisure trips, junks were popular among Hong Kongers eager to explore the territory's isolated beaches and seaside villages.

Lai bought this, the first of several boats he would own over the years, because Judy liked to swim; Lai didn't much care for swimming, but "he could relax, think, and read," says Judy. The Lai family kept theirs in the northeastern town of Sai Kung at a marina in Port Shelter, a popular spot for boaters. On the day they moved from Waterloo Road, with many of their goods still unpacked, they decided to spend the night on their boat. Returning home the next day, they found the house had been burgled and their maid tied up. The burglary provided a sobering reminder of Hong Kong's dangers.

After about a year, they moved to 5 Wiltshire Road, less than half a mile away. Reflecting Hong Kong's status as a British colonial city, their one-block-long street was surrounded by Cambridge, Durham, Hereford, and Oxford Roads. The English names notwithstanding, this densely populated part of Hong Kong was the spiritual center of the city, home to a jumble of factories, restaurants, shops, and residences. It's not the fabled harbor pictured in countless tourist photos, but it's "the most convenient and central area of Hong Kong," says Judy. It was easy to get to their boat in Sai Kung, his factory in San Po Kong (and later in Cheung Sha Wan), and buyers at the Peninsula hotel or Kai Tak Airport. Each was within a few miles.

During the 1970s and 1980s this was still a low-rise area comprising houses, small apartment buildings, and traditional four-story *tong lau*. Common in Hong Kong and Chinese settlements throughout southeast Asia, the *tong lau* featured covered arcades to protect against the rain and small balconies for upstairs apartment dwellers. As height restrictions eased, six-story walk-up apartments sat atop street-level restaurants and shops.

Except for a spell in Taiwan in the early 2000s, Lai would always live within a few miles of the flat on Waterloo Road where he resided when he met Judy. Its restaurants, its shops, and its factories were his landscape. In the mornings, he exercised by swimming at Kowloon Tsai Park or La Salle College, each just a few minutes' walk away, until he joined the prestigious Jockey Club.

The heart of Kowloon also boasted some of the best eating in a food-crazed city. Lai loved food. Now he could afford what he wanted. He and Judy ate out often. He didn't want her to cook. "He said, 'No you don't cook,'" she remembers. "He didn't want to make me unhappy if he didn't like my food." They ate often at Tien Heung Lau and at Fook Lam Moon in nearby Tsim Sha Tsui, both well-known Cantonese restaurants offering dishes like crab roe, double-boiled soups, and suckling pig. "He is obsessed with food," says his daughter Jade. "He loves rich, fatty foods." He eats quickly, finishing a bowl of congee while it is still steaming.

With clothing buyer Bob Aschkenasy he ate at the Spring Deer, another traditional Cantonese restaurant, near the Peninsula hotel. "We used to smoke pot together and go out to Spring Deer," remembers Aschkenasy. "Jimmy says he'll pay double for the next dish coming out of the kitchen [so that he could eat more quickly]. When we first started going there he was unknown. Five years later he was kind of known. Another five years he is known as a pretty hotshot guy. When we would walk in, people would whisper, 'There's Jimmy Lai.'"

Restless and driven though he was, Lai spent a lot of time biding his time in reception areas so that he could meet clothing buyers. Like many successful people with little formal education, he read voraciously. One day in the mid-1970s, while waiting for a Kmart buyer, he read Charles Mackay's *Extraordinary Popular Delusions and the Madness of Crowds*, a classic study of investment bubbles throughout history.

Another salesman ("curly silver hair, tanned skin, and well-dressed . . . more like a professor than a salesman") struck up a conversation. A friendship ensued. Soon Bill Milken and his wife, Kate, invited Lai to stay with them whenever he was in New York. Lai's earnest, genuine manner, coupled with warmth and interest in others, prompted the Milkens to help him find his way in New York City. Lai's openness and enthusiasm made people want to help and mentor him. "I grew up away from home and really had no tutor," he reflected. But he found them in buyers like Joe Papa and salesmen like Bill Milken and the semiretired clerk at his first factory who helped him learn English.

Lai appeared so uncouth to the Milkens that it was almost as if he had been raised by wolves. Once Kate Milken asked if she could privately show him some table manners. He hadn't realized that he behaved boorishly. He had grown up in a Chinese family, where one didn't pass dishes to other people. He had no idea how to hold his silverware. He quickly learned— and he learned to watch others. "Living in their home and having the opportunity to learn the rules and etiquette of getting along with others is a valuable experience." It helped Lai, he said, "avoid many embarrassing situations in the future" and gave him the confidence to "make [others] feel better and more comfortable." From the Canton railway station to the streets of New York, Lai had seen much in his thirtysomething years, but he still had a lot to learn.

The Milkens tried to encourage Lai's quest for knowledge. Kate would regale Lai with tales of the works her book groups were reading—the *Iliad*, Sophocles's *Oedipus the King*, Virginia Woolf's *To the Lighthouse*. She even took Lai to Columbia University to audit a literature class. "That really made me laugh. She didn't let me [stop going to the class] until she knew that I really had no interest in literary novels." Although Lai professed disdain, after a while he picked up a bit of cultural knowledge and "felt that I was noble. Of course, this was just my vanity at work."

In the late 1970s, Lai was becoming "inseparable" from New York, a city that he called his mentor, where he honed both his English and his business skills. Several times a year, he would travel to New York City for two or three weeks at a time to meet his major clients, including the buyers at JCPenney and Kmart. These customers placed big orders, so it was worth waiting around in their offices until he could meet them face-to-face.

"Hey, it's really great, what's your magic?" Lai remembers Tom Higgins, a sweater buyer for JCPenney's Junior Miss line, asking him. "Every time I ask you for a sample, you'll have the goods delivered within a few days, and what you make is what they like." Lai wouldn't divulge his secret—his "magic"—to Higgins. But he later wrote about it.

Lai put his time in New York to good use. He scoured the aisles at higher-end department stores like Bloomingdale's and Macy's to learn what more affluent customers were trying on and what they were actually buying. More important, he got to know the saleswomen, who gave him more information. "I can grasp the sales situation from their mouths; which style sells the best?" he later wrote. "Which style sells the fastest? How have customers responded to these styles?"

Buyers at JCPenney and Kmart believed that what was popular at more exclusive stores such as Bloomingdale's and Macy's would sell at their stores a year later. But Lai thought this assumption was too vague and wanted to better understand the industry and respond to the retailers more accurately.

He dug deeper, taking salesclerks out to fancy places like the '21' club and the Russian Tea Room to impress them. He dressed like an early version of a crazy rich Asian, sporting Valentino suits, Gucci ties, Swiss mercerized cotton shirts tailored by Hong Kong's Ascot Chang, expensive cuff links, and Bally shoes.

"I actually don't like dressing up like that," he later wrote. "However, I am a Chinese from Hong Kong. In order to make friends with the sales-girls, this is the only way I can cover up my old and wretched appearance." Self-deprecation aside, he played to the stereotype of an Asian salesman and used it to his advantage.

Lai plied his salesclerk friends for information on what was hot and what was not. They let him know which items were being restocked, especially repeatedly, and which items were difficult to restock because they were selling so well. He found that midpriced items from high-end retailers were what translated best to the mass market and grew to understand seasonality and the importance of introducing fresh items in the middle of a season. "With these insights, I have a reflexive ability to understand the sweater market," he reflected later. "When I encounter the right style, I will immediately have an explosive sense of enlightenment."

Whenever a buyer wanted him to produce a sample of a new style, he just went to Bloomingdale's or Macy's to collect a few sweaters that his research had told him would sell well in the mass market the following season. He bought every color of each sample item. He transformed the best-looking example of each style into his own sample by cutting off the original label and pasting in his own, including serial number, weight, and price. The other colors for each style would be used as color swatches. "This method is cheap, quick, and simple, and this is my trick." It was a trick backed up by his exten-sive investigation into what shoppers were actually buying. By taking common knowledge and looking deeper, Lai developed an uncanny "magic" ability to pick trends. "I don't have any secrets, I just do more research," he averred.

Was it magic? Was it copying? Or something else? Lai's appropriation of styles from higher-end retailers like Bloomingdale's and Macy's wasn't anything special or unusual. That's what Tom Higgins and his team at JCPenney—and, indeed, their counterparts at mass-market stores around the country—tried to do. Simply copying a style was the easy part. Lai's magic consisted in part simply of working harder and smarter, of digging deeply into real-time sales trends at upmarket outlets by cultivating salesclerks in the pre-computer era, when data was scarce. His success underscored the quip that genius is 10 percent inspiration and 90 percent perspiration. He worked hard and he worked smart. "Any trick contains some special skills; otherwise it wouldn't be a trick, would it?"

Expertise underpinned Lai's success. He could immediately quote prices because he knew every aspect of production and delivery. "I also have one thing that most salesmen don't—I can pick up any sweater and make an offer on the spot. I worked in a sweater factory since I was a child, and I know every process, raw material, and cost well." Not only could he quote faster, but he could do so more accurately—both in figuring out his profit and in ensuring production feasibility and on-time delivery.

Lai also had a strong visual sense; he appreciated design and, above all, color. This would become more apparent at his later businesses in both fashion and media. At Comitex, it meant that he could choose the most marketable color in a sample sweater from Bloomingdale's or Macy's to show a buyer at JCPenney. "He really had a taste for what he was doing," Sandrina Caruso remembers. "If we would be looking at a style and a design, he would pick out the good one. He could pick it out, would know not only how it would look but how it would perform, and if it would be hot. He had that. It was what made him unique."

Hong Kong had emerged as one of the world's most efficient exporters of clothing and textiles. Harnessing inexpensive labor, plentiful electricity, and the profit-seeking drive of thousands of entrepreneurs, Hong Kong in the late 1950s became a major textile manufacturer. This export success appeared all the more surprising because before 1945 the colony had prospered as a gateway to China rather than an industrial center in its own right. Manufacturing had occupied a small niche.

Hong Kong's success in making clothes proved too much of a good thing. The combination of Asia's low labor costs and the savvy of sophisticated entrepreneurs like Lai threatened existing manufacturers in industrialized countries. Textile makers in South Carolina and England's Lancashire, home of the original industrial revolution, found that they couldn't compete when it came to price or quality.

The United Kingdom put limits on Hong Kong exports beginning in 1959 under the aptly named Lancashire Pact. The United States limited textile exports from Hong Kong beginning in 1961 under the Short-Term Arrangement on Cotton Textiles, which morphed into decades-long restrictions on clothing shipments. These measures developed into a wide-ranging set of rules designed to limit imports of clothing from abroad.

Lai found a way to turn these restrictions to his advantage. The quota system set out detailed numerical restrictions on items. For example, it capped the number of women's cotton sweaters that could be exported to the United States in any given year. In Hong Kong, existing suppliers were granted quotas based on how much they had previously exported. For Lai and many others, this system proved a bonanza by limiting competition. Quota holders, moreover, could sell or rent any unused quota. The Star House, just down the street from the Peninsula hotel, housed scores of tiny brokerages that traded in quotas, functioning as a sort of primitive stock exchange.

"Why don't we fuck the quota?" he asked Glynn Manson, one of Lai's closest friends, as well as his partner and the cofounder of British clothing retailer Fenn Wright Manson. "We created a miracle yarn that was not under the quota control." To get around the restrictions on exports of cotton sweaters, Lai introduced sweaters made of 55 percent ramie and 45 percent cotton. Cotton sweaters had a 20 percent duty rate while the ramie sweaters attracted only a 3 percent rate. Bottom line: Lai shipped the ramie sweaters, which were virtually indistinguishable from cotton ones, for \$5 apiece, while the cotton ones cost \$9 apiece. The standard industry practice of quadrupling the factory price meant that Lai's ramie sweaters retailed for \$20 while competitors' cotton ones sold for \$36.

These inexpensive ramie-based products proved popular. So popular, in fact, that the United States introduced quotas on these new fabrics. As the dominant producer, Lai received a generous quota allowance for ramie and for angora wool products, for which he had similarly developed a new fabric that proved so successful that it, too, attracted quota restrictions. As he pulled back from manufacturing in the late 1980s, renting these quota allowances to other textile makers created a financial windfall that netted him \$3.8 million to \$5.1 million annually. Aschkenasy marveled at Lai's ability to profit from the quota system. "I started acquiring Hong Kong textile quotas," he remembered. "Jimmy would tell me when to buy. You could buy it for three dollars and rent it out for one year for one dollar." After three years the original investment had been recovered; every year after that was profit. "It was by far the best investment I ever made," remembers Aschkenasy.

In addition to enriching Lai and polishing his manners, New York City inspired an intellectual awakening, forcing him to think more deeply about the suffering he had endured in China and the freedom he enjoyed in Hong Kong. His intellectual epiphany came in 1977. It was, Lai remembers, a Tuesday night. Bill and Kate Milken took him to "a retired Jewish lawyer's house." The dinner conversation revolved around communism. Lai made his hatred of Chinese communism known. "I bad-mouthed the communists a lot," he remembers. His host got a book from the shelves and gave it to Lai. "'Read this,' he insisted."

The book was Austrian-British economist and political philosopher Friedrich Hayek's *The Road to Serfdom*. Lai devoured Hayek, a Nobel economics laureate who counseled small government and economic freedom. "I was very inspired," remembered Lai. "I read all these books . . . except [the] theory of interest [which I] couldn't understand." Hayek frequently cited Karl Popper, another Austrian-British political thinker who wrote about the dangers of totalitarianism. So Lai plunged into Popper's writings. New York City and this dinner "inspired me to be a useful person." The get-rich-quick books would go. Henceforth Lai would embrace the cause of freedom.

By 1980, Comitex billed itself as one of Hong Kong's largest sweater manufacturers. Lai now counted higher-end brands like The Limited and Polo as major customers. But the restless, probing young man from Shunde was ready to move on. He'd take the knowledge that he had acquired on the Macy's and Bloomingdale's shop floors, in the long hours reading while he waited for buyers, and during his many evenings at the 21 club and the Russian Tea Room. He realized that he didn't need to work through buyers like Tom Higgins. He would take his magic straight to consumers with his own retail shops.

Chapter Three

THE FATHER OF FAST FASHION

Anapkin stuffed into his jacket pocket during a night out inspired the name of Lai's next venture. After a busy day seeing customers in New York City, he was dining alone at Giordano's on West Thirty-Ninth Street, on the fringes of Manhattan's Garment District.

As he later recalled, "One day after seeing a customer in Manhattan, I was very hungry. The whole day I was in the office and I couldn't eat. I went to a pizza place and after I finished, I got a napkin. It said Giordano—it is an Italian name. I said, 'This [is] very good, at least people think my retailing business is an Italian business.' Not that I think I can fool people, but it is a very nice name. So I just went back [to Hong Kong], I gave it to our graphics department and they worked it out. And that was Giordano."

Lai gave a slightly different version of the story to Austin Ramzy of the *New York Times*. He recalled that before going to the restaurant he had unwittingly eaten a marijuana-laced brownie and had the munchies. After his pizza, he put the restaurant's napkin in his jacket pocket, where he found it the next day. Lai's hunger for a pizza that night led to the name of his next venture, one that would take him for the first time into a consumer business.

Comitex had achieved phenomenal success. Five years after its founding, Lai had grown bored with simply running a manufacturing operation. He wanted a new outlet for his creative talents. He had nurtured his suppliers, taking on a more active role than most of his competitors in designing the sweaters, polo shirts, and T-shirts that he manufactured. He sped up production and shipping, working with British fashion merchandiser Glynn Manson to set up a speed sourcing operation. They slashed delivery times for retailers from five months to two weeks. He knew production, design, and the basics of retailing. He also knew that the price of one of his sweaters quadrupled from the time it left Comitex's factory gate until it was sold at an American department store. Lai determined to get some of the profits that now went to retailers for himself.

A retail revolution had just started in the United States. In the immediate post–World War II period, the U.S. clothing market had been neatly divided. On one side stood mass-market national chains like JCPenney, Kmart, and Sears. On the other were exclusive department stores like Bloomingdale's, Macy's, and Lord & Taylor, which charged higher prices and had only a small number of outlets, mostly in major cities. High-end or low-end, these brands sold a wide range of goods.

Manufacturers like Comitex enabled the birth of a new age of mass-market specialty clothing sales. One of its biggest customers was The Limited, founded in 1963 by Leslie Wexner. Unlike JCPenney or Macy's, The Limited did not stock everything from cookware to cardigans. It sold a narrow line of higher-quality women's clothing under its own brand but with midmarket pricing. The chain featured limited styles and colors but changed them frequently.

The Limited contracted with Lai to produce a best-selling ramie cardigan sweater, made with 55 percent ramie and 45 percent cotton to get around the quota on cotton. The company struggled with lead times of five months or more from the time the sweater was ordered until it could be delivered. The dye had to be approved, the fabric knit, and the goods shipped by sea. Lai said he would first make blanks—white sweaters—and later dye them whatever color the company wanted, cutting the production time to thirty days. He also proposed to fly the sweaters to the United States rather than ship them across the Pacific. The quicker delivery times allowed sellers to capitalize on hot trends.

"Jimmy revolutionized the thinking on merchandising," remembers a former Limited executive. "If I am buying fashion stuff and I can replenish it in forty-five or sixty days instead of five months, or six or nine months, that changes everything. That one moment changed everything in retail, everything The Limited did. I bought my first house on that sweater." Soon Lai was chartering jumbo jets and stuffing them with sweaters and polo shirts for shipment to The Limited's Columbus, Ohio, headquarters.

Lai's impulse to develop his own brand—and later to branch into setting up his own chain of stores—sprang in part from weakness. Comitex depended on a small number of large customers. These could choose from a variety of manufacturers, so Comitex didn't have a strong bargaining position when it came to setting prices. Buyers from foreign retailers specialized in playing hungry manufacturers off against each other, haggling over every penny.

Lai termed the situation "very dangerous, because you will be captive. Whether a good price or a bad price you still have to make it, so I felt a constraint being a manufacturer." Although buyers typically quadrupled the price they paid the factory when they put it out for sale in a store, they couldn't count on selling everything, especially at full price, and had to cover the costs of shipping, rent, electricity, sales staff, and their teams of buyers and merchandisers. Still, the apparent prospect of substantial profits appealed to Lai.

More than money, Lai wanted a different challenge. "[B]eing a manufacturer for a long time I felt bored. You cannot be very creative being a manufacturer. . . . At least that's what I thought at the time. Of course, that's not true. You can be creative. I thought, hey, maybe retailing is something I should try."

"Manufacturing itself is not an exciting business," remembers Canadian clothing designer and buyer Sandrina Caruso, who first worked with Lai in the mid-1970s. "For me, seeing my ideas come out and look great is wonderful. But his only role was to make the clothes."

Lai started Giordano in 1981. Originally, he harbored ambitions of building a brand, competing with products such as the Lacoste crocodile polo shirt that defined preppy style at the time. Caruso remembers foreign buyers cheering the start-up. "Giordano was again a new idea—there was nothing like that in Hong Kong. He was manufacturing, but they were his ideas, his design." For a Hong Kong company to establish its own brand proved tough. First, Lai tried wholesaling, with only modest success. Then he turned to company-owned stores. The first Giordano shop opened in 1983.

The 1980s witnessed the emergence of millions of new middle-class consumers in the Asian Tigers—Hong Kong, Singapore, Taiwan, and South Korea—as those economies posted sustained, rapid economic growth of a sort that the world had never seen. Economic prosperity rested on export manufacturing exemplified by companies like Lai's Comitex. But domestically oriented businesses like retail remained stuck in the past.

Hong Kong boasted the Lane Crawford and Wing On department stores, the former started by two Scotsmen and the latter by a pair of Chinese brothers who had returned from Australia. The colony's posh Central business district featured imported brands such as France's Daniel Hechter, a self-described affordable luxury brand. Throughout the city there were plenty of stand-alone clothing stores. And Hong Kong was famous for its tailor shops. But anyone wanting to buy basic stylish casual clothes—itself a revolutionary concept that was just catching on in rich countries with outlets like Gap—didn't have many options. Consumers in Singapore, South Korea, and Taiwan had even less choice because their governments didn't want to encourage consumer spending.

Lai had acquired global manufacturing know-how at Comitex. He would focus on casual clothing—stylish but inexpensive. He had the skill and the eye to anticipate styles and fashion in the competitive American market. He had a good sense of how information—whether obtained using information technology or derived from his own grasp of market trends—could be used in the service of a retail fashion business.

These advantages notwithstanding, Giordano's first five years were, in Lai's words, "a flop." Too many styles, too much choice, and too much complexity. Lots of goods piled up unsold.

Political uncertainties and an economic downturn added to the business challenges Lai faced. Britain had seized the island of Hong Kong in 1841 in the first Opium War. Less than two decades later, following the Second Opium War, Britain acquired a sliver of mainland China known as Kowloon, just across the harbor from Hong Kong Island. The Chinese agreed that the British could rule both Kowloon and Hong Kong Island "in perpetuity." When Britain grabbed an even bigger chunk of land to the north, the New Territories, it settled for a ninety-nine-year lease. That agreement would run out on June 30, 1997. By the time Lai founded Giordano in 1981, the colony's inhabitants had begun looking ahead nervously to that fateful date, just sixteen years away.

British prime minister Margaret Thatcher visited Beijing in September 1982, the first serving British prime minister to do so. Chinese leader Deng Xiaoping bluntly told her that China would take the colony back—all of it. The promise that Britain could rule "in perpetuity" had been made under duress, and Deng now disavowed it. Lai had started Giordano a year earlier. Now he would race against a countdown to the communist takeover.

The question marks around Hong Kong's future prompted a run on the colony's currency. The collapse of an overly indebted property company triggered a wider economic slump. Lai had counted on buoyant consumer spending to power Giordano, but his would-be customers weren't in the mood to splurge at a new store.

"I made a lot of mistakes, I made a lot of assumptions," Lai reflected. He adopted a traditional high-margin, large-selection business model. The new retail business "fell flat on its face." At a board meeting, other directors said that Lai should shut the business if he couldn't fix it. "I was going to close it because I didn't think I was going to do anything good with it," but he couldn't bring himself to make the final decision. "I went in and I just couldn't close it. My heart wanted me to carry on." While mulling his next move, he went back to the factory where he first worked when he came to Hong Kong a quarter century earlier:

> I went back to the same food store, just sat there and ate the noodles. I thought about the first day I came to the factory. I thought, "I'm not going to give up. I am going to try my hand again at retail." Looking at the factory where I first lived in Hong Kong, after the hellish time I had in China, I knew how lucky I was. How thankful I should be. I should not give things up just because I had an obstacle. I couldn't give up.

A trip with his three young children to McDonald's helped him find his way with Giordano. The fast-food chain had opened its first outlet in Hong Kong in 1975. The Hong Kong shops quickly became some of the world's busiest. In October 1981, a McDonald's outlet in the factory district of Kwun Tong broke the world record for most transactions in a single twenty-four-hour period. Lai marveled at the simplicity of the menu and the service speed. "I thought to myself that I can make my retail business as simple as McDonald's."

He slashed Giordano's offerings from as many as four hundred items to no more than fifty. But he gave consumers the illusion of choice by expanding the number of colors. Instead of four colors he ramped up to thirty or forty for a typical item. "Colors don't complicate the business—only items do," he said. To avoid getting stuck with excess stock in slow-moving colors, he made everything in white and dyed the items when orders came in. This inverted the traditional clothes-making method of using dyed fabric to make clothes. It also dramatically reduced the amount of unsold clothes. If lime-green was selling and orange wasn't, Giordano would dye a lot of lime-green clothes—and avoid getting stuck with orange ones. "Simplicity became the theme. Every day I ask myself, 'Can I make it simpler, can I make it cheaper, can I make it better?'"

Lai pioneered fast fashion. His success attracted a Japanese entrepreneur named Tadashi Yanai, who had started out as a kitchenware salesman at a Japanese department store and later worked at his father's clothing shop. Yanai opened the first Uniqlo clothing outlet in Hiroshima in 1984. He was in Hong Kong, and Giordano's polo shirts caught his attention. "The quality was good, despite the relatively low price," Yanai remembered. "I went to meet with Jimmy Lai, founder of Giordano, and learned that there are no borders to trade, and no borders to manufacturing and sales. We're the same age, and I thought, 'If he can do it, so can I.' After that, I started doing business in Hong Kong and was traveling there nearly every week."

Yanai spent considerable time with Lai, familiarizing himself with Giordano. Yanai's Japanese retail network remained small, but he had big plans for expansion. He invited Lai to invest in his business, proposing a $5 million investment by Lai in exchange for 25 percent of the business. When Lai balked, Yanai sweetened the offer, suggesting that he would cede 30 percent of the company in exchange for $5 million. Lai didn't generally like partnering. He also couldn't easily spare the cash needed for the investment. He said no to a partnership with a man who would go on to be one of the world's most successful retailers.

Yanai took Lai's emphasis on simplicity—and his fascination with how McDonald's did business—to build a global powerhouse. He became the king of fast fashion, offering an ever-changing variety of stylish, inexpensive clothing. He now has a net worth of some $38 billion and ranks as Japan's richest man by far. His extraordinary success sometimes prompted Lai to wonder what would have happened if he'd invested with the Japanese entrepreneur. He gives Yanai credit for achieving a level of quality that exceeded what he would have been able to attain. Uniqlo became the global giant; Giordano did not. But Giordano provided a template.

"He never stopped talking about his time with Yanai," says Lai's longtime aide Mark Simon, but he didn't rue not partnering with the Japanese entrepreneur. His real regret, Lai told Simon, was that he hadn't taken the Giordano concept to the United States. The United States, with its massive consumer market, represented an alluring opportunity, but it was too distant from Hong Kong for Lai to have confidence that Giordano could succeed there.

Lai's emphasis on simplicity paid off for Giordano when the company sold its shares on the Hong Kong stock exchange in 1991. That stock market listing brought in additional capital for expansion and gave Lai's stake in the company a valuation of more than $100 million.

The company reported detailed financial information in preparation for its stock listing. Sales tripled from $91 million in 1989 to $295 million in 1993, growing 40 percent a year during most of this period. Even Hong Kong's post-Tiananmen slump barely slowed the company; its sales rose 25 percent in the year following the massacre. Profits more than quadrupled from $3.7 million to $17.7 million in those four years.

Every measure of corporate health looked robust. Debt fell dramatically and shareholders' equity in the company soared. The return on equity—the profit earned in a given year as a percentage of the money shareholders had invested in the business—would make a monopolist envious. In the worst year during this period, the return on equity was 34 percent, meaning that profits washed in so fast that an investor would recoup his entire investment in just three years. (That return is almost double the average for general retailers in the United States in 2023.) In fiscal 1989, a 142 percent return on equity meant that for every $1 a shareholder invested in the company, the company generated a profit of $1.42. Lai had hit on a winning formula.

Giordano used the funds it raised to go on an expansion binge. In 1992, it opened its first store in mainland China. Lai's opposition to the Chinese Communist Party notwithstanding, he remained confident that China would develop into an increasingly market-oriented economy whose growing consumer class would turbocharge the profitability of retailers—and that political reform would naturally grow out of economic development. Giordano also opened in Malaysia and, by 1995, in Thailand, South Korea, and, in the Middle East, in Dubai, Oman, and Saudi Arabia. In 1995, the official Hong Kong Trade Development Council affirmed Giordano's role as one of Hong Kong's international success stories with an export marketing award.

Hong Kongers embraced Lai's brightly colored polo shirts and his affordable prices. In keeping with its value-for-money strategy, Lai cut prices—from $11.40 to $7.60 on its popular polo shirts. Low wages traditionally underpinned economic growth in a city that didn't institute a minimum wage until 2009. Lai doubled staff wages to boost morale and foster Giordano's customer-friendly feeling.

To ensure the high quality of his customers' experience, Lai worked closely with Chinese University of Hong Kong professor Leung Kwok to develop training programs. They taught staff how to greet customers, how to show that they cared about the customer on the way to making a sale. Leung and Lai didn't stop with the sales staff; they organized focus groups where consumers could tell executives what they liked and what they didn't.

Giordano wooed shoppers with its well-lit stores, fresh merchandise, and friendly but not overbearing staff. Part of the appearance of endless product variety was an illusion, because the wide array of colors masked the limited number of products. But the value and affordable style was real, driven by the manufacturing efficiencies Lai knew how to exploit. The journalist Laurence Zuckerman, who profiled Lai for the *International Herald Tribune* in 1991, remembers thinking at first that Giordano was a European brand—not so much for the name as for the modern vibe of the stores, so much at odds with the stuffy feeling of most Hong Kong brands. "You had the sense that Jimmy Lai could have been a global business success" with Giordano, says Zuckerman.

Lai also spent money on technology, especially computer systems that would allow him to track what was selling. He knew the importance of timely, accurate sales and production data. He introduced computerized point-of-sale systems. These instantly transmitted sales data to headquarters. This allowed Lai and his executives to better manage their stock. By the early 1990s, he boasted that it took only five days from the time his staff reordered a hot-selling polo shirt until it reached the shelves in a Giordano shop.

That speed upended an industry that had worked on the seventy-five-day cycles it took to get Comitex sweaters to JCPenney's warehouses. The faster pace allowed Lai to cut markups on goods, an idea he borrowed from British retailer Marks & Spencer. For any particular item, Lai budgeted slimmer profit margins, abandoning the industry norm of setting retail at four times the factory gate price. But by cutting the quantity of clothes that had to be sold at a discount, he kept profitability high.

Lai's success didn't rest only on flashes of stoned inspiration in a New York City pizza parlor or a sudden insight while eating at McDonald's with his children. He continued to read voraciously, relentlessly hunting for ideas. His reading focus switched from how to make a fortune in the stock market to how to build a great business. He subscribed to the *Harvard Business Review* and sent copies of articles that piqued his interest to senior managers. To stay on top of the fashion business, he read *Women's Wear Daily*, a trade newspaper. When Andrew Tanzer profiled Lai for *Forbes* in 1993, he noted how Lai "sprinkle[d] his conversations with quotes from famous U.S. retailers such as Sam Walton and talk[ed] enthusiastically about his reading [and] his study of economics."

Lai invited Tanzer and his wife, Kazuko Ouchi, to lunch at his house. He greeted them wearing denim overalls and cooked them a winter melon soup, remembers Tanzer, and talked about the cooking classes he was taking during this early 1990s period of semiretirement. (His cooking teacher was the renowned Chinese aesthete Wang Shixiang.) Tanzer notes the many books Lai had. "I visited many tycoons at their houses and you didn't see a single book," he says. "He spoke in long sentences, despite having little formal education. I was struck by how different he was from other Hong Kong and Chinese businessmen" who Tanzer noted tend to be "pragmatic, materialistic, and self-interested." Lai, says Tanzer, "has to be one of the most philosophical of all."

Lai inhaled new ideas as naturally as he breathed, determined to make up for the ground he'd lost by not even finishing primary school. He loved to share his favorites with others. Over the years, he gave away countless copies of Hayek's *The Road to Serfdom*. While running Next Digital two decades later, Lai bought fifty copies of a book on the Six Sigma manufacturing improvement process developed at General Electric and distributed them to staff. He also handed out copies of the business bestseller *In Search of Excellence*.

Tanzer noted that what set Lai apart from many tens of thousands of self-made Chinese businessmen was "the careful way he studied, then borrowed from, the formulas that had led others to success in retailing." As Lai told Tanzer, "I went out and picked the best in the market and stole what they had learned by trial and error." Although he hadn't wanted to share what he knew with JCPenney's Tom Higgins, he grew more generous as he became more successful. This was manifested in his mentorship of Tadashi Yanai. Information—sometimes to be kept secret, sometimes to be shared—constituted a currency and a form of power that continued to fascinate Lai.

Chapter Four

"LIKE MY MOTHER CALLING"

Giordano's retail revolution played out against a backdrop of momentous changes in China. In December 1978, paramount leader Deng Xiaoping cautiously initiated what would over the following twenty years become sweeping economic reforms. In 1980, a Special Economic Zone was established in Shenzhen, on China's border with Hong Kong, where the Kowloon–Canton Railway crossed the border.

The establishment of a free-market enclave next to Hong Kong electrified the colony. After three decades of inward-looking Maoist economic policies, a little corner of China next to Hong Kong would be safe for capitalism. The lure of the China market beckoned, just as it had done for centuries. More important for Hong Kong manufacturers like Lai was access to labor. Giordano and Comitex benefited from these reforms, which allowed Hong Kong manufacturers to take advantage of an almost limitless pool of low-cost workers right on the colony's border.

As China opened up in the 1980s under Deng Xiaoping, Lai grew increasingly optimistic about the country's prospects for economic reform. Comitex and Giordano started manufacturing in China. By 1997, they and other Hong Kong companies had created some five million manufacturing jobs in Guangdong province alone. Comitex partnered with a state-owned company, China Resources; the Beijing-owned company bought 30 percent of Comitex in 1987. "He was so pro-China," remembers Bob Aschkenasy of Lai's belief in Deng's 1980s economic reforms. When it came to China's economy, "he was like a Zionist."

While Deng opened the economy and ushered in three decades of supercharged growth, politics remained firmly under party control. When Margaret Thatcher met Deng Xiaoping in 1982, she openly expressed her doubts that China could run Hong Kong as well as the British did. She told Deng that he couldn't understand a city that ran on free-market principles and whose people prized their liberty. She offered to turn sovereignty over to the People's Republic but argued that administration should remain in British hands for a transitional period.

Deng would have none of it. Hocking into a spittoon, the diminutive political survivor told Thatcher that he thought China could run Hong Kong just fine, thank you. Even if it mismanaged the city, he continued, the political importance of recovering a Chinese territory that had been taken during the heyday of imperialism outweighed any damage that would follow the demise of an important trading and financial city. Thatcher didn't think Deng understood how a free society worked or why freedom mattered. She was right. But Deng didn't care.

Lai wasn't involved with politics in the 1980s, but he certainly didn't like the idea of handing Hong Kong over to mainland Chinese rule. His lack of political participation reflected the reality that Hong Kong people counted only as spectators in the negotiations that determined their fate. The British excluded Hong Kongers from the group of diplomats who conducted two years of tense negotiations with China. Deferring to the People's Republic, they ended by betraying their colonial subjects' desire for freedom.

These talks culminated in December 1984, when Thatcher flew to Beijing to sign the Sino-British Joint Declaration. This international treaty laid out the terms of Hong Kong's 1997 handover to China. In exchange for promising a peaceful transfer of Hong Kong rule from Britain to China in 1997, she negotiated a novel arrangement. Dubbed "one country, two systems,"

Beijing's formula promised that Hong Kong's freedoms and its free market would remain in place for fifty years after the Chinese takeover, until 2047. Thatcher went into her 1982 meeting with Deng determined somehow to hold on to Hong Kong, but Deng's forcefulness and her advisors' caution prompted her to quickly back down. She later wistfully wrote that she liked the idea of granting it independence. That was never a realistic option. Instead she settled for China's pledges that it would keep its hands off the territory.

A city made up of people who had fled communism now faced a deadline. In thirteen years, Beijing, with all its unpredictability, would rule their territory. As the clock ticked for Hong Kong's handover, Lai was among many who sought the safety of a foreign passport, obtaining British citizenship in 1992. Although Hong Kong was free—newspapers could publish what they liked and protesters could demonstrate in the streets—the colony was not democratic. Queen Elizabeth appointed the governor, who was always a white British man and who exercised broad powers.

Conservative colonial administrators, Chinese and British businessmen so conservative they would have felt at home in Victorian England, and a government in Beijing that wanted to forestall any sort of democracy all combined to stifle political reform. Only a tiny number of people could vote for the Legislative Council. Legco, as the city council was known, itself had limited power. It couldn't even propose spending money—the request had to come from the government.

Lai, meanwhile, faced trouble on the home front. In 1984, the family had moved to a villa on Tai Po Road in the hills above Kowloon. Although it was only a few miles to the northwest of where Lai had long lived, the spot was isolated. A chauffeured gold Rolls-Royce ferried him into town. Lai had a miniature zoo that included peacocks, a flying fox, deer, a monkey, and a pet bear who liked to drink cream soda. Once, Lai wrestled with the bear as it tried to escape, and got scratched up in the process. The zoo was "a crazy 1980s nouveau riche fantasy," Jade remembers. He invited friends over to take saunas and cold plunges and smoke weed as they looked across the majestic harbor toward the skyscrapers on Hong Kong Island.

None of this could hide the deterioration of his marriage. When the family took vacations, Lai had his own room where he holed up reading; Judy had a separate room with the children. Lai remained consumed by business, though he never talked about company affairs at home. Judy felt he rebuffed her attempts to talk about anything. In 1987, she left Lai after a tearful scene in which he knelt with the children, begging her to stay. The children remained with their father.

Lai had long sought his mother's praise, with no result. When he went with the three children to Guangzhou to tell his mother that he was getting a divorce, she proved surprisingly understanding. "Son, you're a good person. Don't be afraid, believe in yourself, and this will pass."

Jade remembers that he was "always involved" as a father. Lai and Tim, Jade, and Ian had dinner every night together. They swam at the Hong Kong Jockey Club, which Lai had joined in the early 1980s, and often went hiking in Hong Kong's rugged countryside. They went out on the junk a lot. Jade recalls that on one occasion her brother Ian fell overboard; Lai instantly dove in to rescue him. "We spent a lot of time together," says Jade. "He was really cool, really fun to be around." Lai's friends and colleagues repeatedly say what fun he was; the seriousness of his commitment to fight the Communist Party shouldn't obscure his characteristic joy and ebullience. Even in difficult situations, Lai almost always manages to find a reason to be upbeat.

Hong Kong's worst fears were realized in 1989. In April, former Chinese leader Hu Yaobang died. By communist standards, Hu counted as a reformer; Deng had ousted him as general secretary of the Chinese Communist Party two years earlier for being too liberal. Large crowds of mourners in Beijing's Tiananmen Square commemorating Hu's death morphed into a prolonged demonstration by hundreds of thousands of people, who demanded more democracy and an end to corruption. The protests spread throughout the nation. Protesters disrupted the May visit of Mikhail Gorbachev, the first Soviet leader to visit the Chinese capital in thirty years.

The prolonged occupation of Beijing's Tiananmen Square—and similar protests in scores of cities throughout the country—sparked hope for reform in China. Hong Kongers sent supplies and money to Beijing to support the pro-democracy protesters. With China set to take control of Hong Kong just eight years later, Hong Kongers knew that the colony's fate depended on what happened in China. "Today's China is tomorrow's Hong Kong," read a banner hanging from the mainland-owned Bank of China in Central. The slogan summarized the worries of a city where almost every family had someone—a father, a mother, an aunt, or an uncle—who had fled from communist rule on the mainland.

The students protesting in Tiananmen Square inspired Lai. In his early years, he had not enjoyed the luxury of engaging in politics. Politics in China had shattered his family and destroyed his childhood. Lai felt something between embarrassment and shame when he thought of his homeland. He had turned his back on China in the 1960s and 1970s as he worked to get ahead in Hong Kong.

Hong Kong people rallied in support of Beijing's protesters. In 1988, a crowd of a few thousand people was considered a large pro-democracy rally. In May 1989, a million people marched to government headquarters on Hong Kong Island; pro-communist groups walked alongside pro-democracy ones. The colony witnessed a spring of unprecedented democratic ferment.

Lai looked for a way to demonstrate his sympathy. He boosted Giordano's edgy reputation and the pro-democracy movement's coffers by raising $122,000 from the sale of more than 23,000 T-shirts. One Giordano shirt featured a large exclamation point, with "How are you?" written underneath. Below that, in small letters the shirt admonished the old men in Beijing's Zhongnanhai leadership compound: "Please step down!" Lai added another $64,000 from his own pocket and gave it to the Hong Kong Alliance in Support of the Patriotic Democratic

Movement in China. Besides cash, he also sent scores of tents to protesters in Tiananmen Square.

His boldness prompted Odette Heung, a young aide to Martin Lee, to reach out to Lai. Lee had graduated from the elite Wah Yan College, a prominent Jesuit high school in Hong Kong, before studying law at the University of Hong Kong and training as a barrister in London. His father, Lee Yin-wo, was a former KMT general who also enjoyed close ties to the Chinese Communist Party, notably Mao-era premier Zhou Enlai.

Martin Lee headed the Hong Kong Bar Association in the early 1980s. In the late 1980s he sat on the Basic Law Drafting Committee, which was tasked with writing the mini-constitution that would underpin Hong Kong's "one country, two systems" governance after the 1997 handover. Beijing kicked him off the body in 1989 for supporting the Tiananmen students. In 1989 Lee was an aspiring politician but he would soon emerge internationally as the face of Hong Kong democracy.

"We didn't know [Lai] at all—he was a businessman and he wasn't well-known in the political world," recalls Heung of Lai. She remembers thinking, "'Oh, this guy, he has such courage.' A lot of people would condemn the harsh measures against the students but no businessman was doing anything like Jimmy." She cold-called Lai's office and the three of them met at a Beijing restaurant inside the newly opened Pacific Place mall in Admiralty.

"When Jimmy showed up I didn't know he would be so young," recalls Heung. Casually dressed, his Giordano polo shirt contrasting with the barrister's suit, "he was very down-to-earth." Over lunch, Lai wanted to know what he could do to help. "He was very happy to meet Martin," she remembers. "He said, 'I am totally in support of the democratic movement.'" Lee mentioned that his bare-bones operation didn't even have a fax machine. "The next day he sent over a fax machine." Heung remembers Lai as very low-key. "He didn't socialize with people. He would not usually come out to dinner. He was not making the social circles. He was a very private man and a family man—more concerned about raising his children and [running] his business."

Lai emblazoned a second batch of twenty thousand shirts with pictures of student activists. He wanted to give faces to the names, to humanize the struggle for democracy. Lai chose three of the most prominent students—Wang Dan, Wu'er Kaixi, and Chai Ling. The successful T-shirt campaigns drew on Lai's visual sense and his merchandising expertise. He knew how to sell shirts. Now he would sell ideas. "It was very exciting," said Lai of his first foray into politics. "I wanted to get involved. I gave money. I gave T-shirts. I had banners in my shops."

Lai reflected mainstream Hong Kong opinion in his support of the Tiananmen Square protesters. He was older, richer—he was, after all, a businessman—and more of an establishment figure than the protesters in Tiananmen Square. But most Hong Kongers shared his views during 1989. What took place that spring was a spontaneous, organic grassroots uprising by the Hong Kong community. "There must always be someone to take the lead in any campaign," he said at the time. "I guess I felt the same as many others, but I've got the channels to express it."

In Beijing, authorities imposed martial law on May 20. On June 4, Deng struck back, presiding over a massacre that killed hundreds of people, at least, in and around Tiananmen Square. For Lai, as for so many Chinese of his generation, 1989's push for democracy and the Tiananmen Square massacre marked a turning point in his life. Initially, he appeared chastened, telling an interviewer the following month that "[w]e would have been more cautious if we had thought it through. The move was impulsive."

The cause had touched his emotional core. "When I first noticed what happened in Tiananmen, I was very moved," remembered Lai in an interview with Father Robert Sirico, who produced a documentary movie, *The Hong Konger*, about Lai. His optimism about China's economic reforms notwithstanding, "I was always trying to run away from China since the time I escaped. Anything China represented, I wanted to forget. I wanted to keep a long distance, at least emotionally." Lai recounted how "the more I learned about the free world outside, the more I learned about how wonderful freedom is," the more "ridiculous" and "disgusting" communism appeared. "I didn't feel anything about China until Tiananmen Square happened. Suddenly it was like my mother was calling me in the darkness of the night and my heart opened up."

His mother calling in the darkness, his heart opening. Something changed inside Lai during those fateful, emotionally charged months in the spring of 1989. The route China charted after the killings would disappoint the hopes of many, both in Hong Kong and in China itself. Lai's own path would, from then on, be one that publicly and defiantly put him in opposition to the Chinese Communist Party.

Before Tiananmen, Lai had been looking for his next start-up. He had spent a decade building Giordano and he was getting ready to list it on the Hong Kong stock exchange. Money didn't especially motivate him after he'd made his first fortune at Comitex; he loved creating businesses, seeing an idea become a profitable reality. "An entrepreneur is more motivated by the challenge, the creation, by doing something that has never been done, that is new, fresh," he told Sirico.

What could be fresher than fresh food? From Lai's first morning's breakfast in Hong Kong as a twelve-year-old immigrant, the smells and flavors of Hong Kong's fragrant dumplings, steamy congee, and hearty soups had meant more than just a way to fill his stomach. Hong Kong's food symbolized hope and freedom. Now, he saw it could mean business. He ranked most fast-food restaurants in Hong Kong as low-quality. A market opportunity beckoned.

Lai envisioned bringing the same sort of consumer choice to Chinese fast food that Giordano had brought to casual clothes. He would offer fresh ingredients instead of fresh clothing styles. Patrons could customize their meal, much as they could choose among many distinct colors at Giordano. But there would be a limited number of ingredients, just as in reality there were only fifty different items at Giordano. Like the clothing shops, friendly staff at Lai's planned restaurants would provide top-notch service. Lai imagined something like a Chinese version of what the Chipotle chain pioneered a few years later in the United States.

But the Tiananmen massacre changed everything for him, as for so many people in Hong Kong and in China. Lai had been pulled into politics.

Right after the massacre, Lai read about Perry Link, a Princeton University professor who managed the Beijing-based National Academy of Sciences' scholarly exchange program. A prominent scholar, he had been an interpreter for the pathbreaking 1972 trip to the United States by a mainland Chinese Ping-Pong team and had a deep knowledge of China. After the Tiananmen killings, Link helped renowned Chinese astrophysicist Fang Lizhi find refuge in the U.S. embassy in Beijing. Fang had long been a powerful voice for democracy as well as one of the country's most prominent scientists. Link negotiated with U.S. officials, who initially turned Fang away from the embassy. U.S. diplomats reconsidered after receiving instructions from Washington. In the predawn hours of June 5, they found Fang hidden in a hotel and spirited him into the embassy. Fang's stay inside the Beijing embassy, which would last more than thirteen months, worsened already tense Sino-U.S. relations in the wake of the Tiananmen killings.

The National Academy of Sciences told Link to shutter the Beijing operation. Lai read about the risks Link had taken in the operation to rescue Fang and his wife. He thought that the academic was someone he needed to meet. Lai contacted Link through a professor at Princeton that he knew. When Link arrived in Hong Kong five days after the killings, Lai welcomed the professor and his family. A chauffeured car took the group to an amusement park. Lai hosted them at restaurants. He arranged a dinner with Martin Lee. "A man I didn't know at all was generous and solicitous," Link remembers admiringly more than three decades later.

Rich and powerful people don't generally reach out to professors or activists. Lai reached out not only to Link but to prominent Chinese dissidents. These included Wei Jingsheng, an early democracy leader who found refuge in the United States after serving eighteen years in prison, and Tiananmen student leader Wang Dan. "In both cases it was Jimmy who took the initiative," Link says. Wang remembers Lai meeting him for breakfast in Detroit shortly after he had been taken directly from prison in China in April 1998 and put on a plane to the Midwestern American city. Lai encouraged him in his political work, gave him an envelope with cash—and a copy of Hayek's *The Road to Serfdom*. "He told me I had to read it," remembers Wang, who developed a friendship with Lai.

Lai scrapped his plans for a fast-food chain. Passionate, but at the same time driven by a firm sense of the business opportunity, Lai instead embraced the media business. He believed that China would have to get back on the road to reform. He felt certain that economic liberty would pave the way for political freedom. Lai also saw that information was changing. It moved faster, and there was lots more of it than when he sold to JCPenney and Kmart.

With nine-year-old CNN broadcasting from Tiananmen Square during the 1989 democracy movement, allowing a global audience for the first time to watch events unfold as they happened, Lai saw that the world had entered a new age of transparency. He could use technology to champion freedom for Hong Kong and for China. He wanted to use mass media to spread the ideas of democracy and free markets. With his typical confidence, Lai told colleagues that he had read enough publications—*Forbes*, *Time*, the *Economist*—to know how to operate a media business.

Emotionally charged though the decision to invest in media was, it's worth highlighting that Lai always saw media as a business. Fittingly, he hung a Chinese calligraphic scroll bearing the characters *fanmai ziyou* ("selling freedom") in his office. He was a full-fledged entrepreneur, not a political activist. He wooed one potential hire for *Next* with visions of riches. "We are going to get this thing going and then we are going to sell it," Lai pitched the potential staffer. "Who the hell wants to run a magazine? It's too much trouble," Lai concluded.

Giordano had proved Lai's skill at a retail business. Media, too, was a consumer business, perhaps the ultimate consumer business. Newspapers needed to serve something new every day. If it didn't sell, the product was spoiled. Fresh news had a shelf life shorter than fast fashion.

Media attracted Lai because it embodied freedom—specifically, the free flow of information. The idea of information, of knowledge, increasingly fascinated Lai. He'd used information that he'd gleaned in the aisles of New York department stores to propel Comitex to the top ranks of Asian garment manufacturers. He used information garnered from focus groups to make Giordano a success. And now he would use the democratizing power of information to make his media ventures both popular and profitable.

Chapter Five

"TURTLE EGG"

On March 15, 1990, Lai launched *Next*, a weekly magazine advocating for free markets and democracy alongside gossip and business news. It was a fast-fashion approach to news that gave consumers what they wanted. People wanted democracy, Lai knew, but other publishers were afraid to support it for fear of provoking the Chinese rulers who would soon be controlling Hong Kong.

Lai's thinking had matured. He had always hated the Chinese Communist Party. But his had been a raw, unthinking loathing triggered by seeing his mother insulted and humiliated and by his experiences as a boy forced by the police to pen propaganda leaflets. He had a wider perspective after reading Hayek, Popper, and other such thinkers. He now understood that economic and political freedom were intertwined. Rule of law guaranteed property rights and underpinned economic growth. Democracy ensured that bad leaders could be thrown out, making it less likely another leader like Mao could rise to power.

China's 1989 spring of democracy jolted Lai. Until then, he'd been a typical *garmento*, a politically disengaged rag-trade factory owner with his pet bear and his chauffeured Rolls-Royce. He shifted from aversion and avoidance to action. "I was involved in it. I was very moved by those kids who fought for freedom for China," he reflected in 2006. "I was very excited. I asked myself if I made enough money, if I just go on making money, it doesn't mean anything to me, but if I go into the media business then I deliver information which is choice and choice is freedom. I will be in the business making money and also bringing freedom. This is wonderful."

Lai named the magazine *Next* "because I kind of think that the other business was my past life and I want my next life, my next business," to be embodied in the magazine. Lai envisioned *Next* as a new sort of periodical. Most Hong Kong magazines focused narrowly on politics or business or entertainment and had circulations of just 10,000 to 20,000 copies in a city of six million people.

Lai's idea was to combine everything in one. Paparazzi stalked starlets to ensure the magazine would excel in its entertainment coverage. Barely clothed actresses shared the pages with free-market economists. Lai paid lavishly for well-known columnists. The magazine offered in-depth business and markets coverage and employed the most aggressive team of investigative reporters the colony had ever seen. Sex scandals, political scandals, money scandals, *Next* broke every kind of story. It was a guilty pleasure that the elite loved to hate—but found themselves reading.

Lai again showed his marketing savvy, shortly after the first issue on March 15, 1990. To pump up all-important newsstand sales, Lai pioneered the concept of two separate magazines sold together under one name. Beginning with the thirty-eighth issue, at the end of 1990, *Next* split into two volumes. Like most magazines, it was stapled, so there was a natural opening at the exact center of the magazine. That allowed one magazine to nest inside the other, almost as if they were two identically sized Russian dolls. Lai wanted to provide two magazines so that a couple enjoying Sunday dim sum would each have something to read—the "A" magazine featured political and business stories; the "B" contained entertainment and lifestyle features. Two magazines for the price of one gave consumers value for money.

Two covers meant twice the chance of a sale. This seems to have been a first in the global magazine industry. No one had tried to sell a political-economic magazine tucked inside a flashy entertainment one in working-class areas; in the Central business district, the entertainment section would nest inside the business-political issue that featured a cover shot of a business or political bigwig—usually someone in trouble. Some newsstands displayed both covers, giving *Next* double the retail shelf space that a single magazine would enjoy.

Lai set up *Next* using borrowed office space in a building called West-lands Centre, on the site of the old Taikoo Sugar Factory on Hong Kong Island. Lai's businesses had always been across the harbor in Kowloon, but the publisher Albert Cheng had some room to accommodate the first *Next* magazine employees. Cheng, nicknamed *taipan* ("big boss"), was a flamboyant media personality who owned the monthly magazine *Capital*. Lai told everyone that Cheng was his teacher. Lai proved an exceptionally gifted student. *Next* expanded quickly and was soon leasing a half floor in the Westlands Centre. Then it leased a full floor. By early 1994, the young magazine had run out of space and *Next* departed Hong Kong Island for the Garment Centre on Castle Peak Road in Kowloon's Cheung Sha Wan factory district.

The Tiananmen killings notwithstanding, Hong Kong's financial markets had begun a lengthy period of growth in which the city would emerge as Asia's most important global finance center. The American business magazine *Fortune* was said at the time to be in talks to buy *Capital* for almost $13 million. In the early days, at least, Lai wanted to make money even as he worked to change China. "Come work for me and we will sell this and be rich," an early hire remembers Lai telling him over lunch at a Cantonese restaurant in Central's upscale new Exchange Square. "That was the story he tried to sell me." Lai put $6 million of his own money into the venture.

He hired the best writers, the best cartoonists, the best designers that money could buy. He ran edgy cartoons, bold headlines, and provocative editorials. Once he got into a circulation battle with a rival magazine, *East Week*. Senior staff ran some models estimating how much the price war would cost if it lasted three months or six months. Lai wasn't interested in this sort of detailed financial modeling. "He just told me, 'No, this is not how you do business,'" remembers the early hire. Lai relied on his gut and his knowledge rather than spreadsheets. He sometimes seemed to spend as if he had limitless resources. That wasn't the case. He cared about profits but was willing to lose money while he got the product right. His advice: "Don't think about costs. Think about the product. Keep trying, keep experimenting. The money will come in."

The magazine struggled to find readers at first. Lai pared back the press run from its initial 75,000, bottoming at just 30,000. Then the circulation climbed as the magazine found an audience for its eclectic mix of Hong Kong celebrities, crime, politics, company coverage, market commentary, and investigative pieces. By 1994, it was selling 180,000 copies a week with more than nine hundred pages of advertising in a single issue. *Next*'s secret proved to be a relentless emphasis on Hong Kong. In the early years, the magazine focused on rich businessmen and the secrets to their success. Coverage of "Superman" Li Ka-shing, the homegrown entrepreneur with modest beginnings who ended with multibillion-dollar holdings in telecoms, infrastructure, retail, and property, guaranteed big sales.

Ip Yut-kin, who joined *Next* after a career at rival *Oriental Daily News*, got credit for developing the magazine's signature—and aggressive—paparazzi coverage. Ip turbocharged existing practices by hiring even more photographers and making sure they had cars and drivers to get to the scene of the scandal or the crime more quickly.

"My sister and I would fight over who got to read it first," remembers Victoria Tin-bor Hui, who graduated from university the year that *Next* was founded. "Just when Beijing was getting very successful" with shutting down critics, "Jimmy comes along." The magazine had the resources to do serious investigative journalism of a sort that Hong Kong had never seen. "All of a sudden you open your eyes to the secrets of the rich and famous and the powerful," says Hui, who is now a political science professor at Notre Dame. "Those stories were the number one draw."

Next's fearlessness in taking on the city's triads, its notorious organized crime gangs, won it more readers. Photographs documented gang members' birthday parties, organized prostitution, and shooting galleries. The magazine exposed how gangsters controlled the city's fleet of minibuses. Reporters secretly recorded conversations detailing exactly how the system worked—who paid what to whom. *Next* editors found that when they played a triad story straight—no comment, just the facts—they generally remained safe from reprisals. That wasn't always the case, though.

Mobsters broke into *Next*'s Quarry Bay office one morning and smashed up computer equipment. "The damage wasn't too bad," remembers one of the handful of staffers who were there, "but it was sensational. It was the first time a media office had been ransacked." Although there was video footage, the attack in broad daylight remained unsolved.

Next later broke the story of a mysterious disease plaguing Guangdong province, just over the border from Hong Kong. Stores had sold out of vinegar. *Next* ran pictures of factories boiling vinegar, which was thought to kill the vaporous germs. Guangdong authorities told their Hong Kong government counterparts that nothing was amiss, and the territory's leaders accepted the denial. Only when the mysterious disease spread to Hong Kong was it identified. This was SARS. In 2003, as in 2019 with Covid, China's cover-up cost lives. *Next* helped expose the cover-up and in doing so likely checked the disease's further spread. Lai's belief in the free flow of information proved prescient. Media freedom was not a luxury. It didn't just make markets more efficient. The free flow of information could save lives.

Next's libertarian philosophy helped shape Hong Kong governance. It curbed efforts by the last British governor, Chris Patten, to introduce what Lai and the magazine's editors regarded as an overly statist pension program in a city that had prided itself on its small government. After 1997, *Next*'s crusade for the elimination of both the inheritance tax and wine duty bore fruit, as did a successful campaign to block the imposition of a sales tax. The tax cuts helped cement Hong Kong's ranking as the world's freest economy, an accolade it enjoyed for decades.

Media brought the power to shape ideas but it also represented yet another consumer business for Lai. He moved Professor Leung Kwok and the team that had run focus groups for Giordano to *Next* to provide quick, candid feedback. *Next* paid sixty-four dollars to each of the half-dozen or so participants who gathered in the company's office on Thursday evenings, the day after the magazine hit the streets, to say what they liked and what they didn't. Staff watched from behind one-way mirrors. Lai worked on speed of delivery and good customer service. He focused on mistakes, on failure. "Mistakes are only steps in going forward," he later said. "When you can't make mistakes, it's perfect because you are dead. As long as you are still working, mistakes are inevitable. I believe that in every mistake there is a message. We try to correct it through trial and error."

Few people subscribed to publications in Hong Kong. Most simply bought each issue from a newsstand. Some of the handful of *Next* subscribers complained that an issue available on newsstands on Wednesday didn't get delivered to their home by the post office until Friday. So Lai hired pizza deliverymen on motor scooters to deliver the magazine more quickly.

A quiet young student named Teresa Li had spent the summer of 1989 working as an intern at the colony's leading English-language newspaper, the *South China Morning Post*. A few weeks after the Tiananmen killings, an editor dispatched the twenty-four-year-old Li to profile the brash clothing magnate who had made T-shirts to support the Tiananmen students. Lai's personal life had been unsettled since Judy had left him two years earlier. He found himself smitten by this young reporter sixteen years his junior. As soon as Teresa left, Lai told his assistant that he had a crush on the intern. He pursued her with characteristic intensity.

In Teresa he found a woman who came from a world quite different from his. Li, part of a close-knit Catholic family originally from the northern province of Shandong, had five sisters and a brother. A polyglot, she was as at ease in French and Italian as in Mandarin and English. Lai was brash and boisterous, as quick to weep as to shout. Teresa was controlled and poised, centered above all by her Catholic faith.

Enchanted, Lai followed her to Paris when she returned to school that autumn. Lai describes that time in Paris as a crazy collage of cultural mis-understandings. Asians were uncommon, especially in the luxury Hôtel Plaza Athénée, where he had a suite. Once a man asked him to carry his luggage. The ever-helpful Lai grinned and shrugged, then obliged, and pocketed the proffered tip. The guest was Woody Allen.

Another time, a hotel chauffeur refused Lai's offer of a tip. Asked why, the driver responded: "I heard that you are a big boss of the Japanese Yamaguchi-gumi [gangsters], so I don't dare." Lai found humor in the incident: "A Japanese guy with a shaved head has money to live in a suite? Isn't he a gangster?" Fueling the cultural stereotype, Japanese gangsters often cut off their fingertips as a sign of fealty; Lai had lost the top of his right ring finger in the glove-making factory.

He went back to Paris to continue his courtship of Teresa just six months after launching *Next*, in October 1990. He later wrote a love song to Paris in one of his weekly columns, alluding to his successful wooing of Teresa: "Paris, you are unusually sensual, you have made a reserved girl fall in love." Lai married Teresa in a civil ceremony on July 19, 1991, two years after they met. They had a church ceremony in Paris the following year.

On leaving Hong Kong for Paris in autumn 1990, Lai told his staff at *Next*, "Don't worry. This thing is going to make a hell of a lot of money." Although Lai never had any concern about funding or costs, the magazine's suppliers didn't have the same confidence. Bosses of failing Hong Kong businesses often slipped out of the colony, leaving creditors empty-handed.

The day after Lai left, the company's auditor came to the office. Was this business viable, the worried number-cruncher asked? In technical terms, the auditor wanted to know if *Next* was a "going concern," or was it in danger of going out of business in the next twelve months. Shortly after that, the printer showed up. He had just given the company longer to settle its bills, figuring that it was becoming more established, but with Lai gone he worried that he wouldn't get paid. After discussion, the printer agreed to keep the more generous payment terms in place. Meanwhile, the magazine's weekly sales climbed from the trough of fewer than 30,000 to peak at over 200,000 copies a week in the mid-1990s. Lai's confidence proved justified.

Lai didn't simply own *Next* magazine. He wrote for it—a weekly column starting with the first issue in March 1990. The columns displayed his bold, sometimes crude style. Over the next three decades, he wrote some 1,600 columns on everything from politics to his entrepreneurial past to his childhood to food. In the early days, these columns were handwritten. Later they were written on his mobile phone as a text message, often composed when he was alone on his boat.

A column he wrote in July 1994 marked a milestone in his emergence as a critic of the Chinese Communist Party. That month Premier Li Peng made a state visit to Germany as part of a lengthy European tour, the first by a Chinese state leader to Western democracies since the Tiananmen killings five years earlier. Lai and many others saw Li as Deng Xiaoping's chief hatchet man in carrying out the Tiananmen massacre, earning the premier infamy as "the butcher of Beijing."

During Li Peng's 1994 visit, Lai also happened to be in Europe. He was visiting Paris with Teresa, who was six months pregnant with their first child. Thinking about their child's future in a city that would soon be controlled by the Chinese Communist Party prompted Lai to write a column that put him on a collision course with Beijing.

In it, he derided the Chinese premier as "a national humiliation." He criticized the barbarism, corruption, and decay of the Chinese Communist Party and pointed out that the party used people merely as tools, means to an end, rather seeing the worth and dignity of each individual. Lai touched on the themes of information and democracy, telling Li that his "slave-master's face is a laughingstock in today's information-informed egalitarian world." He closed his column with an emphatic throwdown to the premier: "I want to tell you that not only are you a bastard, you are also a bastard with zero IQ." Literally, he called the premier a *gui dan*, or turtle egg, an everyday curse implying that the object of the curse, like a turtle, doesn't know who his parents are.

The column "came completely out of the blue," remembers an editor who handled the piece after Lai faxed his handwritten text from Paris. "We didn't cover mainland politics. From day one our focus was always on Hong Kong. Who gives a hoot about what's going on in China?" Still, the editor didn't give the column much thought. Hong Kong remained a British colony and China had promised that existing freedoms would remain unhindered. "We believed in the promise of 'one country, two systems,' the rule of law, and freedom of speech. It was one column, not even seven hundred characters. Anyhow, who is Jimmy Lai? People wrote much worse things about Li Peng in Hong Kong newspapers every day."

Who is Jimmy Lai? To the Chinese Communist Party, he represented an unusual threat. He was a multimillionaire businessman, a textile magnate turned retailer, and now a successful magazine owner. He had announced plans to start a newspaper. He had three assets that the party feared—money, independence, and influence. From Beijing's standpoint, he needed to be stopped. The party reached into its time-tested playbook and struck back by attacking Giordano. The retailer had opened its first stores in China two years earlier, following its listing on the Stock Exchange of Hong Kong. In August, Chinese authorities went after Lai in the state-owned media and started harassing Giordano's Beijing outlet, abruptly shutting off the electricity, investigating the company for a purported "licensing problem," and shutting its store.

Lai doubled down. In September he wrote another column, defending the first one. While apologizing for his vulgarity, Lai elaborated on why he opposed the Communist Party. He reiterated the importance of the free flow of information and his belief that the Communist Party would wither in the face of more democratic information. These two pieces in *Next* articulate his core beliefs in freedom and transparency as well as his optimism that justice would prevail. They also hardened the Chinese Communist Party's determination to silence him. They set Lai on a course that would define the rest of his life.

Yes, I am anti-communist. I am completely opposed to the Communist Party because I hate all things that restrict personal freedom. The basis of communist ideology is the absolute restraint of individual freedom.

Today, the Communist Party has no place to stand. The transparency of information makes people's consciousness more and more independent. . . . People yearn for more freedom of choice and less constraint. In this new state of consciousness, where will communism still have room to survive? . . . The Communist Party is hopeless, but China today is full of hope. . . .

I have full confidence in China. I [have] decided to stay after 1997 because I am really reluctant to part with Hong Kong, and I believe that my anti-communist awareness would not cause me any inconvenience. I truly believe that the Communist Party today is almost dead, [alive] in name only, and once Deng Xiaoping is gone, it will be even less important. . . . I am anti-communist not because of hatred, but because of knowledge, conscience and conviction. I have no vanity to be a hero, a savior, or a martyr. I want nothing more than to be an honest intellectual.

The more open and prosperous China's economy is, the deeper the people's understanding of the world, and the greater the demand for freedom of personal choice. The Communist Party, as the dominant force in China's political consciousness, will gradually become corrupted and decline.

It was also because of June Fourth [the date of the Tiananmen Massacre] that the Communist Party lost its prestige and revealed its ugliness, which accelerated its corruption and decline, and further guaranteed China's opening up. Today, the Chinese government relies on opening up the economy and improving people's lives in order to maintain power. . . . What is there to be afraid of?

China's economic achievements today are due to the fact that the Chinese Communist Party has become more and more pragmatic. It is an indisputable fact that the more open the Chinese economy is and the more civilized the government is, the less terrifying the Communist Party will be.

I am anti-communist, because totalitarianism disgusts me, and I love freedom too much.

Lai finished with a defense of his original column and a credo: "I will fight for freedom, I will not give up anticommunism, I will never give up my dignity as a human being, never will."

Chapter Six

THE BULLDOZER

Jimmy Lai's next move was to double down on media by starting a newspaper. It was just two years before Hong Kong would be handed over to China. Was he brave—or crazy? *Apple Daily* quickly became one of the best-read and most profitable newspapers in a market crowded with competing titles even as it attracted government attention that spelled trouble for Lai.

The Chinese government harassed Giordano stores in the mainland after Lai's column attacking Li Peng, figuring that Lai would back down. This sort of economic pressure reflected a common strategy of communist control. Virtually without exception, businessmen put profit ahead of principle when faced with such threats. But Lai didn't give way by shutting *Next* or softening its coverage. Instead he resigned as Giordano chairman in August 1994, the month after the column ran; in 1996, he sold his 27 percent stake in Giordano for $185 million, helping defray costs associated with *Apple Daily*'s launch.

Next, launched nine months after the 1989 Tiananmen killings, was both popular and profitable. But it only came out once a week. A daily newspaper would give Lai and his staff an opportunity to push an anti-corruption, freedom, and democracy agenda every day of the week. Lai knew that the newspaper represented a solid business idea. Although his media ventures became a crusade, his investment in *Next* had started as a business decision.

Hong Kong had one of the world's most competitive newspaper markets, with more than half a dozen major Chinese-language newspapers and three English-language dailies. Media in the mainland was controlled by the Communist Party. In Hong Kong it was a free-for-all. But other newspapers were increasingly afraid to take on China. Even those media owners who had supported the 1989 Tiananmen pro-democracy protests and mourned the crackdown on China's political reform movement had dialed back their support of democracy as the 1997 takeover of Hong Kong loomed.

Hong Kongers overwhelmingly supported more democracy. In 1991, in the first-ever popular elections for seats on Legco, about six of ten Hong Kongers voted for pro-democracy candidates. Lai knew, therefore, that the paper could count on a ready market. Governor Chris Patten was pushing for sweeping democratic reforms. Not only would there be lots of news, but also a chance for the paper to play an important role in Hong Kong's democratic struggle.

Lai dubbed his newspaper *Apple Daily*, thinking of the Garden of Eden. "Eve ate the apple," the fruit of knowledge. "Without the apple there would be no news." "One night after prayer," he told Father Robert Sirico, "the idea came to me to call it 'Apple' because I thought if Eve did not bite the apple we would still be in heaven, there's no need for a newspaper." Lai did not meet Steve Jobs and never admitted that his publication's names had anything to do with a then-struggling California-based computer company with the same name; if so, it is a remarkable coincidence that Apple founder Steve Jobs had also started a company called NeXT in 1985.

The paper hit the market on June 20, 1995, just two years and ten days before Britain would be handing colonial Hong Kong back to China. The entrepreneurial Lai used familiar techniques from his time at Giordano— low prices, savvy marketing, bold graphics, and feedback in the form of consumer focus groups—to give readers what they craved.

He'd hired pizza delivery people on motor scooters to speed distribution of *Next*. At *Apple Daily* he quickened the tempo by putting many of his reporters and photographers on scooters. At one point, *Apple* had thirty cars and fifteen motorcycles for reporters and photographers. Ip Yut-kin moved over from *Next* and ramped up the paparazzi culture at *Apple Daily*. When a woman who had arrived from one of the territory's outlying islands went into labor on the ferry pier in Hong Kong's Central district, an *Apple* photographer arrived at the scene before the ambulance. Another time, as police pursued two armed robbers, an *Apple Daily* photographer joined the chase, snapping frames as the drama unfolded.

Flush with cash from selling his stake in Giordano, Lai invested $90 million of his own money in the start-up to make sure the venture had the resources to succeed. From the start, he printed the entire newspaper in color, paying top-dollar to print on high-quality paper. Print media was still in black and white. The *New York Times* didn't print its first color illustration until 1993 and didn't feature color on the front page until 1997. High-quality color printing on every page in a newspaper meant that *Apple Daily* could command a premium from advertisers. The newspaper's use of more expensive paper and top-of-the-line printing presses echoes Lai's use of costlier yarn for the original JCPenney order two decades earlier.

The premium color printing attracted luxury goods advertisers, a coup for a high-circulation newspaper. *Apple Daily*'s success sparked a price war that saw market leader *Oriental Daily News* drop its price to just 25 cents per copy from 65 cents. Competitors that could afford to make investments in new presses went all-color. Others dropped out. *Express News* and pro-Taiwan *United Daily News* folded at the end of 1995.

Jimmy Lai was a hands-on publisher. In addition to writing columns, he served as *Apple*'s chief spokesman and marketer. He posed for countless pictures featuring apples to promote the newspaper's launch. A memorable television advertisement showed masked archers ringing Lai and riddling his body with arrows before successfully skewering an apple on his head, William Tell–style. (Or perhaps, given the birth of his son Sebastien a few months earlier, he had the martyrdom of St. Sebastian in mind.) Lai then nonchalantly took the apple and ate it. "That ad defined Hong Kong in the 1990s," remembered Dennis Kwok, a lawyer who later became a Legco member. "The ad, the newspaper, Jimmy Lai—they were game changers."

Richard Lam, a popular Cantopop lyricist and a columnist for the magazine, helped develop the marketing strategy. One of its slogans was "An *Apple* a day keeps the liars away." Lai's close friendship with Lam—and his professional reliance on him—highlighted his ability to tap people outside of his circle for help. Lam helped Lai connect with mainstream new-generation Cantonese culture at a time of change in Hong Kong. Lam's sister Eunice was a prolific book and newspaper writer who lived for many years with another well-known Cantopop lyricist, Wong Jim, the lyricist for the *Below the Lion Rock* theme song. Lai had the big ideas. Lam made up part of the creative ecosystem that made Lai's media ventures work.

"We are making a newspaper for Hong Kongers. As long as readers choose us, support our reports, and agree with our stance, we will certainly be able to stand tall no matter how strong the pressure," vowed the inaugural editorial. The newspaper sold 200,000 copies on its first day and quickly became the number two newspaper, trailing only the mass-market *Oriental Daily News*. Lai later reflected on the public enthusiasm for *Apple Daily*.

> It was two years before the Chinese takeover of Hong Kong. Most of the media was so scared of the way communists control media. They all went into self-censorship. . . . All of a sudden somebody came up who didn't care about the communist takeover and was not afraid of it. People find some strength there. Seems like some crazy guy but the crazy guy gives them something to lean on.

It wasn't as easy as he made it sound. *Next* magazine's aggressive approach and the mainland attacks on Giordano after the Li Peng column had already made Lai radioactive. Other businessmen didn't want to be seen helping him. *Apple Daily* initially subcontracted printing to the Premier Printing Group, which already printed a giveaway paper distributed in subway stations. But its quick success meant Lai needed a printer who could easily accommodate the newspaper's growing print run. His team reached out to the *South China Morning Post*.

The Malaysian-born commodities king and hotelier Robert Kuok had just bought the paper from Rupert Murdoch, and it had a plant in the New Territories town of Tai Po. "The *SCMP*'s business manager was a low-key British guy," remembers the *Next* editor, who approached the *Post* about a printing deal. "We met at the Jockey Club. The Brit was noncommittal. *SCMP* had just built a new printing plant in Tai Po, clearly with excessive capacity. But given Kuok's Beijing ties, there ain't no way he was going to do us any favors." Lai had to stick with Premier Printing until *Apple* built its own printing plant several years later at its new headquarters.

Oriental Daily News, the largest-circulation paper, also felt the competitive pressure from the price war and *Apple Daily*'s aggressive coverage. *Oriental* was pro-Beijing and unabashedly mass market and its circulation had dwarfed all rivals until *Apple* launched. The newspaper had been founded in 1969 by brothers Ma Sik-yu and Ma Sik-chun; both men fled to Taiwan in the 1970s following charges that they had smuggled a staggering seven hundred tons of opium into Hong Kong from Burma's Golden Triangle. As competition with *Apple* heated up, *Oriental Daily News* tried to force vendors to take more newspapers than they could sell, with no refunds. A female newsstand agent who refused to accept the allocation was hacked to death with a meat cleaver.

Apple Daily innovated by creating Chinese characters for Cantonese slang that had previously not been written. The newspaper's bold headlines, big color photos, and the barely clothed starlets gave the chattering classes plenty to snigger at. Officials, business executives, and professionals found *Apple Daily* an easy target. People claimed to hate *Apple Daily* but they read it; several people typically read a single copy of the newspaper, so *Apple*'s readership numbers rivaled those of *Oriental Daily News* but its readers were better educated and wealthier than *ODN*'s. No one could ignore it.

As early as the 1997 handover, rumors circulated that Lai headed a secret list of people who would be rounded up as soon as China asserted control. In June 1997, he broke down in tears before hundreds of people in the ballroom of Hong Kong's Grand Hyatt hotel as he confessed to his interlocutor, *USA Today* founder Al Neuharth, his fears that he would be jailed.

Lai focused on exposing wrongdoing and corruption and pushing for more transparency and accountability. *Apple Daily* shook up what had been a cozy press world, breaking story after story. In 1999, *Apple* revealed that the director of Hong Kong's tax department secretly owned shares in his wife's accounting firm. He lost his job. The next year the paper broke the news that a pro-Beijing legislator, Gary Cheng, had passed on confidential government information to his public relations firm's clients. Cheng was sentenced to three years in prison.

Next magazine specialized in long-form investigative stories, while *Apple Daily* was famous for its take-no-prisoners, tabloid-style approach. It was a broadsheet newspaper in size, but it had a tabloid's scurrilous bent. "I always thought of *Next* as the sword and then *Apple Daily* was the bulldozer that drove it home," observes Mark Simon, who served as the paper's general manager from 2004 to 2006. They had different cultures. *Next* was more cerebral, more collegial, as weeklies tend to be. *Apple* was freewheeling and chaotic, as dailies often are.

Apple Daily's aggressiveness led to errors. The first edition of the paper contained a serious front-page mistake after relying on a lousy tip. Two years before the handover, *Apple Daily* conjectured that the territory's first chief executive under Chinese leadership would be someone surnamed Leung or Neo. The newspaper wasn't even close: it would turn out to be Tung Chee-hwa. "On the first day they were wrong about the new chief executive," snipes the longtime *Next* editor. "We thought *Apple* was a joke."

The two publications occasionally took opposite positions on a particular issue. *Next* fought a political reform bill in 2010; *Apple Daily* supported it. The split confused readers and staff alike. "I said, 'Who cares?'" remembers the *Next* editor. "We are *Next*, they are *Apple*." Lai encouraged this diversity, even competition. Whatever their differences, the two publications packed a powerful one-two punch fighting for freedom and transparency, united in their editorial commitment to democracy.

Lai's editorial choices were idiosyncratic. He hired Li Yi, a controversial journalist who had close ties to both the CCP and KMT. Li, who died in 2022, was the highest-profile of several journalists from the communist press whom Lai hired. Jin Zhong, a dissident journalist who had earlier worked with Li Yi, thinks that Lai hired Li and gave him a prominent column to tap into the communist press's broad and deep intellectual Chinese roots. Critics, including some on Lai's staff, believed that Li remained a communist agent and couldn't understand why Li was hired.

The simplest explanation is that Lai wanted talent. "A lot of leftist journalists were very literate compared to the average Hong Kong journalist, who was brought up under colonialism," says Jin, who had himself moved from the mainland to Hong Kong. In order for Lai to "build up a good stable of writers and editors it made sense for him to extend his relationships into that world." Whatever the reason—and Li Yi's close ties with Taiwan could have been an added motivation—it provided yet another example of Lai's out-of-the-box thinking and unwillingness to be handcuffed by traditional ways of doing business.

Apple Daily and *Next* both ran stories that reflected Lai's willingness to take on the most powerful people in the colony. It was *Next* that reported the suicide of the former wife of Li Ka-shing, Hong Kong's wealthiest and most powerful businessman. Li was famous for controlling news about his family and his companies—and his companies were aggressive and litigious in dealing with the press. Li got wind of the story about his former wife before it ran. He summoned Lai to his office and tried to get *Next* to kill the article. Lai refused. Word of his courage in standing up to Li Ka-shing quickly circulated throughout the region, cementing a corporate ethos of not backing off even when faced with threats from powerful people.

Lai didn't hold any personal animus toward Li: he later spurned an attempt to target Li in what turned out to be a blackmail scheme. A source pitched the magazine's editors with unfounded tales of Li's purported wrongdoing; then he went to Li claiming that *Next* had damaging information on him but that with payment he could prevent the article from being printed. Lai told *Next* editors to stay away from the character, a well-connected figure. Only in retrospect, though, did editors see the plot for what it was.

Hong Kong's coterie of powerful businessmen and government officials had long exercised vetoes over stories they didn't like. Lai's boldness in standing up to Li Ka-shing overrode that veto power. Lai's stance toward Hong Kong's richest man emboldened his reporters and editors. Li and his companies stopped advertising in Lai's publications. Lai benefited from not being part of Hong Kong's elite social circles. "I have the advantage that I don't go out," he told journalist Tim Ferguson in 1994. "I don't associate with people. I'm a loner—an absolute loner, because I don't need anybody."

Tycoon or dissident—Lai and his team went after anyone. Lai had featured Tiananmen student leader Chai Ling on one of his 1989 Giordano T-shirts. She fled China after the crackdown, escaping to Hong Kong and then Paris, where she became friends with the Lais. She subsequently thanked Teresa and Lai in her 2015 book, *A Heart for Freedom: The Remarkable Journey of a Young Dissident, Her Daring Escape, and Her Quest to Free China's Daughters.* Later, at what she imagined was a private dinner with Lai at his house, she had confided that her marriage was breaking up. Lai's friendship with Chai didn't stop *Apple Daily* from breaking the news of her impending divorce.

Apple Daily courted controversy from the outset. The most notorious feature at the paper's launch was a daily column purporting to be a consumer's guide to Hong Kong's Portland Street—a red-light district in the Kowloon area—with critical reviews, much like restaurant reviews, listing each prostitute's specialties. (Prostitution is not illegal in Hong Kong, though pimping is; as a result, hundreds of ostensibly one-woman establishments that were in reality controlled by pimps proliferated.) The author or authors penned the consumer guide under the name "Fei Long" ("Fat Dragon"), the nickname given to Hong Kong's sybaritic treasury secretary Rafael Hui.

The idea of a consumer's guide to prostitution using Rafael Hui's nickname epitomized *Apple*'s buccaneering style and garnered the attention Lai wanted. *Apple Daily* kept pushing against the edge of journalistic ethics and often passed beyond it. Lai conceded that the paper's focus on sex was "despicable" but noted that when he cut off the Fei Long feature, circulation dropped 30 percent. That left him with the choice of running "a small newspaper that no one reads" or continuing with its salacious approach. "It is a cross I have to carry," he told Sirico. "I know I am a sinner."

The paper's most serious ethical misstep came in 1998. A young mother threw her two young children off a roof and then jumped after them. The widowed husband, Chan Kin-hong, showed no apparent concern at his children's deaths or his wife's suicide. Instead he slipped across the mainland border to anything-goes Shenzhen. Fueled by $650 from an *Apple Daily* reporter, Chan partied with his prostitute-mistress—a spree chronicled by the newspaper. Two weeks later, Jimmy Lai wrote a full-page apology, saying that he and his team had gone too far, that they were "deeply sorry" and would "learn from this regrettable experience." He also had to apologize after *Apple Daily* doctored photos to exaggerate bruises and cuts suffered by publisher—and former mentor—"*taipan*" Albert Cheng in a knife attack.

Lai's swashbuckling style permeated the company. Salesmen celebrated an advertising order by blasting a horn mounted on the office wall. "What a contrast that was to Dow Jones, where we were happy to get an ad but it never dawned on me to put a Klaxon on the wall," says Gordon Crovitz, the publisher of the *Far Eastern Economic Review* and, later, of the *Wall Street Journal*.

Lai bears comparison with William Randolph Hearst. As press barons, both combined sensationalism with hard-hitting reporting, banner headlines, and provocative editorial cartoons. Technology allowed Lai to take sensational journalism further than Hearst had been able to, with full-color photos of everything: car crashes, women giving birth on the street, and politicians slipping into hotels with their mistresses. Brain splatter, amputated limbs, corpses, and car crashes. *Apple Daily* showed them all in graphic color photos.

Where Hearst pushed Americans to fight for an overseas empire, beating the drums of war during the Spanish-American War—a conflict that resulted in the United States acquiring the Philippines and Puerto Rico—Lai promoted democracy in Hong Kong. "He had everything," says Crovitz. "Editorials that could have appeared in the *Wall Street Journal*, gossip that went well beyond *People* magazine, political coverage that was quite sophisticated, and pictures of actresses. He cared about what Hong Kong people wanted to read. He had a big advantage as a media innovator, which is that he didn't grow up in the industry, so he could do whatever he wanted."

Brad Hamm, the former dean of Northwestern University's Medill School of Journalism and, from 2015, a member of Next Digital's board of directors, believes that Joseph Pulitzer provides a better comparison. Pulitzer, like Lai, built his newspapers by shrewdly combining sensationalism with crusading investigative reporting. Like Lai, Pulitzer too faced legal challenges. The federal government indicted Pulitzer for criminally libeling President Theodore Roosevelt in his exposé of a Panama Canal corruption scandal, though the publisher prevailed in court.

Lai threw free-market economics into the mix too. In the early 1990s, he met Nobel Prize–winning economist Milton Friedman through University of Hong Kong professor Steven Cheung. Cheung had worked with Friedman at the University of Chicago and had returned to Asia to help further China's economic reforms. In 1993, Lai traveled to China with Friedman and his wife, Rose, on a trip organized by Cheung. In their memoirs, Friedman singled out Lai and the *Next* magazine editor, Yeung Wai-hong, as "the two most interesting of those whom we had not met before."

After summarizing Lai's background and Giordano, Friedman describes Lai: "More remarkable, on his own, he acquired a liberal education and became a libertarian, absorbing all the classic literature, from Adam Smith to Ludwig von Mises and Friedrich Hayek."

Friedman also noted Lai's adventurous eating habits on the trip to mainland China. One memorable evening, after a long drive to the restaurant, the meal appeared. "The first dish served was puppy. It was cut up but it was laid out with what looked like a little tail coming out of one end and ears out of the other. The second dish was a camel's hoof, followed by a snake. They were a most exotic and unusual assortment of dishes that we and most of our group had the good sense not to eat." Lai, "undoubtedly the most adventurous among us, sampled everything and ended up by throwing up after we returned to the hotel."

Milton and Rose Friedman and Teresa and Jimmy Lai became close friends. In 1998, the Friedmans visited Hong Kong for two weeks as guests of the Lais. The Lais often visited the Friedmans in California. The two couples continued to meet most years until Milton died in 2006. The Friedman children, after their parents' deaths, presented the Lais with a blanket that Milton and Rose had bought on their honeymoon as a token of friendship.

Lai was determined to preserve free-market ideals in Hong Kong—a city that he worried risked losing its small-government, low-tax, and light-touch approach. In addition to Chris Patten's attempt to introduce mandatory pensions and other social support measures, the social welfare tendency of Hong Kong's democrats alarmed Lai. He inaugurated a series of private economic seminars led by University of Hong Kong economics professor Richard Wong, who had also been on the China trip with Milton Friedman.

Attendees at the dinners, usually held at the elegant Victoria Restaurant overlooking the harbor, included *Next* and *Apple Daily* journalists as well as politicians in the pro-democracy camp. His friendship with the democrats deepened after Teresa's sister Irene married Democratic Party leader Yeung Sum in 1995, but he distrusted their economically interventionist approach. "The idea was to undercut their socialist economic policies," remembers an editor who attended. Featuring structured presentations and discussion topics, the dinners "went on for a couple of years, maybe more, but gradually lost steam."

Hong Kong government and business leaders, as well as the Chinese Communist Party, watched Lai with fear and frustration as *Apple Daily* and *Next* magazine exposed wrongdoing even as they opposed social spending and pushed free-market solutions for social problems like housing. The combination of a radical freedom agenda (free people and free markets) coupled with often prurient photos and reporting that went after some of the city's richest and most powerful people shook up a staid, conservative elite in a city that was preparing for—and later coping with—a takeover by the Chinese Communist Party.

Apple Daily gave its journalists unusual freedom. Reporter Cori Wong had previously worked at the *Oriental Daily News*, a rigid hierarchical operation that "was like working with a really strict father. You cannot say anything—cannot even take pictures in the office." (The paper's owners, the Ma family, prohibited mention of horses because the character representing their name—*ma*—meant "horse.") "At *Apple*," she says, "you could write anything, any story." There was proofreading and light editing, but no censorship. "There was no sense of 'cannot write this' or 'cannot report that.' There was never this sort of thing ever." The only forbidden area was commentary that smacked of socialist economics.

In 1998, the fast-growing Next Media secured a long-term lease from the government-owned Hong Kong Science and Technology Parks Corp. for a plot of land to build its headquarters in the Tseung Kwan O industrial area. The company included a swimming pool on the top floor of the newspaper's new five-story structure. The few Hong Kong companies that had swimming pools typically restricted their use to executives. At Next Media, everyone from security guards to editors could use it. The pool, however, stayed off-limits to one group—Lai's family. He didn't want them using company assets.

Staff largely admired Lai but he was often tough on his employees. In meetings he could be quick-tempered, brusque, even harsh. He acted quickly, whether it was a decision to invest in a new publication or to fire someone. When longtime staff member Simon Lee says Lai thought about a proposal "a long time," he meant "more than thirty seconds." Sometimes Lai's decision-making appeared impulsive, even reckless. Behind his back, some staff called him "the Chairman Mao who speaks English."

Being decisive didn't make Lai a dictator. He shared Mao's penchant for sudden, bold moves but lacked his cruelty and malice. At times he involved himself closely in operations, even running daily sessions where he and senior editors critiqued the previous day's newspaper. He also went for long stretches, sometimes for years at a time, with little daily involvement at *Apple Daily.* "He was not too involved as a boss," remembers Ip Yut-kin. Most of the time, "he let people do their own thing."

After the 1997 handover, Lai's publications continued reporting stories that no one else in Hong Kong would touch. *Next* had broken the story of the SARS outbreak in Guangdong. In March 2003, while people were still preoccupied with SARS spreading through Hong Kong (it would kill 299 people there), *Apple Daily* revealed that Financial Secretary Antony Leung had avoided $24,000 in taxes by buying a Lexus shortly before announcing that he would steeply raise registration fees on new cars. Leung's misdeeds were quickly dubbed "Lexusgate."

China had promised democracy for Hong Kong. Instead it lurched toward repression, attempting to put forward a national security law in 2003. The Basic Law's Article 23 required Hong Kong to institute legislation in this area. Critics worried the law would instead criminalize political dissent. Lai used his newspaper and magazine to stoke opposition to this move by an undemocratic and unpopular government. Opposition to the legislation and support for a protest march on July 1 permeated the newspaper. Public unhappiness over SARS and Lexusgate fused with fear of new restrictions by China under the proposed national security law.

Apple Daily had spent its first eight years exposing scandals and shattering the cozy relationship between journalists and politicians. In the popular mind it was associated with gutter journalism, from its Portland Street prostitute reviews to paying for Chan Kin-hong's Shenzhen orgy. "In the 1990s he was not embraced by a lot of journalism organizations," remembers

Tim Ferguson, who first met Lai in 1994 as a *Wall Street Journal* columnist. "He came across as kind of rough—a big husky guy whose English was rough, too. . . . His journalism was seen as the tabloid exploitative sort."

Lai's fight against the national security law in 2003 marked a sea change in Next Media's political engagement. For the first time, *Apple Daily* and *Next* took a leading role in catalyzing opposition forces and motivating people to take to the streets. *Apple Daily* and *Next* took on a role akin to an opposition political party in a city where a rigged system meant pro-democracy politicians had no route to power.

The week before the march, *Next*'s cover showed a photoshopped picture of Chief Executive Tung Chee-hwa being smashed in the face with a cream pie; on July 1 itself, *Apple Daily* featured mocking photos of Tung designed to be cut out and displayed as protest signs by marchers. The paper exhorted people to join the gathering.

Lai spent an unprecedented amount of his own money to support the anti–Article 23 movement. In the two weeks leading up to the march, Lai personally paid for advertisements in *Apple Daily* and all other major non-communist newspapers in the territory, calling for people to take to the streets on July 1. "He paid for these out of his own pocket, as he didn't think it right to ask shareholders to kick in," says aide Mark Simon. (That act itself represented a departure from practice in Hong Kong, where many business owners treated their companies as private piggybanks.) Lai went further and adopted a policy of personally paying 50 percent of the cost of any *Apple Daily* political ad that someone wanted to run, providing that he agreed with its content.

He also bought protest materials. "Jimmy was ordering everything," marvels Simon, who paid for advertisements and bought posters, banners, and other protest material for Lai. "I was a cash machine," he remembers, with $1.3 million in stacks of cash piled up in the safe in his office. When guards in an armored truck would deliver cash to the Next Media offices, "the finance department would get one small bag and I would have two large bags." Simon estimates that Lai spent over $1 million of his own money for the 2003 protest. The ads that Lai paid for in *Apple Daily* alone cost him $770,000.

Since the late 1980s, Lai had provided most of the pro-democracy movement's funding. From the time he first sold T-shirts in support of Tiananmen to the day he went to jail, Simon estimates he contributed at least $140 million.

The government predicted some 30,000 people would turn out in protest. On July 1, half a million people took to the streets on a brutally hot day. They marched two miles from Victoria Park to the Central Government Office complex, in the heart of the city. The government's flawed estimate of the turnout showed its lack of rapport with the city's people.

Public protests had long been important in Hong Kong. But large protests had been infrequent. The most notable exception was the million-strong march in support of China's pro-democracy protesters in 1989. Since then, every year tens of thousands, sometimes more than one hundred thousand, had attended the annual June 4 commemorations of the Tiananmen killings held in Victoria Park. Certainly, 500,000 protesters marching in a city of seven million people constituted an unmistakable rebuke to the government.

"Without Jimmy and *Apple Daily*, I don't know if you'd have half a million people protesting in 2003," says Notre Dame professor Victoria Tin-bor Hui. "The Chinese Communist Party fears his mobilization capacity. He was so dangerous [from the CCP's standpoint] because he brought different people together. When you can talk to people who care about cooking and horse racing and football you get everyone in Hong Kong."

The frontal opposition to national security legislation enraged Beijing. The support that Jimmy Lai and other Hong Kongers had shown for the 1989 democracy protests had already stoked China's fears that the territory's democratic fever would infect the mainland. Beijing worried that the city might become a base for China democracy activists. When the government had announced the Article 23 national security legislation the previous October, only a few dozen people had attended an initial protest rally. Lai's central role in nurturing an issue that at first had attracted little attention and making it into the biggest challenge the post-1997 government faced worried Beijing.

The protest achieved results. The Article 23 national security legislation was withdrawn. Secretary for Security Regina Ip, who had pushed the bill and mocked protesters, stepped down. So, too, did the Lexusgate finance minister, Antony Leung. In March 2005, Chief Executive Tung Chee-hwa left office, two years early. With Tung's resignation, Lai's campaign to block the national security legislation had succeeded beyond any reasonable expectation. Ten years after *Apple Daily*'s launch, it had spearheaded a campaign that toppled the city's leader.

But the Chinese Communist Party couldn't tolerate effective resistance of the sort that Lai and his journalists had mounted. Lai's success increased Beijing's ire. At its heart, a communist system is specifically designed to ensure that dissent is not vocalized; when it appears the party roots it out. The CCP insists on "correctness," notes professor Perry Link, where *correct* means "supportive of the Party's interests."

In Lai's case, dissent was coupled with significant financial resources. That made him even more dangerous, especially because he used his money to build a media platform that could oppose the government. Beijing took journalism seriously. It equated media with propaganda and insisted that newspapers and magazines—and their owners—should serve the government and the party. He was also incorruptible. He was happily and faithfully married, so not susceptible to sexual blackmail, thus denying the party another common tactic it used for keeping people under control. He was unconcerned with money: he had made so much that he simply couldn't be bought off. And he was spending that money globally.

Half a world away from Hong Kong's high-rise cityscape, the Prince of Wales Hotel in Canada's Niagara-on-the-Lake, Ontario, evokes the glory days of the British Empire. With horse-drawn carriages that deposit guests at the front of the redbrick Victorian building, it would be hard to find a more extreme contrast with Hong Kong hotels. In Hong Kong only the 1920s Peninsula, where Lai had met so many clothes buyers, projected the same air of colonial grandeur.

Built in 1864 and renamed after a visit by the future George V at the beginning of the twentieth century, the lakeside resort has hosted a parade of royals over the years. Visitors from nearby Toronto queue up with tourists from the United States, Japan, and China for scones and cucumber sandwiches served as part of the hotel's high tea service. The top-of-the-line "His Royal Highness" offering features twelve-year-old Islay scotch along with a selection of local cheeses and charcuterie and a selection of tea. It's all part of the hotel's promise that guests at the five-hundred-dollar-a-night hotel will "live like royalty."

The Prince of Wales Hotel became the flagship property in Lai's expanding hotel empire. The resort town's 18,000 residents live downstream from the eponymous falls and just a few hundred yards across the Niagara River from the United States. Niagara-on-the-Lake embraces its history. A historic fort and buildings remind visitors that it was here that U.S. troops invaded Canada during the War of 1812 as part of a failed attempt to capture Toronto. Most of today's American visitors are simply looking for a low-key alternative to the commercialism on the U.S. side of the border.

The clutch of more than a dozen luxury hotels, restaurants, and spas that Lai owns represents his largest and perhaps most improbable investment. Yet it's weirdly apt that a Hong Kong Chinese entrepreneur imprisoned for upholding British ideals of freedom he learned as a colonial subject now owns Victorian-era hotels built at the height of Britain's imperial era. Lai's hefty investments have been key to making the once-faded town an internationally recognized center for food, wine, and the arts. In 2023, *Condé Nast Traveler* singled out the Prince of Wales Hotel in naming Niagara-on-the-Lake one of the fifty best small towns in the world.

The hotels represent the antithesis of Lai's business successes in mass production. He had specialized in large standardized operations—Giordano's fast fashion, the mass-market sweater production for JCPenney and Kmart, the hundreds of thousands of copies a day of *Apple Daily*. But Lai has always loved retail. Niagara-on-the-Lake's charm lies in its uniqueness. The Prince of Wales Hotel and its famed tearoom don't exist anywhere else in the world. As with all his ventures, Lai got intensely involved. His obsession with food and design found an outlet, above all in his attention to the cuisine in the dozens of hotel restaurants and stand-alone outlets that he owns.

Things weren't always so idyllic in Niagara-on-the-Lake. Longtime residents remember when women would cross the street to avoid walking by the scruffy, biker-hangout, bar scene at the Prince of Wales Hotel. Lai's twin sister had escaped China four years after him, making a perilous swim to freedom across Shenzhen Bay. Lai initially helped Si-wai when she arrived in Hong Kong. She had a daughter, Celia, in Hong Kong in 1972 and moved in the late 1970s to San Francisco, where she gave birth to a second daughter, Erica, in 1979. The family then moved to Ghana, where her husband was involved in the textile business. The marriage didn't last and Si-wai and her daughters moved to Canada in 1982. Si-wai started work at a hotel in Niagara Falls and saved enough money to buy a souvenir shop and then a motel near the falls. "My childhood was spent between these two establishments working any minute we were not in school," remembers Erica Lepp, as she is now known.

On Sundays, Si-wai and her daughters would drive to Niagara-on-the-Lake for brunch. Si-wai dreamed of having a house there someday. "In 1994 she took me to the Pillar and Post [hotel] and we had brunch," says Erica. "I'll never forget where we sat. She asked me if I liked the brunch and I said yes. She told me her and Uncle Jimmy were going to buy this place."

For the better part of a decade, Lai funded an investment spree. Three decades and many tens of millions of dollars later, the Lais dominate the town. Lais Hotels owns the three best hotels—Queen's Landing and the Pillar and Post as well as the Prince of Wales—along with a sushi restaurant featuring fresh seafood flown in from Tokyo, a Thai restaurant, and a handful of boutique hotels. There's a new spa hotel in nearby wine country and a pair of hotels farther along Lake Ontario.

Back in Hong Kong, Lai had deflected the initial round of attacks from Chinese authorities by selling his stake in Giordano. Diversifying his holdings—getting money out of Hong Kong—seemed wise, and Lai lavishly backed Si-wai. While a desire to help his sister drove the initial investments, Lai also demonstrated shrewd business sense. As the sun set on the British Empire in Hong Kong, investment in a Commonwealth country with a strong commitment to rule of law—including protection of property rights—constituted a sensible strategic bet.

Lai had put up the cash for the purchases Si-wai made in Niagara-on-the-Lake and had given her 10 percent of the company as a reward for building the business. The twins decided they wanted to go their separate ways. Lai assigned Mark Simon the delicate task of negotiating a business separation with Si-wai. Successful mediation between the siblings ended with Lai paying his sister $12 million and giving her a handful of the smaller properties and established Simon as Lai's most important aide.

Lai made Simon chairman of the hotels and, with 3 percent of the company, a shareholder. He had been an offensive lineman at East Carolina State University, and he would play a similar role for Lai—blocking and protecting his boss. Besides handling family issues and overseeing the Canadian operations, and running various parts of the newspaper's business operations and its animation unit, he developed a Taiwan property business and ran Lai's equity portfolio. Simon had served in the U.S. Navy, and his father was a career bureaucrat at the CIA, fueling rumors in Hong Kong, which he denies, that he was a U.S. spy.

In Canada, Simon hired a team of professional managers and let them grow the operations. As with Giordano and the media businesses, Lai took pains to find out what would appeal to customers. He pioneered weekly burger nights at the flagship Prince of Wales Hotel to make locals continue to feel welcome as the hotel moved upmarket. On Wednesday evenings, the

Mark L. Clifford

hotel's cozy English-style Churchill Lounge serves as many as 350 generously sized hamburgers with soup or fries for just $3.75 (C$5). It's a hotel meal for less than the price of a cup of Starbucks coffee.

Rising food costs after the pandemic prompted hotel executives to ask if they could raise the price. Writing from Stanley Prison, where hamburger is not on the menu Wednesday night or any night, word came back from Lai—the $3.75 burger must stay. What started as a way to get some business during the long offseason now appears on the Wednesday night menu throughout the year.

Lai isn't just serving his guests burgers and fries or high tea. He's also displayed much of his art collection for hotel guests to enjoy. He has a significant collection of paintings by Walasse Ting, the fruit of a decades-long friendship. Lai displayed dozens of Ting's fluorescent-colored acrylics and watercolors—featuring cats, birds, and women—in Next Digital's Hong Kong and Taiwan offices. As authorities moved to shutter the company in late 2021, Lai gave orders for the paintings to be moved. Although police only had the right to seize corporate assets, and the paintings had been loaned from Lai's personal collection, they likely would have been taken in the chaotic 2021 raids that swept up virtually everything in the company's buildings.

These paintings now hang on the walls of the Niagara-on-the-Lake hotels. Many are displayed in the Queen's Landing, where they don't have to fight with the rococo Victorian ambience that characterizes the Prince of Wales Hotel. Other paintings by Burmese, Canadian, and Filipino artists also grace the walls of the hotel. There's something almost dissonant about museum-quality art hanging on the walls of a hotel that caters to attendees at corporate meetings. But it's fitting for anyone who's aware of Lai's strong visual sense.

Si-wai's taste tends toward the decorative and ornate, but she also possesses a strong sense of design. The Prince of Wales Hotel today still features baskets and porcelain pieces she bought from Hong Kong's Hollywood Road antique shops. She commissioned a larger-than-life copy of Michelangelo's colossal *David* statue for a terrace overlooking Lake Ontario at the Queen's Landing hotel. Until Lai took over from his sister, *David*'s oversized genitals featured in the background in countless bachelorette-party pictures. Si-wai commissioned unique décor for each of the hundreds of rooms in the main hotels. Her obsession for detail ensured that she remembered what belonged in each one. Once, spotting an unfamiliar vase, she ordered it removed from the room. It turned out to be an urn holding funeral remains. Staff quickly restored the vessel to its owner.

Si-wai still lives in Niagara-on-the-Lake and owns several of the smaller properties. She can be seen many afternoons slowly riding an adult-sized tricycle down Main Street, trailed on foot by her Filipina domestic helper as she pedals to or from the Shaw Café or the Oban Hotel, two of her remaining properties.

The Lai twins' investments helped catalyze a local renaissance. Three decades after Si-wai's pioneering purchases, Lais Hotels employs some 900 people year-round in the area and is the town's largest taxpayer. The Shaw Festival, whose theater Queen Elizabeth opened, ranks as one of Canada's most renowned. Inniskillin Wine, famed for its extra-late-harvest ice wine, sparked a boom in wineries; the region now supports more than forty. Lai tapped into the popularity of wine-country tourism with the purchase of the Cave Spring winery facility in the nearby village of Jordan, where Lais Hotels has swallowed much of the tiny town center. Though Lai hasn't gone into the winemaking business, he owns everything but the grapevines: his holdings there include Cave Springs' underground storage cellars, a tasting room, a spa, and a restaurant.

His success in the comparatively low-tech hospitality world reflects Lai's obsession with providing memorable consumer experiences. For all his fascination with technology, Lai knows what's needed to make a good consumer business. "He has a deep, profound understanding of people," observes Thomas Crampton, a former journalist who joined Lai's empire to grow his digital media business. As a businessman, Lai focused on three things—the consumer experience, operational efficiency, and the adoption of the best available equipment and techniques. From Comitex and Giordano, through *Apple Daily* and *Next*, Lai used technology as a competitive weapon. His willingness to spend on tech set him apart in Hong Kong. The parallel successes he and Si-wai have had in revitalizing a struggling resort demonstrates his feeling for how to profitably provide what consumers want.

Chapter Seven

"GOD SUFFERS WITH ME"

The first time Jimmy Lai attended Mass he walked out midway through the service. Teresa, a devout Catholic, had invited him to go to church with her shortly after they met in 1989. They went, aptly, to St. Teresa's Church in Kowloon, built in 1932 and one of the colony's most important Catholic churches. The imposing building, a mix of Early Christian, Byzantine, and Romanesque architecture, had been financed largely by the colony's sizable Portuguese community. By 1989, Hong Kong's Portuguese had largely disappeared, the older generation dying out and the younger ones having emigrated to the nearby Portuguese colony of Macau or to Portugal itself. Cantonese now made up most of the parishioners in Hong Kong's vibrant and politically important Catholic community.

Neither the architecture nor the history—nor even his interest in Teresa—could hold Lai. Impatient, restless, he was bored. Church felt too much like school—"'stand up, sit down, be quiet,' like somebody was trying to grab him," Teresa says. He bristled at the idea that he should submit to God and to the church's rigid hierarchy.

Eight years later, Lai had found God and submitted. He converted to Catholicism in 1997, at a baptism ceremony at Hong Kong's Cathedral of the Immaculate Conception in the Mid-Levels district of Hong Kong Island.

Conversion represented both the culmination of his thinking about his place in the world and the beginning of a new phase of his life.

In 1989, Lai had wanted to remain neutral when it came to religion. By 1997, he had decided to take a stand throughout his life. Pushed by Beijing, he had chosen *Next* rather than Giordano. He had chosen Hong Kong rather than exile. He had chosen Teresa rather than bachelorhood. He had chosen to resist the Chinese Communist Party rather than to abase himself before an evil government. Now, on July 1, 1997, the day that China took control of Hong Kong, he made the decision to put himself in the hands of a higher power. He later described his thinking in an interview with Father Robert Sirico.

> My wife is a very devout Catholic so I went to church for a long time but I don't know how I came to faith. It is like how we fall in love. You don't know why. Maybe it is the pressure when Hong Kong was taken over by communist China. I was one of the few guys who was outspoken, who had a media business here. Obviously, I had a lot of passion. Was I [living] in fear? I don't know, I never seem to have a sense of fear. Definitely I was a bit apprehensive about what was going to happen. A lot of people rumored that I would be arrested. Maybe that kind of [quest for] security crept into my psyche. I made up my mind to be baptized.

Apprehension and a functional desire for protection, rather than pure faith, drove the conversion. Teresa sums up Lai's thinking at the time: "He knows that a fight is coming and that he will need God's help for this fight." At a time of uncertainty over the arrival of the Chinese Communist Party, he turned to faith in a higher power for ballast. "My faith gave me such a certainty. Faith makes so many other things so clear. This is something wonderful . . . I definitely feel I have a god for protector. . . . Whenever I am in difficulties, whenever I am in crisis, I feel His presence. I am very calm. I feel that I am going to be OK."

Lai's conversion followed years of casual conversation with Father Dominique Li in Paris, a mainlander who left China in the 1940s and spent the following half century in Europe. He officiated over the Lais' church wedding at the Church of Notre-Dame de Clignancourt in Paris, where he was a priest, in 1992. "They talked about communism and religion in a very casual way," remembers Teresa. "Little by little he saw the beauty and the freedom" in Catholicism.

Lai's decision to convert reflected, above all, Teresa's importance in his life. When she married Lai in 1991, Teresa remained relaxed about his agnosticism. She had two overriding goals for their life together. First, she vowed to raise their children in the Catholic faith. Second, in a presentiment of the difficult road her husband would walk, she promised never to abandon him, declaring that she would walk with him no matter what difficulties came their way. She maintains she never pushed Lai to convert to Catholicism, saying later, "I knew it would come. For me he was already there, he just needed to formalize it."

Teresa credits David Aikman, a longtime reporter for *Time* magazine, with catalyzing Lai's conversion. Aikman joined Lai and Teresa for a dinner at their Cox's Road apartment in Kowloon just a few days before the British relinquished Hong Kong. (They had moved to the penthouse apartment at Highview, 1A Cox's Road, in the heart of Kowloon, following a 1995 robbery at the Tai Po villa.) Teresa remembers:

After dinner David said, "Shall we pray for the Holy Spirit to come?" and we knelt around the table. I think something special happened at that moment. I think it was the presence of the Holy Spirit. It was David who initiated the prayer. It was in the presence of the Holy Spirit that [Jimmy] decided to become a Catholic. The handover triggered him. . . . He must have [had] a feeling of helplessness and [so] he has to give everything to God. He always knew there was a superior power. He surrendered himself to God, to that superior power.

Like so much of Lai's life until that time, the conversion process took place at high speed. The circumstances verged on chaotic, against the backdrop of the handover and a swarm of global visitors who descended on Hong Kong. Teresa had asked journalist Bill McGurn to urge Jimmy to convert in the week before the handover. Lai declined McGurn's invitation, the second time he had asked. At the dinner, "I told Teresa, 'No, we have to leave it,'" remembers McGurn.

The night of the handover he appeared despondent. *Business Week* journalist Sheridan Prasso met him for the first time that evening, at a party at his Cox's Road apartment.

> He said, "This is terrible. The communists are going to destroy this place." He was very, very negative and very, very pessimistic. It struck me because it was so much in opposition to the excitement and cautious optimism among a lot of other Hong Kong people that we were encountering at the time. It was as if he had already seen what would happen twenty-three years later, that this was the end of Hong Kong. He foresaw on that night that this was the end of Hong Kong's freedoms as we know them.

A couple of days after the handover he called McGurn into a side room in the family's sprawling apartment. "He said, 'I want Jesus Christ in my life,'" remembers McGurn. He wanted McGurn, a close friend but more than a decade his junior, to serve as his godfather.

Unless there's an emergency—such as imminent death—Catholic conversion consists of an extended process that generally takes about a year. Lai did it in one week. A long-standing friendship with Bishop Joseph Zen jump-started the process. Zen gave Lai a stack of books to read. In his characteristically intense style, he quickly worked through them, beginning his ongoing study of Catholic theology.

A photo taken inside the cathedral just after the baptism shows Lai in a black suit, the trousers too long, wearing a white shirt and a red-and-gold patterned tie. Teresa and Lai stand with their arms around one another. Teresa wears a magenta dress cut a couple of inches above her knees. She is smiling unreservedly, almost giddily. Lai, too, is smiling, but uncertainly. Martin Lee, also a Catholic and the godfather of Lai's son Sebastien, stands just behind him. Godfather Bill McGurn stands in the front row with his wife, Julie, and two-year-old daughter, Grace. Beside them, an *amah* holds the Lais' year-old infant, Claire. Three-year-old Sebastien, Catholic missionary Audrey Donnithorne, and a handful of foreign journalists also attended.

McGurn had first met Lai nearly three years earlier through the *Wall Street Journal*'s Gordon Crovitz. In August 1994, Crovitz had penned a note to McGurn suggesting that Lai was the only other person in Hong Kong who had read the complete works of Friedrich Hayek. Lai and McGurn quickly found that their worldviews coincided. They shared a belief in the power of free markets and regarded Hong Kong as an exemplar. McGurn wrote editorials for the *Far Eastern Economic Review*, owned by *Wall Street Journal* publisher Dow Jones. The *Journal*'s long-standing motto, "Free men; free markets," dovetailed with Lai's own philosophy.

McGurn marveled at the commitment to economic and political freedom by Lai, who had a businessman's instinctive aversion to government control. During an earlier stint living in Hong Kong in the 1980s, while working as an editorial writer at the *Asian Wall Street Journal*, McGurn had written *Perfidious Albion*, a stinging indictment of Britain's betrayal of the Hong Kong people. The consequences of that betrayal for people like Lai intensified as the handover to Chinese rule approached.

The two shared more than an intellectual connection. Teresa Lai and Julie McGurn formed a strong bond. They had similarly aged children— Sebastien Lai was born in late 1994 and Grace McGurn early in 1995. The McGurns, half a world away from their family in the United States, spent most weekends with the Lais until they returned to the United States at the end of 1998. Julie was godmother to Claire Lai, who was born on May 13, 1996, the date of the Feast of the Lady of Fatima, a saint revered for her anticommunism. In turn, Teresa served as godmother to the McGurns's second daughter, Maisie, who was born in 1997.

The friendship between the two families was strengthened by their shared faith. "It was a Catholic house—we liked that," remembers McGurn. Teresa filled the Kadoorie Avenue house, where they moved two years after the handover, with religious iconography. An exquisite four-foot-high wooden crucified Christ, carved in northern Europe around the fourteenth century, dominated a living room wall above a fireplace.

Even a close friend and sympathetic Catholic like McGurn wondered about the suddenness of Lai's conversion. Several years earlier, when he had first asked Lai if he "wanted to join the team," Lai demurred. "He had said no because he wanted to be independent, to appeal to all religions," McGurn says. A quarter century later, McGurn reflects on his concerns. "On the day of his conversion, I didn't doubt his good faith. It wasn't bad intentions but I did wonder how much he understood and believed what he was getting into. He had social reasons—Teresa, Martin Lee, he liked Cardinal Zen. So many people in the democracy movement were Catholic. But I thought, 'How much of this does he really believe?'"

A clutch of prominent Catholics stood at the core of Hong Kong's democracy movement. Jimmy particularly admired Martin Lee and Joseph Zen. Though Lai looked up to Lee, the lawyer initially didn't appear so certain about Lai. In the early 1990s, *Next* magazine wanted the best barrister in the colony to defend against a libel lawsuit brought by Larry Yung, a powerful and politically well-connected mainland businessman who had set up shop in Hong Kong. "I had to meet Martin Lee, to see whether we should proceed or admit defeat and pay up," remembers the senior *Next* editor. "We met for maybe thirty minutes. He kept asking me, 'Are you sure Jimmy is going to pay my legal bills? Are you really sure?'"

Given that Lai and Lee had first encountered one another in the 1989 Tiananmen spring, the editor remembers feeling "a bit taken aback—does Martin really know Jimmy?" Or was it snobbery? "He was a top, top barrister in Hong Kong, pretty much nobility. Martin looked at Jimmy as *chaang luo*, a factory guy, sort of unkempt."

In the following years, the two forged a close friendship—the erudite Queen's Counsel and the rough factory guy. Lai long deferred to Lee, ten years his senior, especially in public forums. More than age, Lee's educational credentials and his high-powered legal career in the service of democracy gave him a status that Lai felt he did not share.

Cardinal Joseph Zen became another close friend in the early 1990s. Born in 1932 in Shanghai, Zen fled to Hong Kong ahead of the communist takeover of China. Zen had a long-standing involvement with social justice issues. Five decades of teaching and visiting China had intensified his opposition to the Chinese Communist Party and strengthened his belief in the importance of democracy. Having escaped communism in China, he rejected the strain of faith known as liberation theology that prompted many priests to work with leftists, notably in South America. Zen and Lai both felt that Pope Francis, who was elected in 2013, too often ignored the dangers communism posed. Indeed, in 2020, Zen publicly attacked the Vatican for ceding too much to China in its attempts to reestablish relations with Beijing.

Zen's fast-tracking of Lai's conversion underscored the intimacy of their relationship, a friendship that deepened after Lai's baptism. Testifying to those ties, Zen later celebrated a private Easter Mass at the Kadoorie Avenue house. More publicly, Zen demonstrated the depth of that friendship when he chose Lai, along with Martin Lee, to join him in meeting Pope Benedict when he became a cardinal in 2006.

Lai donated generously to the church through Zen. In 2011, Zen said that he had received $2.56 million from Lai since 2005, much of which went to helping the underground church and the poor on the mainland. "I received millions and spent them for the church and the poor," said Zen, who was speaking to counteract a smear campaign alleging that he had enriched himself at Lai's expense. Zen noted that the money funded scholarships for 170 students from both the official and underground church to go abroad. The money helped "a long list of priests, nuns, and bishops in China and elsewhere." Zen also used the money to fund translations, including a lengthy compendium of the church's social doctrine. It was originally published by the Vatican in 2004 and Lai's friend, missionary Audrey Donnithorne, had championed its translation into Chinese.

Lai's brother-in-law Yeung Sum constituted another important Catholic member of the pro-democracy movement. Like Lee, Yeung graduated from the University of Hong Kong (HKU) and studied in England. He returned to Hong Kong and earned a PhD from HKU, where he taught for many years in the Department of Social Work and Public Administration. A year older than Lai, and born near him in Guangzhou, the longtime party activist and Legco member succeeded Martin Lee as the second chairman of the Democratic Party in 2002.

In converting to Catholicism, Lai didn't just strengthen ties with people like Martin Lee, Yeung Sum, and Joseph Zen. He joined a church that had an influence in Hong Kong far beyond these elite pro-democracy Catholics. Hong Kong's archdiocese counts almost 400,000 Catholics among the city's residents, a little more than 5 percent of the total. (This doesn't include more than 200,000 Catholics, most Filipino domestic servants, who live in the city but aren't considered permanent residents.)

Catholicism plays a role in Hong Kong far beyond the 5 percent of the population that practices the faith. This outsize influence partly reflects the importance of Catholic schools. As of 2022, Hong Kong had 242 Catholic schools, with over 136,000 pupils. New York City, with a million more people, in 2023 had 148 schools, with 50,000 students. The legacy of Catholic schools reflects the hands-off attitude toward education that characterized most of the 156 years of British colonial rule. (Notably, primary school education wasn't compulsory until 1971.) Catholic schools offered a high-quality, reasonably priced choice for parents—believers and nonbelievers alike—forced by a lack of places in government schools to make their own arrangements. The church was a contractor; it ran the schools—and other social services—and received subsidies for four-fifths of the cost.

The Catholic Church took a more robust stance on social issues beginning in the late 1960s. Bishop Francis Hsu, who headed the church in Hong Kong from 1969 to 1973, adopted the spirit of the modernizing Second Vatican Council of the early 1960s. He folded social concerns into Church teachings and activities, to the displeasure of the colonial government.

As the handover approached and concerns about religious freedom mounted, the Catholic Church became more involved in the struggle for democracy. Hong Kong held the first two citywide Legislative Council elections in 1991 and 1995. Catholics turned out to vote at a rate double that of the electorate as a whole. Over eight of ten Catholics voted in each of those first two Legco elections, compared with fewer than four of ten voters overall. Most Catholic voters chose pro-democracy candidates like Martin Lee and Yeung Sum.

Chris Patten, the last British governor and himself a Catholic, first met Lai with Martin Lee and a few other prominent Catholics in the pro-democracy movement shortly after he moved to Hong Kong in 1992. Lai appeared so close to Lee and the other Catholics that Patten assumed he was a Catholic when they met. (Lai and Patten subsequently developed enough of a friendship that Lai presented the departing governor with a painting by the Chinese American artist Walasse Ting as a farewell gift. Patten keeps it behind his desk in his house in France.)

Patten quickly noted the political and social engagement of Hong Kong's Catholic community. "[I]t was their belief, which was related to their Catholic faith, in human rights, in the dignity of the individual, and the importance of personal choice. All of those things mattered to them, but it was interesting across the board how many of the figures we now think of positively in terms of the future of Hong Kong—Chinese but [who] define their patriotism not in favor of the communist party, quite the reverse, Chinese who were Catholics partly because of the social teaching of the Catholic Church and [who were] naturally attracted to politics or law and very active in both."

Hong Kong's Catholics aren't all democrats. The ranks of the Hong Kong church include establishment stalwarts such as chief executives Donald

Tsang, Carrie Lam, and John Lee. Like Martin Lee, John Lee also attended Wah Yan College, though he did not go on to university. A 1999 survey found that 76 percent of senior officials had graduated from Catholic or Protestant secondary schools; Christian schools made up 250 of the city's 512 secondary schools around the time of the handover. Although there were exceptions, even after the 1997 handover, the Anglican clergy in Hong Kong didn't markedly change their long-standing colonial-era policy of buttressing government power.

Catholicism's importance in Hong Kong and its democracy movement helps explain McGurn's initial skepticism about the depth of Lai's faith. "The social circles of the pro-democracy movement in Hong Kong are so Catholic, there is such a nucleus of Chinese Catholics in the more liberal side of Hong Kong. So many of Jimmy's friends and the people he admired were Catholic. . . . I wondered how much was becoming part of the club of people that he admired rather than doctrinal belief in Christ," McGurn notes. "He knew it would make him closer to Teresa. I don't think it was bad intentions but I did worry about [how deep his faith was]. After all, his paper was still printing reviews of whorehouses." Even after Lai's baptism, *Apple Daily* continued to feature reviews of the prostitutes on Portland Street.

In the initial years after Lai's conversion, not much seemed to change. His columns had little reference to religion. Guests on his yacht or at one of his dinners typically didn't hear about God. Conversations still mostly revolved around politics and economics. How corrupt had the Chinese Communist Party become? How long could it last? When would the United States wake up to the threat that China posed? What were the CCP's latest provocations toward Taiwan? And endless discussions on local Hong Kong politics.

For the next decade or more, religion seemingly remained peripheral in Lai's life. Columns like the 2008 Christmas column for *Next* magazine, where he wrote how an angel had saved him as a young boy afraid and lost at a train station on the outskirts of Guangzhou, constituted a rare exception. McGurn's fear that Lai had converted for practical reasons, and for the social cachet, appeared to have been realized. As his godfather, McGurn took some comfort in the fact that Lai appeared more at ease. "Before his conversion he was restless. After his conversion he was no longer restless. He was comfortable."

Lai's friendship with missionary Audrey Donnithorne suggests that beneath his ever-bluff exterior he was undergoing a spiritual journey. Lai counted Donnithorne, born in 1922 in a Quaker hospital in rural Sichuan province to Anglican missionaries, as one of his closest and most enduring friends. She had led a colorful life. At two and a half years old, bandits kidnapped her, along with her parents and six others, and secured the group with halters as they marched them into the mountains. Donnithorne studied at Oxford, where she became close friends with the chemistry student Margaret Roberts (later Margaret Thatcher). Donnithorne's 1967 book, *China's Economic System*, represented one of the first comprehensive attempts to understand the Maoist economic system.

Donnithorne enjoyed close ties with the aboveground "patriotic" church in China as well as the underground priests who professed loyalty to Rome. Lai, Zen, Donnithorne, and a handful of others would strategize over dinners about how to get the word of God into China. "She was the mule," says Mike Gonzalez, who recalls Donnithorne smuggling Bibles and cash from Lai into China for believers. (She was often accompanied by a Filipina friend of the Lais who masqueraded as her maid.) Gonzalez, a Catholic who during his time in Hong Kong headed the *Asian Wall Street Journal*'s editorial page, adds, "Audrey was the perfect person to do this—who would suspect an older woman with an upper-crust British accent?" Even as Jimmy Lai's legal woes mounted in mid-2020, Teresa and Claire Lai sat with Donnithorne hour after hour, day after day, in the months before her death in June 2020, praying and wiping sweat from her body.

Lai's spiritual journey has deepened in the more than a quarter-century since his conversion, especially during his time in prison, providing needed sustenance and even nurturing a sense of freedom. Lai has embraced his fate as a political prisoner, even making the most of solitary confinement, which keeps him alone in a cell twenty-three hours a day. Authorities permit fifty minutes of outdoor exercise a day.

Lai has taken to heart Soviet dissident Natan Sharansky's admonition that a prisoner can choose to live freely. When in prison, Sharansky told him in a conversation shortly before Lai was jailed, "whether I will survive physically or not does not depend on me. It depends on the KGB. As long as I live, I will live as a free person. Every day I live, I will enjoy my freedom." Lai's prison writings display a sense of freedom and a belief that his imprisonment has meaning.

> I adapt well with prison life. I'm always at peace and have joy occasionally when reading theology that touches my heart or while I see myself improve my drawing or spiritual realization. I sometimes wonder [if] I might have been forgiven of my sins to be so adept in prison life. I pray every day for God's forgiveness. I hope He has heard.

Prison regulations allow Lai only six books a month. He has used his time behind bars to study Catholic theology. The books he read during his first two years in confinement reflect the breadth of his interests. They range from *The Collected Works of St. John of the Cross*, by the sixteenth-century Spanish mystic, to the early-twentieth-century Catholic apologist G. K. Chesterton's *In Defense of Sanity*. He reads many books by Pope Benedict but none by his more liberal successor, Francis. Lai draws courage from *The Cost of Discipleship* by the Lutheran theologian Dietrich Bonhoeffer, who was hanged by the Nazis. McGurn marvels: "I don't think Jimmy read much Catholic theology or philosophy before he went to prison, but he devours things."

In October 2022, Lai's daily entry included a brief reverie about food, after which he admonished himself.

> I'm trying to dispossess myself to enter in communion with God. I should not think of food or anything I like. I should forget myself and think of God and know Him and carry His cross with Him.

May God help me on this. For now, I try to draw good pictures, the best I can. . . . I draw very carefully and thoughtfully and correct often. I should take this opportunity of not being allowed [out of prison] . . . to improve my skill with greater discipline.

The following day, Lai struck a similar note. "Now it takes me two days to draw a picture of Pietà. Good. I want to draw a really good picture, whatever time and patience it takes from now on. I will show people only my good pictures. At least the best I can master that moment. Only with discipline could I [become] a good painter. May God help me."

Having strengthened his faith in prison, Lai turned to proselytizing. He counseled conversion to Catholicism for a variety of relatives and friends, especially those suffering difficulties. Writing after a visit by his daughter Jade, he noted: "She needs a new life, a new life reborn in God's love and grace. Only then she will be saved. May God have mercy on her." On a subsequent visit he noted, "I pointed out all the causes of her problems and she knows they were true. I shall use subsequent visits to evangelize her to convert to Catholicism."

Lai observed the effect of Christian faith—and the lack of it—on other prisoners. Lai noted approvingly that former Next Digital chief executive officer Cheung Kim-hung already practiced Christianity when authorities jailed him. Editor-in-chief Ryan Law, to Lai's dismay, initially did not. After nearly two months' detention, Lai heard disturbing reports about Law's well-being.

He was greatly ruffled, could hardly compose himself. When Pastor Lee visited him, he was angry, miserable, even cried in front of him. His family was much alarmed. His sister, an evangelist, used to work here and now evangelizes in Canada, gathered pastors, friends throughout the Christian community to give him support and console him. It works. Now he is at peace, even cheerful, and ready to be baptized.

115

Lai struggles to balance the sense that he had chosen a noble action in going to prison with the Christian dictate of humility. In the difficult circumstances he endures, he needs to find meaning in his suffering without being swept up in his own sense of importance. He struggles consciously—and almost constantly—in prison to become a more perfect person. He castigates himself for gluttony, even when just thinking about food. (Gluttony is one of the seven venial, or lesser, sins in Catholicism.) Lai didn't have a problem with most of the other ones—greed, lust, envy, and sloth. But he struggled with pride and occasionally anger. In October 2022 he described his mixed emotions to news that he had not received the Nobel Peace Prize, for which he and other Hong Kong activists had been nominated.

> I woke up with exalted happiness. It was a strong feeling. So happy. I was full of hope and promise. Though not knowing why. Later I read in the newspaper three Russian freedom fighters were awarded this year's Nobel Peace Prize. [Was my exalted happiness] the foreshadow[ing] of the news I was so happy with? A few movement comrades who are in prison were nominated with me for this year's Nobel Peace Prize. Now, we did not get it. That means I've been saved being exalted by vainglory. That I may stay humble to serve the Lord. This delivery from temptation of fame and glory was the reason I was happy.

Earlier, Lai told Robert Sirico about the power of ideas that remained as a legacy of the century and a half of British colonial rule. "We inherited Western culture and values and institutions. The British did not give us democracy but they gave us rule of law, private property, freedom of speech, of assembly, of religion. This is why China is very afraid of us. The values we share with the West are very dangerous to Chinese in China. That's why they want to clamp down on us. We are a small island but we have big ideas."

Lai's belief in the power and strength of the idea of freedom ruled by law, coupled with his Catholic faith, gives him the strength to endure for far longer than he expected would be necessary. "I think when he went in, he didn't think he would be in for long," says McGurn. "Jimmy is more at peace after four years in prison than ever before in his life. He never complains about anything."

McGurn, his initially somewhat skeptical godfather, believes that Lai has finally found his purpose in life. He always felt that he was marked out as someone special, but he didn't know what form that exceptionalism would take. Now he is becoming a focus of opposition to the Chinese Communist Party. "He is driving them crazy because he won't go along with the lie." One man in a country of 1.4 billion people who uses his considerable moral and material resources to fight the lie.

Chapter Eight

"CRAZY HYPE
AND ARROGANCE"

Ihad a midlife crisis and I lost more than one hundred million dollars."
That's how Lai sums up his first dive into e-commerce. He had set up
Admart, an online grocery shopping site, in June 1999 during the dot-
com boom. Using technology to do away with physical stores and deliver
directly to consumers struck the experienced retailer as a sure winner.
Amazon, founded five years earlier, had shown the commercial promise
of an e-commerce platform. Dozens of other young companies peddled
everything from pet food to groceries in America. Lai figured he would
get out in front of the competition in Hong Kong.

Lai thought that at Admart he could replicate the success he'd had with
Giordano and *Apple Daily*. By buying in bulk, Lai calculated he would
have a low-cost model that could dominate the market. Hong Kong's small
size would keep delivery costs low. Geographically Hong Kong is a bit
larger than New York City. With 70 percent of the city set aside as parks or
agricultural land, most of the territory's seven million people are jammed
into high-density neighborhoods in Kowloon, Hong Kong Island, and a
handful of satellite cities in the New Territories. Almost everyone lives in
apartment buildings.

Lai's success at his previous businesses prompted him to invest on a large scale and ignore warnings from associates. Admart's flop revealed the downside of Lai's character, showing how his strengths could lead to failure as well as success.

Admart marked the first of several setbacks over the next decade. Although Lai had a strong understanding of technology's business potential, and his entrepreneurial vision led to important insights, he sometimes failed to capitalize on his ideas. Sometimes his thinking proved to be too far ahead of the capabilities of commercially available products. Or it relied on an overly optimistic assessment of the market. In other cases, the problem was stiff competition from deep-pocketed and powerful rivals.

Three factors contributed to the online delivery company's collapse.

Unlike most entrepreneurs, Lai had too much money and too few restraints on his decision-making. He set up Admart as a private venture, separate from the publicly traded Next Media. Flush with cash, he didn't have to go to a banker, so he didn't endure the sort of hard questioning that might have forced him to evaluate the business more dispassionately. He invested too much, too quickly. In addition to buying 350 delivery vans, Admart leased sixteen warehouses around Hong Kong and employed 850 people. "I was so rich that I didn't have to borrow money or even stretch my resources," he told journalist Thomas Crampton.

The downside to strong leaders, especially well-funded ones, is that employees tend not to be able to question the strategy. Nobody could stop Lai until he had racked up big losses. A longtime associate teamed up with Chinese University of Hong Kong Professor Leung Kwok, who had played a pivotal role in the success of Giordano, Next, and Apple Daily, in trying to dissuade Lai. "He got very annoyed when both of us tried to tell him it wouldn't work," remembers the close associate. "He was very stubborn about the whole thing. He somehow lost any sense of proportionality."

Hong Kong's small size and density proved as much a curse as a blessing. A market of seven million wasn't large enough to sustain a business model focused on bulk grocery deliveries. These carried lower profit margins than perishable food, like expensive beef and fresh fruit. "We didn't have the economy of scale to sustain it," says colleague Simon Lee, who joined *Apple Daily* in 2004 as a columnist and later worked for Lai in a variety of different tech-focused roles. "The per-delivery cost was too high, over twenty-five dollars." Hong Kong's density, viewed as an advantage, proved too much of a good thing—delivery vans couldn't park near enough the apartments where most people lived, so delivery people had to make time-consuming drop-offs by foot in vast housing complexes. That also raised delivery costs.

Third, rival grocery stores struck back in a way that newspaper rivals wouldn't dare. Two big companies, part of larger business conglomerates, dominated Hong Kong's grocery market. Jardine Matheson, heir to the traders who had prompted Britain to seize Hong Kong in the first Opium War, owned grocery store chain Wellcome. Hutchison Whampoa, controlled by Li Ka-shing, counted rival PARKnSHOP in its stable of businesses.

"Admart crushed PARKnSHOP and Wellcome every single day with the price of goods," maintains Mark Simon, who had been a shipping industry executive when Lai hired him in May 2001 to straighten out Admart's logistical problems before dispatching him to untangle the Canadian hotels and later assigned him to a variety of roles at *Apple Daily* and Next Media. Admart advertised in *Apple Daily* so everyone in the city knew what the company was charging for, say, Coca-Cola. "People were marching in to Wellcome and PARKnSHOP and asking why they had higher prices."

Rival grocery giants had the resources needed to match Admart on price and service. PARKnSHOP started a home delivery offering. Wellcome and PARKnSHOP both cut prices to maintain market share. They also dissuaded local distributors from selling to Admart. So Admart had to source gray-market products from as far afield as the Philippines and South Africa. That made Admart vulnerable to supply-chain problems. When a shipment of Bordeaux wine proved counterfeit, competitors jumped on the news.

The competition proved great for consumers. Simon Lee points to an economic analysis done at the time calculating that Admart alone lowered Hong Kong's inflation rate by several percentage points: "Its impact on the inflation rate was quite phenomenal." Lai could take satisfaction in knowing that he had made Hong Kong's retail economy more competitive. Admart showed how existing business models could be upended by the internet.

By the time Lai decided to shutter the operation in December 2000, after just eighteen months in business, only fifty of the 350 delivery vans he bought had been driven. And no more than one of four customers used the internet to place orders; most people phoned or faxed. "I was blinded by crazy hype and my own arrogance," Lai told Crampton. It was an expensive lesson, but Lai shrugged off the losses. He willingly paid the price to learn how the internet and other new technologies were upending business.

With newspapers and magazines, he offered an eye-catching product that promoted freedom and democracy—a product that consumers wanted and his competitors proved afraid to provide. The unwillingness of other newspaper and magazine owners to compete with Lai politically meant that his publications had no real competition. To use a concept popularized by legendary investor Warren Buffett, Lai's media products were protected by a moat, a barrier that made it difficult for competitors to breach. The grocery business didn't have the same sort of bulwark against competition that the city's tense political environment guaranteed for Lai's media. Grocery sales largely depended on low prices. And Wellcome and PARKnSHOP would match Admart's to keep the upstart from succeeding.

The technology-induced "hype and arrogance" that led to Admart's failure sobered employees at Next Media and set back Lai's effort to integrate digital operations into the print magazine and newspaper business. "After Admart shut down, no one ever wanted anything to do with digital again," remembers Mark Simon, whom Lai put in charge of the company's digital operations in 2006. A small team of four people uploaded the newspaper every morning at 10 a.m., but the website remained static, unchanged until the next day's paper was uploaded. "Nobody would touch digital because it had bad mojo from Admart," said Simon. It would take the better part of a decade before *Apple Daily* journalists embraced the internet and mobile technology.

Lai's focus shifted to Taiwan, where the country's first opposition president had taken power earlier in 2000. "After building a base here in Hong Kong for my publications to enter Cantonese-speaking China from the south, I will build a Mandarin-speaking base in Taiwan from which to enter the north," Lai told Thomas Crampton at the end of the year. "China is the future, not the Internet."

In both Taiwan and Hong Kong, Lai invested in a clutch of technology ventures, some sensible and many quixotic. Crampton later joined Lai's private company, where he worked on a number of such ideas. Lai knew that new high-speed broadband would give content providers new power. "He saw that the day was coming when we would be able to break the cable TV's monopoly [on distribution] through the internet," says Crampton.

Crampton worked with Lai to develop a small device, about the size of a deck of cards, that people could plug into the back of their television set and directly access streaming services, thus bypassing cable. In 2007 and 2008, when Crampton tried to develop Lai's idea, the product to do this didn't yet exist. Soon afterward, when internet services improved, U.S.-based Roku succeeded with a virtually identical offering. "The challenge was the bandwidth," remembers Crampton, with internet speeds too slow to allow streaming services of the sort Lai had in mind.

For a time, the idea of virtual reality captivated Lai as a new business area. His idea foreshadowed what Mark Zuckerberg would later dub the metaverse. He fitted out a large production studio on the northern edge of Taipei for virtual reality and animation. "His vision was that everyone could create their own avatar and have a presence in alternate space like a movie avatar," says Simon Lee. "He thought about having this immersive experience for people." Computing power at the time proved inadequate. Commonly available technology just wasn't ready for a 3-D world. Lai's prized avatars looked comedic. He quickly shelved most of his ideas for virtual reality.

Lai challenged Lee, who had originally joined as a free-market columnist, to make a commercial success of virtual reality in a more modest business codenamed Homebuyer. Lee used aerial photography and three-dimensional imagery to create an immersive virtual reality experience of viewing a model apartment. Many developers in Taiwan and Hong Kong sell apartments before they are actually built, using buyers' down payments to fund construction costs. A virtual reality apartment viewing could have helped boost sales. The company applied for a patent on a phone camera that could create the illusion of three-dimensional space by tracing the lines of a room. The venture proved modestly profitable but never took off.

Lai also wanted to build hyperlocal websites. HomeBloc allowed local businesses—and individuals—to sell to a very targeted group. "People could invest a small amount of money advertising services like piano lessons, tutoring, babysitters," remembers Simon Lee of the thinking in 2006, the year before the iPhone was introduced and upended consumer-oriented technology businesses. "We wanted to build that kind of relationship with advertisers. We wanted to get advertising from these small-timers. We were thinking of that way before the smartphone." Again, the internet was too slow to make the idea successful.

Monitoring police chatter in real time allowed *Apple Daily* photographers and reporters to get to the scene of a crime or a fire at the same time as cops and firefighters—often, because many of Lai's paparazzi rode motorcycles, ahead of these first responders. *Apple Daily*'s dramatic photos had helped make the paper successful. Lai and his team struggled to adapt when the Hong Kong police force moved their communications onto a secure closed-circuit system around this time, doing away with open radio channels. Now Lai's people weren't there to snap the photos. "The new system took away our ability to report," says Mark Simon.

Eager to find a solution, Lai took inspiration as he watched his son Sebastien, then a young teenager, glued to a screen watching cartoons. Simon remembers Lai's insight: "We can't show the news, but we can animate it." If *Apple Daily* couldn't photograph the news, Lai figured that his team could use cartoons to tell the story as it could have happened. "Jimmy's concept was that the current generation's language is that of video games," notes Crampton, who headed the new operation. "We need to bring that language of video games and marry that with the newsroom." So he hired "a bunch of smart video game people and a bunch of journalists" to produce a different kind of nightly news.

The team worked behind unmarked doors in a secret location in the Neihu district of northern Taipei beginning in mid-2009. They toiled for weeks to produce a single three-minute video. Lai liked what he saw. "Give me three of those every night," he ordered. Lai urged the team to think about showing events like an unfolding auto accident. "Show me what happens three seconds before the car crashes," he told Crampton.

The most famous—or infamous—bit of cartoon news Next Media Animation produced featured golfer Tiger Woods storming out of his house after a Thanksgiving fight with his then-wife Elin Nordegren, crashing his car, followed by Nordegren smashing the back window with a golf club. Or at least that's how Next Media Animation portrayed it. The core of the incident was real—Tiger Woods left his house late on Thanksgiving night in 2009 and crashed his car. Next's animated version was largely speculative.

Global media took notice. *Wired* admired the effort. The *New York Times* worried about the blurring of fact and fiction: "Welcome to the new world of Maybe Journalism—a best guess at the news as it might well have been, rendered as a video game and built on a bed of pure surmise." The Tiger Woods video showed how an imagined, re-created version of the event could define how the public thought about it. When *Sports Illustrated* wrote about the incident in 2017, eight years after it happened, it provided a link to the Next Media Animation video.

The 1.7 million views it garnered in its first week was impressive in the early days of YouTube and mobile online viewing. The early success prompted a staggering $300 million investment in a full-scale production studio and the animation group's quick expansion. Michael Logan joined the Taiwan team in March 2010 as international content director from Hong Kong, where he had been running the *South China Morning Post*'s website. Logan had one colleague on his team when he showed up in Taipei. Lai tasked Logan with growing the international business following the success of the Tiger Woods video. Next Media Animation signed a contract with Reuters to distribute its content to subscribers around the world. Lai hit the accelerator on the business. Logan had sixty people on the international team when the venture peaked a few years later.

Next Media Animation specialized in satire. Shortly after Logan joined, a clip featured Steve Jobs releasing the iPhone 4. Critics had complained that the phone had poor reception. Jobs, known for his tendency to bend reality to his way of thinking, had countered that consumers should hold the phone differently. Next Media Animation cast Jobs as Darth Vader, immune to consumer complaints, using his light saber to amputate three fingers from the critic's iPhone-cradling hand. Now, with just the thumb and a single finger holding the phone, full bars, signaling strong reception, magically appeared. "We had one and a half million views in less than a week," marvels Logan. "I realized we had something special."

Daily operations resembled a mash-up of a traditional newspaper editorial meeting, a Ford Model T automobile assembly line, and a 1920s Hollywood production studio. The group would initially pick a story with international resonance, like the iPhone launch. Then a team of writers would go to work, tossing around ideas with a view to wrapping up a script within about an hour. The script would be translated from English into Chinese and go to a storyboard artist. She would sketch panels and present the animation to the production team.

The modelers would go to a database and pull what images they could while getting actors ready for the motion-capture machine. Actors, dressed in what looked like full-body diving suits dotted with Ping-Pong-ball-like motion sensors at their joints, played the Darth Vader light-saber scene on a motion-capture stage. Finally, a team of animators and editors would finalize the clip and set it to music. The visual vocabulary had to work because the clips were usually in Chinese.

These clips were done at high speed—six an hour in the motion-capture studio. Next Animation Media bought top-of-the-line equipment that would have met Hollywood standards. Everything was off-the-shelf, rather than custom-made. "What was novel was the arrangement of workflow, the idea that you would animate something in three hours and assemble the parts," remembered Logan. "You can't do Pixar in three hours." At its peak, the studio operated around the clock, turning out more than one hundred animation clips a day.

Lai calculated that he could sell each thirty-second clip to multiple subscribers around the world for $50 each. But the production costs added up to $700 for each clip. Lai's assembly-line approach meant relatively low production costs. Relatively cheap, yes, but it still cost $84,000 to produce an hour of animated news. Far too much of the output went unsold. "Our capacity was huge," said Logan. "I had several hours a day of animation that needed to be monetized."

YouTube paid more than $100,000 a month at the peak but after it changed its algorithm, that amount dropped to almost nothing. Reuters paid more than $30,000 a month but there weren't enough other big-ticket subscribers. Contract work, mostly for *Apple Daily* and *Next*, helped cover the overheads but was done on a low-margin, cost-plus basis. "The debate I always had with him was who your market is," Crampton remembers. "He said, 'There are so many American newspapers and they need material.' I said that these American newspapers don't have any money." Crampton proved correct.

"To set up a news animation studio was a crazy thing to do," reflects Logan. "But it was a lot of fun to see [our work] on *Late Night with Conan O'Brien*, to see it on BBC, to see it on *The Daily Show* and to be able to put a spotlight on Taiwan. Even though ultimately the economics didn't work, I always feel that wasn't the only reason Jimmy did things." Lai ultimately bought the animation unit for $100 million from the public company, selling an investment he had made in Taiwan's E.SUN Bank to finance the purchase for his private holdings. He later folded it.

His enthusiastic adoption of technology extended throughout his media empire. Just as he had invested heavily in point-of-sale data systems at

Giordano to create a better customer experience, he continued to experiment and spend lavishly at *Next* and *Apple Daily*. From the early days of the print businesses, Lai's editors and designers worked with best-of-class software and computers. The paper rolled off world-class Goss printing presses. *Apple Daily* quickly adopted all-digital printing, and the paper won numerous awards for its production quality. In November 2009, Lai started Apple Action News to produce videos that could be viewed on a computer or one of the increasingly popular iPhones that had been introduced just two years earlier. The product won the loyalty of a new generation of young Hong Kongers.

Over the course of three decades, Lai's embrace of technology allowed him to transform a print-based media empire into a successful multimedia conglomerate. His adoption of innovative products proved more successful when they were integrated into existing businesses than in futuristic start-ups. He had succeeded at Comitex with an endless stream of small improvements. Giordano's point-of-sale systems and the high-quality color printing presses that *Apple Daily* and *Next* used paid for themselves with increased profits. The string of early successes may have given Lai a feeling of invincibility and contributed to the arrogance that he confessed to Crampton. His visionary ideas, reflects Logan, are "always a decade or two ahead of the technology."

His best ideas reflected a tendency to learn by doing. "The way that he works, he wants you to try [an idea] to the point of failure," says Logan. "He'll have one hundred ideas and he only needs one of them to work. He wants to go through all one hundred and you have to fail those ninety-nine times. . . . He is the kind of person who wants to try things and fail rather than have some consultant tell him why it isn't going to work."

Chapter Nine

"I WANT TO BE TAIWANESE"

On March 18, 2000, Jimmy Lai glimpsed the future of Chinese democracy. It was in Taiwan. That day, the island's 22 million people threw off five decades of authoritarian single-party rule and elected longtime pro-democracy lawyer Chen Shui-bian as president. The same evening, "I told my wife, 'let's move to Taiwan,'" Lai remembered. "When he was elected, it was obviously a true democracy."

Lai moved to Taiwan with Teresa and their two children and spent much of the next decade in the island nation. Son Sebastien and daughter Claire attended the French elementary school in Taipei. Lai loved the food, the arts, and, above all, the sense of freedom. Taiwan showed what a modern Chinese society could look like. "I love Taiwan," he told friends. "I want to be Taiwanese."

The shock wave from Chen's election in 2000 reverberated throughout Asia. His victory led to the first peaceful transfer of elected power in more than two thousand years of Chinese history. Chen's election repudiated the idea that Asians invariably favored strongmen. "This was a landmark," marvels Antonio Chiang, who for decades had been a dissident journalist in Taiwan. In a sign of how much had changed, Chiang joined Chen's National Security Council as deputy secretary general. "We always had one sky and one sun,

129

Mark L. Clifford

but now we had two or three suns. They said Asian values were authoritarian. We proved them wrong. That's what excited Jimmy Lai," says Chiang, who developed a friendship with Lai and later wrote for *Apple Daily Taiwan*.

Martial law in Taiwan had ended in 1987, setting the stage for a political thaw that quickened after the 1988 death of Chiang Ching-kuo, the son of the country's autocratic founder, Chiang Kai-shek. Liberalization in the late 1980s gave Chen Shui-bian an opening to start climbing the rungs of the national political ladder. In 1989, he was elected as a national legislator. In 1994, as Lai prepared for the launch of Hong Kong's *Apple Daily*, Taipei voters elected Chen their city's mayor. Although he lost a mayoral reelection bid in 1998, he took advantage of his increased prominence to run for president in 2000. When the ruling Kuomintang (KMT) party split, Chen squeezed ahead of the other two candidates and ended more than a half century of one-party rule on the island.

Chen, the son of peasants from southern Taiwan, had a background every bit as modest as Lai's. He had begun in politics by defending dissidents in 1980 and soon found himself drawn into the pro-democracy movement. In 1985, authorities jailed him for his work editing a pro-democracy magazine. While Lai struggled to build Giordano in Hong Kong, in Taiwan Chen Shui-bian, Antonio Chiang, and a small group of determined democrats were pushing back against the military government.

Chen's election diminished the chance of a rapprochement with the mainland and threatened the official "one-China policy," which envisioned an eventual merger between the mainland and Taiwan and had guided China-Taiwan relations since 1949. That's when Chiang Kai-shek, faced with defeat on the mainland, evacuated some one million KMT soldiers and their families to the island. He continued to cling to the fiction that he would one day rule China. Taipei had a provisional feel because the KMT viewed the city merely as a temporary home: the party didn't invest in what it regarded as a temporary seat of government. Whatever their ideological differences, both the Chinese Communist Party and the Kuomintang agreed that there was only one China—they just didn't agree on who should rule it.

Chen ran on a pro-Taiwan platform that barely mentioned reunification with mainland China. This reflected voters' growing disenchantment with the idea of a political union. In electing Chen, Taiwan's voters repudiated both the Chinese Communist Party and the KMT's insistence on the one-China policy and the idea that Taiwan should be ruled by a one-party state. Chen came from a family that had long called the island its home, and he and his supporters focused on democracy rather than reunification.

Taiwan's recent political history was almost as dismal as China's, making its embrace of democracy even more encouraging to Lai. The KMT had taken control of Taiwan, for five decades a Japanese colony, after Tokyo's surrender in 1945. Its rule was authoritarian. In a 1947 bloodletting, the so-called February 28 (or "228") incident, thousands of civilians were killed in an uprising.

While Hong Kong remained politically frozen following the 1997 handover of the former British colony to China, reform in Taiwan surged forward. In 1997, a continuing political thaw permitted the opening of the commemorative 228 Memorial Park. For almost fifty years, Taiwan had prohibited mention of the incident, much as mainland China has banned discussion of the Tiananmen massacre. Chen's election as president in 2000 reflected more than two decades of political struggle and change.

By the time Lai moved to Taiwan in 2000, Taiwan had reinvented itself: the Japanese agricultural colony had become a poster child for economic growth, one of the four Asian Tigers. Along with Hong Kong, Singapore, and South Korea, Taiwan had gone from rice paddies to riches in a generation. Its hardworking, entrepreneurial, and scientifically skilled labor force transformed the island into a key global electronics producer. Taiwan's factories produced semiconductor chips, keyboards, monitors, laptops, desktops, phones, and virtually all the components that went into manufacturing them.

By the time Chen was elected, Taiwan had emerged as a one-stop shop for the electronics industry—it would produce anything and sell to anyone.

At first this was low-end, labor-intensive manufacturing. Increasingly, Taiwanese companies moved into more sophisticated areas of the electronics business. Homegrown giant Taiwan Semiconductor Manufacturing Co. (TSMC) spent billions of dollars every year on new factories to make chips for Apple and other leading global manufacturers and was already one of the world's most important chipmakers.

Meanwhile, authorities had begun liberalizing Taiwan's domestic economy in preparation for entering the World Trade Organization. No longer would Taiwan simply be an exporter, selling to the world and buying little in return. It would be a free market, officials promised. Taiwan might never be as economically open as Hong Kong but it looked set to adopt more global, market-oriented standards.

Taiwan's raucous political scene gave the lie to the Chinese Communist Party's insistence that Chinese people—whether they were in Taiwan itself, in Hong Kong, or on the mainland—weren't ready for freedom. Everyone from filmmakers, painters, and dancers to chefs and restaurateurs showed the world—and Chinese on the mainland—what a free, modern, cosmopolitan China could look like. Importantly for Lai as a businessman, a new generation of Taiwanese consumers had money to spend on food, travel, and entertainment, ensuring a solid advertising base for *Taiwan Next* and *Apple Daily Taiwan.*

Still, Taiwan did not look like an obvious place to start a magazine and newspaper. The market was crowded, with three major newspapers already competing for readers in a country of 20 million. Lai had made *Apple Daily* stand out with innovative characters representing Cantonese slang. But he and his senior team of Hong Kongers didn't speak the local language of the democracy movement, Taiwanese.

Lai believed that his formula of hard-hitting news and no-holds-barred investigative stories, coupled with what a friend termed the "sex, skin, and scandal" tabloid aspects of his papers, would prove as popular in Taiwan as in Hong Kong. He later recalled that "a lot of people thought this was crazy. Go into a market you don't know and it was saturated." He continued:

I was not looking at it this way. What tempts me is the monopoly these newspapers were practicing. When you go into a monopolist market, they don't know how to react to you. They never thought readers were anything you have to take care of. . . .

For us going into a market like this is very easy. We figure out what people need. We are market-driven or reader-centric in the market, which [our competitors] cannot understand because they cannot understand the readers. We have to follow what the people need.

Lai launched *Taiwan Next Magazine* in May 2001, a year after Chen Shuibian took office. Almost immediately, it became the country's best-selling weekly news magazine. A year later, it had a circulation of 140,000 readers. *Taiwan Next* proved that Lai could find a new market for his bold, colorful journalism. He had developed a competitive formula that would transcend the narrow confines of the Cantonese-speaking city of Hong Kong.

He spent the next two years setting up *Apple Daily Taiwan*. Newspapers are significantly more complex and expensive to run than weekly magazines, so this sequential strategy made good business sense. Still, money appeared to be no object. Lai had always compensated his journalists well. In Taiwan, he rewarded his staff with the highest salaries and the best equipment in the industry. Hong Kong native Ip Yut-kin, the first editor-in-chief of *Apple Daily Taiwan*, marvels at Lai: "He's very generous. He doesn't care about money. It's very interesting." Lai single-handedly pushed up journalists' salaries across the board in both Hong Kong and Taiwan.

China joined the World Trade Organization (WTO) in December 2001 after years of negotiations. Taiwan entered the following month. Although Taipei had been ready to enter for some time, the Geneva-based trading body deferred to the mainland's growing power and gave it precedence.

Lai had correctly predicted that WTO entry would help lead to direct links, such as air travel, between China and Taiwan as well as more generally spur trade and economic growth for both economies. The momentum for economic reform in the mainland, followed by more political openness, appeared inevitable to him. Taiwan would be the springboard for Lai's push into the People's Republic. Next Media would be poised to take advantage when China opened to free media. In 2003, Lai wrote shareholders, "I want to assure you that when that day comes—and it will come—we shall be ready and prepared."

In May 2003, three years after Chen's inauguration, the first copies of *Apple Daily Taiwan* rolled off the presses. Lai exuded confidence. In just thirteen years, Lai could justifiably boast, "we have grown to become one of the most comprehensive—and largest—Chinese media groups anywhere in the world." The group now had two newspapers, five magazines, and a commercial printing operation.

The newspaper proved another overnight success. It sold an average of 406,599 copies a day in the second half of 2003. By way of comparison, the *New York Times* had average weekday sales about three times as high (an average of 1,118,565 in the six months ending September 30, 2003), in a country with fourteen times the population.

A year later, circulation had jumped to more than 500,000. In just two years, *Apple Daily Taiwan* had established itself as a top-tier player in Taiwan's crowded media market. "We took over the market," remembers Ip Yut-kin. Ip says that *Apple Daily Taiwan* was "easy to set up—we just followed the Hong Kong model, like we were McDonald's." A handful of Hong Kongers like the Taiwan-educated Ip ran the operation, with hundreds of editors and reporters from Taiwan providing the editorial content.

Competing dailies "were used to martial law–style newspapers," notes Antonio Chiang, who worked closely with Lai even after he joined Chen Shui-bian's National Security Council. During martial law, the government had limited the number of press licenses, removing the incentive to compete. Before *Apple* burst onto the scene, advertising space in local newspapers was so limited that advertisers had to queue up to place ads. As in Hong Kong, *Apple Daily Taiwan* had top-notch presses and high-quality paper and ink: this allowed it to win advertising from luxury brands like LVMH, which typically bought space in magazines rather than newspapers. "If we want to run LV ads, we need high-quality printing," says Ip.

Existing newspapers looked boring, with long articles and few graphics. Before *Apple Daily Taiwan* introduced its flashy, colorful layout, papers had virtually no color printing. Journalists didn't compete on scoops. Each beat had a so-called journalists' club. Reporters covering, say, the presidential palace would agree what would be quoted and what wouldn't—and which stories would run and which wouldn't. Each of the three major incumbent newspapers was linked to a political party and thus partisan.

A sensitive story could be killed by a phone call from a powerful business backer or politician. Not with Lai. "He had no friends," one of the country's most powerful businessmen tells me. "We rely on our friendships to soften the news. We try to make friends and use our influence if it is negative." The Taiwan business community knew of his refusal to back down in the face-off with Li Ka-shing. "We will never be more powerful than Li Ka-shing, so if he will not yield to him, he will not yield to us," says the businessman. As a result, "We didn't need to make friends with Jimmy."

Lai banned cozy relations with businessmen or politicians. He fired a reporter who took an all-expenses-paid junket to China. "The way he ran newspapers was just so different from others," remembers Antonio Chiang. "He didn't socialize. He gave reporters total freedom and he was not afraid of any pressure because he didn't know anybody. That was very new. The reporter is responsible for himself. You cannot blame censorship or your boss's friend [if your story doesn't run the way you want it to]. You are responsible. That was why people in *Apple Daily* were so proud of their independence."

As they had in Hong Kong, *Next Taiwan* and *Apple Daily Taiwan* broke story after story, scandal after scandal. Photographers managed to insert their car into the motorcade for Chen Shui-bian's daughter's wedding. Paparazzi snapped shots of a judge taking his mistress into a motel. Drones captured evidence of illicit activity at a luxury villa. In another case, reporters waited in a hotel room across the hall from where a minister had taken his girlfriend. The photographer took pictures of the aftermath of the tryst even before the hotel staff had a chance to clean the room. In a more serious vein, investigative reporters exposed secret payments by the Taiwan government to U.S. and Japanese scholars.

Lai ran into plenty of opposition. Civic groups, journalism professors, and media watchdogs protested. Ominously, gangsters skinned a dog and nailed it to the door of Lai's house in the exclusive Yangmingshan area, north of the city. Taiwanese call paparazzi *gouzaidui* ("dog packs") and the gangsters wanted to intimidate Lai. "You can see if a man is doing the right thing by who he is angering," says Lai's son, Sebastien. "If you're not afraid of the CCP, you are probably not afraid of gangsters."

In Hong Kong, *Apple Daily* took an antigovernment stance. *Apple Daily Taiwan* adopted a dramatically different approach. In democratic Taiwan, it studiously refused to take sides. *Apple Daily Taiwan* prided itself on its political independence and its willingness to go after anyone. In the Taiwan media, "either you are aligned with some business tycoon or some party powers or the government," said Lai. "We just criticize anybody [and] expose everybody."

Former employees, independent journalists, businessmen, and ordinary readers—even those who felt that he coarsened the journalism scene—back up Lai's assertion. "When *Apple* and *Next* attacked politicians, they never cared about their political background," said Wu'er Kaixi, one of the most prominent dissidents in the Tiananmen demonstrations (and one of the three student leaders whom Lai featured on his T-shirts), who later moved to Taiwan. "Taiwanese all believed in Jimmy's political independence."

The prominent businessman tells me, "Eventually *Apple Daily* became the only newspaper or traditional media most people trust," because other media had affiliations with political parties. "Many people think it's the only neutral newspaper." This executive credits Lai, who he said was "really the chief of the editorial page," for the paper's tone. "He had ideas and knowledge and observations that are right to the point—not just about Taiwan." Lai and this businessman weren't friends and in fact clashed over Next's attempts to get distribution for its television programming in Taiwan.

The long-established newspaper companies pressured their distributors not to carry *Apple Daily Taiwan*. Lai responded by embracing the challenge, showing his entrepreneurial ability to turn setbacks to advantage. "I told people I don't want anything delivered at home. I only want our newspaper to be sold at the newsstand. If the newspaper is delivered at home the guy doesn't have to make a decision to pick up the newspaper and read it." By 2005, Lai could boast that more than 98 percent of the 500,000 daily copies and 600,000 weekend copies were bought at newsstands and convenience stores.

That put even more pressure on the staff to ensure that each day's news would compel readers to buy a copy. "By making the decision to buy it, they are active readers—they are active members of society, at least [for] today," said Lai. "Advertisements are a lot more effective than [in] the other newspapers. That worked very well for us."

Taiwan became a new growth center for the company. It had a population triple that of Hong Kong. Its democracy was becoming firmly rooted. New technology provided more opportunities. "[W]e believe that the island's fundamentals remain strong and that the outlook for its free and democratic society, and particularly for its enfranchised and open-minded citizens, presents us with a special opportunity to provide the kind of publications and products that meet the needs of its readers and advertisers," Lai wrote shareholders in 2007.

Even friends sometimes looked askance at the journalism. Ambassador Raymond Burghardt, a longtime friend of Lai's and formerly the chairman of the American Institute in Taiwan, summarized *Apple Daily Taiwan*'s strategy as "a formula of scandal and sex and skin." An unapologetic Lai countered Burghardt's quip: "That's part of human nature." Lai contended: "A lot of people ask me why you make your news so sensational. It is because you cannot make it a very intellectual product. Nobody wants to go to school every day. They want to enjoy life. They want to have the news relate to their life, to their spending. I think this is something that a lot of people in the media have missed."

Longtime journalist Antonio Chiang remembered Lai pushing him to "simplify and exaggerate." Lai urged his reporters to cover daily life—the price of sugar in the local market, rather than politics or policy that had no emotional appeal for readers. Lai insisted that every column "amuse or educate or inspire," and admonished Chiang, "'Don't talk about nonsense. Every article must have some hook, some catch. You have to amuse people.' It was difficult. Sometimes it drove me crazy." Lai wanted short, jargon-free columns, ones that could be read by a middle school student. He limited columnists like Chiang to just five or six hundred words compared with the pieces running four or five times as long that other papers ran.

Lai ridiculed the dry, dull news served up by his competitors. Many traditional newspapers and TV stations believe "people need something they don't want. This is ridiculous. It's like my mother told me when I was young, I need to eat vegetables though I don't like [them]. My mother had the right to force me to eat vegetables because I was a kid. But we are dealing with adults. How can you treat your readers as kids? If they don't want something you don't force it [onto] them."

While Lai peddled "scandal and sex and skin," he always pushed political freedom and market freedom. He felt that the sexy, salacious skin wouldn't obscure the serious message tucked inside. Worldwide he may have been unique as a media magnate marrying tawdry, eye-catching content to a serious message about liberty. Rupert Murdoch would have to meld the *New York Post, Wall Street Journal*, and London's *Sun* to approximate what Lai did with *Apple Daily* in both Hong Kong and Taiwan.

Murdoch and Lai never met. Their similarities and differences as media owners are striking. Both are important political figures and highly divisive. Lai espouses many of the same free-market ideas as Murdoch and his *Wall Street Journal* and is friends with many of Murdoch's editorial writers. Both Murdoch and Lai peddled scandal in pursuit of market share.

But while Murdoch craves power as a kingmaker, Lai doesn't. Where Lai stood up to China, Murdoch cowered. A 1993 speech by Murdoch boasting that technology has "proved an unambiguous threat to totalitarian regimes everywhere" led the Chinese to retaliate against his Hong Kong–based satellite television operation, Star TV, by banning the sale of satellite dishes on the mainland. Murdoch kowtowed, repeatedly, publicly, in an attempt to get the ban lifted. He removed BBC and its uncensored news from Star TV, canceled Chris Patten's memoirs, and bought a hagiography of paramount leader Deng Xiaoping.

In Taiwan, the business results suggested that Lai was putting out a paper that readers wanted. By 2008 Lai was able to boast that the newspaper was both the island's best-selling and most expensive. "When I first went into the Taiwanese market as someone who comes in from the outside I was not burdened with the past, the connections, the friendships, the business connections. I can publish anything, any scandals. Taiwan was a more conservative place. People didn't do that."

Despite all his hopes for Taiwan's emerging democracy, Lai soured on Chen Shui-bian by the end of his second and final term in 2008. *Apple Daily Taiwan* broke a series of scandals that engulfed Chen and his family. The president, moreover, refused to embrace a more market-oriented economy. Lai bristled at what he saw as an overregulated economy in Taiwan. Companies needed to get many more approvals in Taiwan than in freewheeling Hong Kong. A slow-moving bureaucracy allowed local business interests to keep new competitors out. Antonio Chiang faults Lai, though, for a "very shallow and simplistic" understanding of government and governance. "He thinks the free market will [triumph] over everything."

Though Lai lambasted Chen Shui-bian for his policies, he lauded the longtime opposition politician for his role in strengthening democracy.

Such a bad government is a test [of] democracy. Democracy still stands and is working very well. That is a true democracy. By default Chen Shui-bian has reinforced the strength of the democracy in

Taiwan. Making the Taiwanese a lot more confident with their democracy. Taiwan is next to a dictatorship that was a zillion times more powerful. Taiwanese were very insecure about their democracy whether it is going to work under the threat of the communists. . . . [In focus groups,] we see people . . . having more confidence in their democracy, more confidence in deal[ing] with China. They have never had the sort of self-esteem they have now.

The election of a more market-oriented president, Ma Jing-jeou, buoyed Lai. Ma wanted closer economic ties with the mainland. Lai cheered Ma's commitment to a freer economy. He met with Ma and also arranged for economist Robert Mundell, a Nobel laureate, to visit Taiwan to urge a more free-market-oriented economy. He paid for other acquaintances to visit, including former U.S. government officials like James Cunningham, whom Lai had met during his time as consul-general in Hong Kong from 2005 to 2008. He became friendly with another frequent visitor to the island, former World Bank president Paul Wolfowitz—seeking him out, says Wolfowitz, when not many others were. He hoped that these sorts of contacts could push Taiwan in a more pro-American, free-market, democratic direction.

These attempts to intervene in the political process didn't work any better with Ma Jing-jeou than they had with Chen Shui-bian. Antonio Chiang saw Lai as overly ideological in contending that a free-trade agreement would solve Taiwan's problems. For example, opening Taiwan to agricultural imports would hurt the country's farmers. "We are talking about social justice and welfare. He doesn't buy this. He thinks as long as we open up and are close to the U.S. and are friendly to China, it's the best of both worlds. C'mon, trade is always very political."

The Chinese Communist Party continued to monitor Lai's activities, though his Taiwan business didn't seem like a focus of concern. In Taiwan, the paper concentrated on local news. "The CCP didn't hate *Apple Daily Taiwan* because it didn't have much mainland news," notes Ip Yut-kin. That's something of an overstatement, but it does highlight the difference with Hong Kong, where *Apple Daily* and *Next* were alternate centers of political power.

Mainland Chinese officials tried to co-opt Lai, resorting to tried-and-tested CCP tactics. From 2003 to 2006, two powerful mainland media groups wooed Lai. Shenzhen Press Group and the Shanghai Media Group each put forward proposals giving Lai the chance to partner with one of them to run a newspaper in China on the condition that he limit coverage to sports and entertainment—no business and, of course, no politics. "I would be stupid" to accept this offer, Lai commented two years later. "If I have a business in China, I am captive. The more successful I am the more I am [a] captive." That's because authorities could punish the China business if he didn't modify his coverage in Hong Kong and Taiwan.

Officials in the relatively open border city of Shenzhen largely ignored the stacks of *Apple Daily* newspapers that crossed the Hong Kong–China border every day. (Strict border controls remained in place even after Hong Kong's 1997 handover.) "Every morning thousands of newspapers would leave our printing presses and make their way into China," says Mark Simon. "Some went by boat, some crossed on trucks, and there was actually a guy who used to pick up three or four hundred copies and send them by mail." Shipments into the mainland spiked on Wednesdays and Saturdays, Hong Kong's horse-racing days. Gambling on horse racing in Hong Kong was a lucrative business in China and *Apple Daily* excelled in its racing coverage.

By 2008, Lai's optimism about the ability to use Taiwan as a launching pad into the mainland had waned. He now had little hope that anything would change under the Communist Party. "As long as the regime is still there, it is still a dictatorship. You cannot expect media freedom. Sometimes [they] loosen, sometimes tighten. It is so erratic," he told Burghardt in January. Lai said that he planned to send reporters to China, under the guise of tourism, to cover the Beijing Olympics in August. Sometimes they were arrested, he noted matter-of-factly, and questioned about what Jimmy Lai was doing.

Apple Daily and Lai played a cat-and-mouse game with the Chinese

Communist Party. If Lai needed an example of the dangers of doing business in China, his experience in getting squeezed out of Giordano showed him the folly of an independent-minded businessman doing anything in the mainland. Further evidence that the company would be under tight control surfaced when Lai's right-hand man, Mark Simon, went to meet Shenzhen Press Group executives. Government authorities detained Simon for four hours at Shenzhen's Shangri-La Hotel to find out more about who he was meeting and why. Lai noted that security officials displayed particular curiosity about Mark Simon. "Why would a Chinese hire an American, is he CIA?" they wanted to know. The harassment was a nuisance rather than a threat to business.

The period from 2008 to 2010 ranks among Lai's happiest times personally. His mother had finally left China in the late 1980s and lived for a time in Niagara-on-the-Lake. But she grew bored of being one of the only Chinese in a small Canadian town and in 2008 he brought her to Hong Kong. That same year his oldest child with Teresa, fourteen-year-old Sebastien, had started boarding school at Ampleforth College, a Catholic school in England. *Apple Daily Taiwan* was doing well.

He split his time between London, Paris, Taipei, and Hong Kong. He initially had high hopes that the 2008 Beijing Summer Olympics would further open China's economy, however disillusioned he had become about political reform. Although the global financial crisis deepened throughout 2008 and into 2009, the turmoil didn't seem to bother him.

This first decade of the new millennium saw a more open and increasingly confident China. The country's 2001 WTO entry had succeeded beyond the most optimistic expectations, drawing in unprecedented foreign investment and further fueling a phenomenal multi-decade run of economic growth averaging more than 10 percent annually. Polls showed even wary Hong Kongers warming to Beijing. Increasing numbers identified themselves as "Chinese" rather than as "Hong Konger" around the time of the Olympics.

By 2010, Lai employed more than 4,600 people. Taiwan, with 2,614 staff, had more employees than Hong Kong's 2,040. Daily readership of the Taiwan and Hong Kong editions topped four million. Profits in the fiscal year ending March 2010 totaled $41 million. Twenty years after starting out in media, no one could dispute Lai's claim that the company counted as one of the most powerful and diversified private media groups in the Chinese-speaking world.

Despite his success in Hong Kong and now Taiwan, Lai worried. He knew that print newspapers and magazines had peaked as a business. He believed that video represented the way forward. Lai kept experimenting to find new businesses to fill the place of the declining newspaper business. In Taiwan, he tried TV.

He wanted to get into TV as a technology that would bridge the gap until Next truly became a multimedia company. So he set out to buy a TV station. In November 2008, he had made a deal to buy *China Times*, one of the three main existing newspapers, largely to acquire its TV station. A banquet was planned to celebrate the formal completion of the deal. The very day of the dinner, the deal was canceled. Pro-Beijing businessman Tsai Eng-meng, owner of the Want Want food company, swooped in to buy control of the company for $621 million. The order, it seems, had come straight from Beijing: don't let Jimmy Lai buy a TV station.

Lai found a route using different technology. Next Media set up two internet channels (both using IPTV, or Internet Protocol TV), distributing set-top boxes to 100,000 households in 2010. The cable television boxes allowed users to watch Lai's TV programming. The team ramped up its activities with a news channel. What Lai tried was innovative at the time; it combined the sort of exclusive content that Netflix later developed and on-demand delivery. The team also funded its own productions, just as Netflix later did. To meet Lai's demand for even more video content, executives at the Taiwan TV station spent $7.7 million on movie rights.

Lai confidently set about shaking up the TV market, just as he had done with print. He derided the "technological backwardness and uninspiring content" of the incumbent players. By mid-2012, he had won licenses to launch news, sports, and movie channels on the set-top box channels and secured permission to broadcast an old-style, over-the-air news channel in the southern part of the island. The TV team "spent money like crazy," remembers Simon Lee, whom Lai put in charge of approving purchases. TVBS, a major competitor, had five satellite news vans for broadcasting live from the scene of news events. Next's TV team wanted forty-seven. "I had all these purchase requisition orders on my desk," marvels Lee. "They said, 'These are Jimmy's orders, he wants us to produce news that gives people a real-time, movie-like experience.'"

Lai was just a bit ahead of what was technically feasible. He also had the misfortune to be in a small market where powerful players ganged up to see that he would be frustrated in his attempts to get a broadcasting license.

Despite initially appearing receptive to a more international and liberal economy, Ma's unwillingness to open the economy disappointed Lai. Most damaging for Lai, despite the heavy investments in content and new technology, he couldn't win approval to broadcast in the Taipei area. Although he secured a license, he couldn't get the needed broadcast spectrum. The cable TV providers, for their part, refused to carry his programs. "He didn't realize that our TV is very political," says Antonio Chiang. "The license is controlled by the government and [the process has been] hijacked by a lot of business tycoons."

Both competing broadcasters and the Chinese Communist Party benefited from Lai's failure to get into Taiwan television. The defeat constituted one of the biggest business setbacks he ever suffered. He wrote shareholders in June 2013 that "regulatory authorities and entrenched business interests there have frustrated our efforts." It took a personal toll on Lai in a way that the Admart failure had not. Most of the time he looked at setbacks as an opportunity to learn something. Not with the TV failure in Taiwan. He didn't talk to colleagues about lessons learned. He thought he had done everything right, yet he didn't get the license. "*Apple Daily* and *Next* were so successful that it made Jimmy arrogant," says Ip. "He thought everything was easy."

Lai had hit a dead end. He turned sixty-four at the end of 2012. Hong Kong politics seemed stuck. So too did the media business. He had long prophesied the decline of newspapers and he struggled to find a profitable business model for his existing print publications. Meanwhile, he searched for a new way forward in print. He had long rejected the idea of a free newspaper. In 2011, he abruptly reversed course, launching *Hong Kong Sharp Daily* in September. Five months later, Lai bragged that the newspaper had a daily circulation of more than 900,000 copies. In his annual letter to shareholders, written in June 2012, Lai predicted that the newspaper would soon have one million daily readers, which would make it the city's most-read free newspaper.

His gamble on *Hong Kong Sharp Daily* failed. The paper cannibalized *Apple Daily*, taking readers and advertisers from the flagship newspaper, and degraded editorial standards. His plans to move into video and TV had also flopped. He had intended Apple Action News as a transition product. But a transition to what? For once, Lai seemed at a loss about what to do next. Restless, beginning in 2012 he took voice lessons so that he could sing better in church.

Following his mother's death in the spring of 2011 at the age of ninety-eight, he took a lower public profile. She had lived with him for the last several years of her life. They had always been close, never more so than in these final years. His relationship with her was one of his most important. Her death hit him hard, but only after a delay.

> The moment she gave up her last breath everyone cried. I was numb—could not cry or feel anything. Only after ten days, when I was mindlessly watching TV, all of a sudden I cried out loud. I had to hide in my study. I shut the door and cried most of the day. It felt as if the world just collapsed outside the windows. I went down for dinner. The family knew what happened. Nobody said anything. Dinner was like the scene of a funeral. It took a long time for my mood to recover, or [it] never did. Something died in me.

He put his Taiwan operations up for sale and reached a preliminary agreement in November 2012 to sell them for $600 million to a group of local businessmen, including Want Want's Tsai Eng-meng. Largely because of staff opposition, the deal never went through.

From early 2011 to early 2014 he largely dropped out of sight. He and Teresa traveled extensively, spending most of 2013 in France and Italy. Many of his weekly columns were about the restaurants he patronized. He watched Netflix a lot. "He had no idea what he could do with *Apple Daily* or *Next*," remembers Simon Lee. "After the TV debacle, he was kind of lost." Even his new ideas were small-bore ones. He ate in good restaurants around the world and considered starting an Anthony Bourdain–style television show. It was the low point of his career. He centered his energy on his family, especially his young son Augustin, who had been born in 2006.

Chapter Ten

UMBRELLAS AND
TEAR GAS

A protester enveloped in a cloud of tear gas defiantly holding two umbrellas became one of the defining images of 2014. And it provided the name for a nascent protest movement. Useless though an umbrella was in the face of tear gas, water cannons, and baton-wielding riot police, it morphed into the symbol of Hong Kong's peaceful resistance and the David-versus-Goliath nature of the struggle. Idealistic, naïve, mostly young demonstrators stood up against China's relentless party-state.

Demonstrators surged across a busy motorway and stopped traffic in front of government headquarters late on the afternoon of Sunday, September 28, 2014. Lai, who in 2014 began taking an increasingly active role on the streets, was near the front of the crowd of thousands of fired-up activists. As night fell on a hot, humid evening, police fired eighty-seven rounds of tear gas. It marked the first time in almost half a century that police had fired tear gas at Hong Kongers.

An iconic *Time* cover photo featuring an umbrella-wielding protester captured the start of Hong Kong's open revolt. Coincidentally, the photo also caught Lai at the edge of the frame in a protective crouch, his eyes stinging from the tear gas that largely obscures him.

The Umbrella Movement sprang from a January 2013 newspaper

column on civil disobedience by a mild-mannered sociology professor at the University of Hong Kong named Benny Tai. Tai used the pages of the staid *Hong Kong Economic Journal* for his column, "Civil Disobedience, the Most Lethal Weapon," to lay out a plan for nonviolent protests coupled with a citizen's referendum that would force the government to agree to free elections. (What became the most significant challenge to Beijing's authority since the 1989 Tiananmen protests started as Tai's Occupy Central with Love and Peace but became the Umbrella Movement after the students took leadership; the two names are often used interchangeably.)

The Basic Law, the mini-constitution that the People's Republic of China itself had promulgated in 1990, promised that Hong Kong under Chinese rule would adopt universal suffrage and that its people would be able to elect their chief executive and Legislative Council members—effectively, the mayor and the city council. Chinese officials vowed that Hong Kongers would be "masters of their own house" and held out visions of a postcolonial paradise where freedom would reign. Those promises had come to seem like a cruel joke.

In March 2013, Tai joined longtime pro-democracy campaigner Reverend Chu Yiu-ming and another sociology professor, Chan Kin-man, in kicking off a campaign that they dubbed Occupy Central with Love and Peace. The trio called for civil disobedience to force the government to negotiate a road map for universal suffrage by 2017. Tai thought that ten thousand protesters engaged in an occupation of the business district would force the government to talk seriously. After all, students led by teenage activist Joshua Wong in 2012 had persuaded the government to back down on a proposal to introduce pro-communist course material in high schools.

Lai, who had been slow to back Wong, enthusiastically supported the Occupy plan. He signaled his willingness to jump back into Hong Kong politics in a March 2014 column. "We cannot resist the trend of the times, but we must resist evil," he wrote. "Even if we fail, we should not let this period of history go by without leaving a mark. Even if we fail, we would have fought for universal suffrage, cried, and tried our best, otherwise we will only be mediocre in the history books."

That spring, seeking to engage more with ordinary Hong Kongers, Lai went on long walks throughout the territory, often with Martin Lee and Cardinal Zen, to build support for a citizens' referendum on democracy that would be held in the run-up to Occupy Central. The three men typically walked in the evening, often with a handful of other pro-democracy activists, sometimes with hundreds, talking to ordinary people and rallying support throughout the territory.

Authorities tried to prevent the popular plebiscite. China's State Council, the cabinet, issued an unprecedented official white paper asserting that the central government had "comprehensive jurisdiction" over the city. Any rights that Hong Kong enjoyed, intoned the State Council, stemmed solely from the munificence of the central government. Beijing ordered Hong Kongers to be alert to "a very small number of people who act in collusion with outside forces to interfere with the implementation of 'one country, two systems.'" Both Hong Kong and mainland Chinese officials warned Hong Kongers against taking part in the referendum. Hong Kong police held an exercise to intimidate voters.

Two days before voting began, a massive hacking effort aimed to disrupt the poll. Directed against *Apple Daily* and referendum organizer PopVote, the distributed denial-of-service (DDoS) attack—where hackers direct a stream of spurious messages to flood a target's computers—bombarded the sites with an astounding 500 gigabits of data a second.

The traffic directed at the *Apple Daily* and PopVote servers equaled that of all other internet traffic worldwide. "We're seeing over 250 million [Domain Name System] requests per second, which is probably on par with the total DNS requests for the entire Internet in a normal second," said Internet security provider Cloudflare CEO Matthew Prince, who said it was "larger than any attack we've ever seen." The newspaper's website was shut down for about twelve hours.

Staff at the paper fought back. "At *Apple* we had a special kind of momentum," journalist Cori Wong remembers. "The atmosphere—we cannot find anything like this outside *Apple*. If anyone needed help we always gave it. They hacked us and tried to block us from publishing, but everyone pitched in—we uploaded everything to YouTube and social media," so that readers could have access to information. Having beaten back the attack, the paper ran advertisements defiantly boasting, "You can't kill us." Said Lai: "Whoever is behind [the attack], it is clear that he wants to suppress the call for a referendum."

Despite the threats and harassment, the plebiscite attracted strong support. Nearly 800,000 of the territory's 3.2 million registered voters took part. The referendum asked the public to vote on electoral arrangements as the city moved toward the promised goal of universal suffrage. A plurality backed a plan to allow for open nominations by political parties. Lai and the Occupy Central organizers also had a more radical goal for the plebiscite: the establishment of a secure voter registry. They believed that a citizen-controlled voter list would pave the way for frequent polls. If Beijing wouldn't introduce real democracy, Lai and others would use technology to give voice to the popular will.

For decades, Hong Kong loomed much larger in the Chinese leadership's thinking than its small size or economic clout might merit. As the first bit of Chinese territory lost to a Western imperial power, the city's recovery by the People's Republic had enormous symbolic importance. Reabsorbing a colonial possession, especially one of global importance like Hong Kong, strengthened the communist regime's domestic legitimacy in showing that it could uphold national honor. What was called in the West a "handover" Beijing called a reversion of sovereignty, as if the 156 years of British colonialism represented only a brief pause in Chinese rule.

As badly as China wanted to take Hong Kong back, it worried that the colony's tradition of freedom would pose a threat to the mainland's dictatorial system. The colony had harbored many dissidents over the years. Hong Kong was regarded by Beijing as a haven for dangerous ideas and dangerous people. In 1989, a million Hong Kongers had marched in support of the Tiananmen protesters. After 1989, national security became an ever-more-important issue for the paranoid and secretive regime.

Before the Tiananmen killings, China had set up a committee to draft the territory's post-handover mini-constitution, the Basic Law. To win support among local elites, many of whom remained suspicious of Beijing's intentions, the drafting body included a range of Hong Kong business, political, and religious leaders. Among them were barrister and pro-democracy advocate Martin Lee and another well-known democracy advocate, teachers union leader Szeto Wah. Beijing quickly expelled Lee and Wah from the committee after they announced their intention to resign in the aftermath of the Tiananmen massacre.

Stoking China's fears that foreigners wanted to undermine the communist government, Operation Yellowbird smuggled fugitive dissidents out of the mainland and into Hong Kong after the June 4 killings. British intelligence and the CIA worked with local activists and criminal gangs to evade the communist crackdown and get protesters to safety. One of the key figures in the movement was Reverend Chu Yiu-ming, who played a prominent role in Occupy Central. Yellowbird rescued two of the three Tiananmen leaders featured on Lai's T-shirts, Wu'er Kaixi and Chai Ling. Lai provided financial support for some of those who made it out of China, including Chai. He and Teresa found her in Paris after she escaped from China via Hong Kong, paid for her initial stay in a hotel, and developed a friendship.

Chris Patten had taken office as the last British governor in 1992 and pushed through political reforms in the face of intense opposition from Beijing and the local business community. He widened the political franchise, bringing more popular representation to the Legislative Council. He was a retail politician who had begun his career on the streets of New York City working for John Lindsay's 1965 mayoral campaign and had run British prime minister John Major's 1992 reelection campaign. Patten represented genuine change after the series of colonial administrators and foreign office professionals who had previously served as governor; his popular touch included regular walkabouts, unique among the colony's leaders, where he strolled the streets without a security detail, ate egg tarts and other snacks from small shops, and spoke with ordinary Hong Kongers.

Beijing had consistently fought the introduction of any move toward democracy since the 1950s, correctly reasoning that it would be more difficult to bring a democratic enclave under its control. Patten's changes left the territory a long way from universal suffrage. Yet Beijing protested that they were excessive. To the CCP leadership, the changes looked like a British plot to leave trouble in the wake of its departure.

Patten didn't just give more people the right to vote. He made Hong Kongers justifiably proud of the city they had built. He bowed out of being president of Legco, letting members elect one of their own to run the city council. The Chinese had promised to let "Hong Kongers rule Hong Kong" but Patten moved more in that direction in five years than the Chinese did in twenty-five. He said that Hong Kong had the best civil servants in the world and he largely kept the team of senior local administrators intact rather than bring in his own from London. "That was quite a vote of confidence," notes a senior *Next* editor.

He believed so much in the excellence of Hong Kong that he sent his daughter Alice to Island School, a local—and decidedly unposh—institution at a time when much of Hong Kong's elite sent their children to boarding schools in Britain. Underscoring his lack of pretension, he lined up to meet class teachers just like everybody else did on parents' evening. Hong Kongers nicknamed him *fei pang*, "Fatty Patten," a moniker he accepted with good humor.

The changes that Patten wrought helped create a flood of news that buoyed the media sector, including *Apple Daily*. After his departure in 1997, he remained a cheerleader for the Hong Kong people and for the city's core values: openness and the rule of law. "I think that Hong Kong represented all the aspects of an open society that the communists are terrified by," he said in a 2019 livestream session with Lai. "That is an existential threat."

After 1997, Hong Kong was the only place on Chinese soil that publicly commemorated the June 4 Tiananmen killings. Victoria Park in Causeway Bay hosted an annual evening of remembrance, a solemn occasion attended by people of all ages and often attracting crowds of more than 100,000. Speakers at these events included student activist Wang Dan—the third of the three Tiananmen heroes on Lai's Giordano T-shirts—and mothers of students killed in the massacre. Martin Lee and other Hong Kong politicians often spoke. Jimmy Lai invariably attended but he rarely spoke and when he did it was brief. He preferred to converse in small groups, and he regularly assembled such at his home.

China believed that foreign forces led by the United States had instigated the 1989 protests. Deng Xiaoping excoriated the United States for fanning discontent. "The aim of the counter-revolutionary rebellion," as Deng termed the country's pro-democracy activism, "was to overthrow the People's Republic of China and our socialist system." He maintained that Washington wanted to "add fuel to the fire" and told a Japanese delegation that "Western countries, particularly the United States, set all their propaganda machines in motion to fan the flames, to encourage and support the so-called democrats or opposition in China, who were in fact the scum of the Chinese nation."

The British colony of Hong Kong looked from Beijing's perspective like a subversive fifth column that might encourage mainland dissent. Articles by Beijing-based dissidents such as Wang Dan appeared in *Next* in the mid-1990s. Mainland dissidents who set up in Hong Kong expressed themselves freely. These included Han Dongfang, an electrician at the Beijing zoo who had been jailed after Tiananmen and then expelled from the country. He settled in Hong Kong, where he obtained permanent residency—which would make it difficult to expel him—and set up a labor rights group while hosting a popular radio show.

Singapore resembled the best approximation of Beijing's idea for what

Hong Kong should look like. There, a British-trained lawyer and former leftist named Lee Kuan Yew had turned a swampy equatorial island into a politics-free haven for foreign capital and manufacturing. Business in Singapore, also a former British colony, remained firmly under the control of the government. Civil society and nongovernmental organizations operated within tight confines set by the ruling party. The press functioned as a lapdog rather than a watchdog. A newspaper like *Apple Daily* and a media personality like Jimmy Lai would not have been tolerated.

Beijing evidently believed that only money and pleasure mattered to Hong Kongers. Deng Xiaoping summed up this approach when he reassured Margaret Thatcher that China would not try to impose its system on freewheeling Hong Kong. "Horses will still run, stocks will still sizzle, dancers will still dance," promised Deng, as if that would be enough to keep Hong Kongers happy.

In 2014, seventeen years after the handover, any prospect of electoral reform, let alone real democracy, was receding. Beijing's unwillingness to allow genuine elections even for local officials proved the hollowness of its promises. The State Council's heavy-handed white paper in June wasn't the last word from Beijing. On August 31, the National People's Congress laid down rules for the 2017 chief executive election. Rather than allowing for open nominations along the lines of the winning plebiscite proposal, a pro-Beijing nominating committee would continue to pick candidates. Officials had recently added a new requirement: candidates must "love the country," code for supporting the Chinese Communist Party. The one-two punch of restrictive policies from the State Council in June and the National People's Congress in August shattered any remaining hope of reform.

Lai's personal involvement in the Umbrella Movement emboldened the paper's editorial staff to put the newspaper squarely behind the movement. *Apple Daily*'s support marked a turning point, both for the publication and for the pro-democracy movement, giving the paper a new veneer of respectability and drawing a broader section of the population into the protest movement.

Protesters took over three areas of the city at the end of September, setting up tents and building encampments in the Admiralty/Central area outside government headquarters; the Causeway Bay shopping area; and the working-class district of Mong Kok. *Apple Daily* legitimized the occupation by highlighting the protesters' many civic activities—such as the study groups, the lessons that university students gave to high schoolers, and the gardens with flowers and vegetables that activists established in the heart of the city. The paper downplayed Umbrella's rougher side, notably the occupation site in Mong Kok where working-class protesters repeatedly scuffled with police-backed gangsters. Yellow became the symbolic color of the movement, something that *Apple Daily*'s pages made clear. The newspaper used more yellow ink—in photos of yellow umbrellas, yellow banners, and yellow stick-its on large protest walls—during the seventy-nine-day occupation than it had used in all the time since its founding two decades earlier.

The movement catapulted *Apple Daily* to a newfound importance in Hong Kong. People who had previously been skeptical of its scandal-mongering came to admire the paper's courage. Dennis Kwok, a Canadian-born barrister, was one of those converts.

Kwok had cofounded the Civic Party, made up largely of middle- and upper-middle-class professionals in 2006. He only got to know Lai after he was elected to the Legislative Council, where he represented the legal services sector, in 2012. Growing up in 1990s Hong Kong, he had previously considered *Apple Daily* "a trashy newspaper." But he had watched in dismay as other newspapers increasingly fell under Beijing's sway. By the time he entered Legco, "*Apple Daily* remained almost the sole flame of media freedom, the only independent media in Hong Kong," he says. "Jimmy allowed [his staff] to work freely. He created the environment where journalists could be open supporters of democracy and staunch defenders of freedom in Hong Kong."

When the Umbrella Movement started, Lai and many others pitched tents at the site. His tent stood near government headquarters, across from a KFC restaurant on Harcourt Road. He sat there during each of the seventy-nine days of protest, reading, talking to passersby, and generally showing his support. (He slept at his home.) He skipped a planned boat trip to celebrate Sebastien's twentieth birthday on October 1 to bear witness as the students fought for democracy.

Young activists led the Umbrella uprising. Although they built on Occupy Central's ideas, a new generation steered the protests. Lai did not try to take a leadership role. Lai, Martin Lee, and Occupy leaders Benny Tai and Chan Kin-man had even been booed off the stage early on the morning of September 28, at the start of the 2014 protests, by students concerned that the old guard was trying to hijack their movement.

Lai mostly sat reading in front of his tent or in a chair in front of the main stage. Ellen Bork, the U.S. human rights activist, visited Hong Kong at the time and found him amid the crowd. "I'm roaming around and he's in a lawn chair just sitting there," she marvels. He wasn't treated specially. "Whenever I went to Admiralty," one activist remembers, referring to the district where the government has its headquarters, "I would see him. Sometimes he was staring into space. Sometimes people were talking to him. He was just a bloke." When Lai wanted to have a more private conversation with a journalist, he would move to a nearby McDonald's.

American diplomat Raymond Burghardt, who had first met Lai more than a decade earlier in Taiwan, recalls bumping into him at the protest. After lunching at the nearby Hong Kong Club during a short visit to the city, Burghardt walked through the encampment. "I was walking along, listening to someone harangue the crowd," he says. "I was about to walk away when I looked to my left and Jimmy was sitting there. He waved hello and beckoned me to sit down. I walked over and said, 'Do you think that's a good idea?' He was sitting by himself on a bench. So I sat down and we chatted for a while."

The chance encounter caused a minor contretemps. A photographer from *Oriental Daily News* snapped a picture of Hong Kong's preeminent pro-democracy publisher and a senior American diplomat sitting together. (At the time, Burghardt was chairman of the American Institute in Taiwan, overseeing the U.S.'s Taiwan policy and reporting directly to President Obama's national security advisor.) The meeting typified the open, easy-going environment that prevailed during the Umbrella Movement. Lai's connections to high-ranking American officials such as Burghardt would later be used against him at his National Security Law trial.

Chief Secretary Carrie Lam, the number two in the government, and four other senior officials held a televised debate with five student leaders on October 21. That was their only meeting. But it wasn't a negotiation, nor was there any attempt at a compromise. *Time* wrote that the students "represented the sort of young people any nation would be proud to call its own: intelligent, informed, and impassioned," while government officials "spoke mostly to utter legal sophistries and to tell the students what they have been saying for months: give up your fight and do as Beijing asks, because the decisions that have been made about Hong Kong's political future cannot be changed." Despite the energy and determination and sheer numbers of protesters, the Hong Kong government refused to budge.

Security guards straightened up and a heavy metal gate slid open as Jimmy Lai arrived at the quiet Kadoorie Avenue house where he'd moved in 2001. The area includes eighty-five residences owned by the Kadoorie family, one of Hong Kong's wealthiest clans. The houses sprawl across the spine of a low hill above the Mong Kok district, one of the most densely populated places on the planet. Michael Kadoorie rented the house to Lai, an arrangement that suited Lai even though it cost him almost $40,000 a month. (The house was old and needed work, and constituted a relative bargain in the exclusive neighborhood.) Lai never owned any residential property in Hong Kong. It was too risky, he said—if he ran afoul of authorities, they would seize his house.

Photographers jostled outside the entrance for the chance to snap a picture of him in the back seat of his chauffeur-driven Mercedes 500 S as it pulled into the driveway. In the foyer of his elegantly furnished house, he brushed past a vase of orchids and greeted his twenty-year-old son Sebastien with a quick account of the day and saying, "I'm going to take a shower."

Lai certainly needed to wash off. He'd been sitting in front of his tent at the pro-democracy encampment near government headquarters on the afternoon of November 12, 2014, as he had every day for the previous six weeks. Three men had assaulted him without warning, dumping a foul-smelling slop on him. When he turned away, they hurled more of it—pig organs, it turned out.

The attack represented one of many that Lai suffered in a city whose officials routinely claim it is one of the world's safest. Assailants repeatedly tossed Molotov cocktails over the gate at his Kadoorie Avenue house and, years earlier, had done the same at his Tai Po Road residence. (He also earned a scar on his head after tussling with robbers who had tied Teresa and him up at the Tai Po villa, after they tried to wrench Teresa's wedding ring off her finger.) Thugs trashed *Next*'s office at Westlands Centre. Police had foiled a murder plot against Lai and Martin Lee in 2008. Pro-Beijing protesters and intrusive photographers harassed him and his guests outside his house. A car had rammed the gate of his Kadoorie Avenue house the previous year; the attackers had left an axe and a machete at the scene.

Guangdong authorities sent his older sister, Li Biying, to stage a sit-in outside the Kadoorie Avenue residence, using a common communist tactic: they had threatened to hurt her son's prospects at school if she couldn't convince Lai to give up his support for protesters. (Lai wouldn't meet her, reasoning that authorities would treat her more harshly if she met her brother and still couldn't get him to back down; he sent his longtime driver to talk with her.)

Anonymous agents tried to disrupt distribution of *Apple Daily*. The month before the pig offal attack, demonstrators came to the company's facility in the industrial park of Tseung Kwan O in the middle of the night protesting the newspaper's coverage of the Umbrella Movement. Believed to be paid for by a business rival seeking to curry favor with Beijing, the rent-a-crowd built barricades from wooden pallets and swarmed around the compound's two gates to prevent newspapers from leaving the facility. The newspaper's staff used cranes to hoist the newspapers over a fence surrounding the facility and onto waiting trucks. The trucks, too, were blocked by disruptors; at 5 a.m. they dispersed as if they had been paid to make a point and then leave. Separately, at newsstands, thugs dumped soy sauce on copies of the paper.

A Beijing-orchestrated advertising boycott added to the pressure. Two major British-headquartered banks with long ties to the city, HSBC and Standard Chartered, had traditionally been among *Apple Daily*'s biggest Hong Kong financial advertisers. The two banks had spent $3.6 million in 2013 before both suddenly ended all their advertising in the middle of the year. HSBC told an *Apple Daily* executive that a Chinese official ordered the banks to yank their ads. Around the same time, two more local banks, the Bank of East Asia and Hang Seng Bank, also pulled their ads.

On arriving home after the November attack, though he felt sticky and smelly, Lai was otherwise unscathed. "He was pretty lighthearted about it," remembers Sebastien, then a student at the University of Hong Kong. But the assault on Lai was serious. Coupled with the computer hacks and the ad boycott, dumping pig organs suggested that pro-Beijing forces were intensifying their harassment of Lai.

Lai refused to have a bodyguard and chastised aide Mark Simon when he stepped up security around the Kadoorie Avenue house. "I don't want them to think I'm afraid," he told Simon. The defiant attitude persisted in the face of more threats. "I am fine. I am not scared," he said two months later, in early 2015, when yet more firebombs were thrown over the wall of his house. "These things always happen. They are only provocations."

The seventy-nine-day occupation of three key spots in the city echoed Beijing's Tiananmen occupation of 1989 and similar mass events that took place around the country that spring. In 2014, as in 1989, a large-scale mass movement tried to dismantle the Chinese Communist Party's monopoly on power. Hong Kong's challenge lasted longer but ended without violence. The protesters had lost support from a public weary of the disruptions to their daily lives. Lai was among several people—including Benny Tai, Reverend Chu Yiu-ming, and Chan Kin-man—who offered themselves up for arrest when police cleared protest sites in the first half of December. He was booked but never prosecuted.

Lai was despondent at what he saw as the failure of the occupation. Yet the 2014 Umbrella Movement marked a watershed in Hong Kong's history. It also marked a turning point for Lai and for *Apple Daily*. The paper's reputation for trashiness faded; it was increasingly respected for its political independence and clout.

The events of 2014 reenergized Lai's interest in Hong Kong politics. He had struggled to find a larger purpose outside of his family after his setbacks in Taiwan. He and Teresa had enjoyed traveling among their residences, visiting friends and museums and eating well wherever they went. But it wasn't enough to satisfy his hunger for something more meaningful. His democracy walks across Hong Kong in the spring, his teargassing in September, and the seventy-nine-day occupation that followed opened a new chapter in his activism. Since 1989, he had donated money and written articles in support of democracy. Now he was putting his body on the line.

Chapter Eleven

"WE JUST HAVE TO EAT THEIR MEAL"

Inside the *Apple Daily* newsroom at the end of 2014, senior editors worried that they had lost control of the paper. The daily's embrace of the Umbrella Movement made it look like an opposition publication. The company's new CEO, Cassian Cheung, shared their concerns about journalists taking the newspaper in a more radical direction. Days after the Umbrella Movement ended, on December 12, 2014, Lai stepped down as chairman of Next Media. His political engagement and potential legal troubles were proving too time-consuming and distracting for the chairman of a publicly listed company. Still, his resignation did not eliminate his influence at a company where he owned more than 70 percent of the shares.

Next Media's new CEO had joined the company after serving as president of Walmart China and did not share Lai's commitment to political activism. Lai's resignation gave him and the newspaper's top editors a chance to reestablish authority and move the newspaper away from being too much of a cheerleader for the protesters. Besides ensuring a more restrained editorial line, Cheung also needed to quickly move the firm away from a reliance on revenues from its print publications and develop moneymaking digital ones. Reflecting this transition, Next Media was renamed Next Digital in 2015.

The company's future looked precarious. "Advertisers were being called and getting direct threats," remembers Brad Hamm, who joined the board of directors in 2015. "If they advertised with *Apple* they wouldn't be able to do business on the mainland." Political pressure on the paper had intensified after C. Y. Leung, a hard-line pro-Beijing figure, became Hong Kong's chief executive in 2012. The paper's full-throated support for the Umbrella Movement prompted pro-mainland newspapers and government officials to forcefully attack *Apple Daily* and *Next*. Older readers began deserting the newspaper. In the six months from October 2014 to March 2015, the company's advertising sales dropped 25 percent and earnings plummeted 85 percent compared with the previous six months.

"The political environment became very adversarial and the government very hostile to media organizations," remembers Ted Hui, a former legislator who later fled Hong Kong to avoid jail. "People understood that the political situation had changed and they started worrying about *Apple Daily*'s future. People started counting how many years organizations like *Apple* could survive—was it one year, three years, five years, ten years?"

Young activists pushed for Hong Kong to go its own way even as pressure from Beijing intensified. In 2016, the city ushered in the Year of the Dragon with its most violent conflict in five decades. The Fishball Revolution, as activists called it, occurred during Chinese New Year. Grassroots groups tried to protect unlicensed hawkers selling traditional Hong Kong food like fishballs against an official crackdown. Police fired warning shots; in the melee, ninety officers and about thirty protesters suffered injuries. Authorities arrested sixty-one protesters. The era of nonviolent opposition was over.

Apple Daily and Lai came down hard against the protesters, echoing the government's claim that they were "rioters." These weren't just word games. When proven in court to have "rioted," demonstrators could receive heavier sentences than those who engage in nonviolent forms of protest. The rift widened between *Apple Daily* and the youth movement.

"*Apple Daily* had the resources to destroy lives," complains one activist about the newspaper's stance toward Fishball participants. "They had that power, and they were willing to use it and they wouldn't care. It felt like they were so powerful, almost gangsterlike. In 2016, Jimmy's attitude was still like 'young people, you will have your time,'" remembers this protester, who was in his midthirties at the time: "Jimmy thought we were too young and naïve." Lai believed, according to this demonstrator, that "the serious business of politics should be left to the older generation."

While younger activists explored fundamental ideas about Hong Kong identity and built grassroots support for the previously unthinkable idea of independence, *Apple Daily* couldn't break away from the long-standing pan-democratic effort to advance electoral reform. Even as Beijing ratcheted up pressure on the democracy movement, Lai and his newspaper found themselves squeezed between a fundamentally conservative old guard of pan-democrats and a more impatient and radical younger generation.

The Fishball Revolution represented only the most visible sign of simmering political tensions that persisted following the end of Umbrella occupations. The years between the Umbrella uprising and the passage of the National Security Law in 2020 were a period of increasing political stress. Beijing regarded itself as fighting an unremitting plot by hostile foreign forces to instigate a revolution in Hong Kong. Beijing regarded Hong Kong's political upheaval as part of a shadowy global conspiracy.

China had tried to make the Hong Kong Chinese feel that they belonged to the People's Republic. For the first decade after the handover the policy appeared to be working. In the run-up to the 2008 Beijing Olympics, the people of Hong Kong increasingly saw themselves as Chinese. But more aggressive and authoritarian Chinese behavior, in the mainland as well as in Hong Kong, nurtured a separate Hong Kong identity. After 2008, Hong Kong people more and more saw themselves as distinct from mainland Chinese.

Hostility toward Chinese from the mainland increased. In 2012, *Apple Daily* ran an advertisement decrying mainland Chinese as "locusts" overrunning the city. "Hong Kong people, we have endured enough in silence," said the ad, which pictured a locust looking at the Hong Kong skyline. Mainland mothers filled maternity wards in the territory so that their children could enjoy Hong Kong residency, making it hard for Hong Kongers to find a hospital to deliver their babies. Mainlanders swept baby formula off grocery shelves after a deadly adulterated baby formula scandal shook the mainland. Hong Kongers couldn't get formula for their children, forcing the government to enact restrictions on purchases for everyone.

In 2019 and 2020 two pieces of legislation pushed Hong Kong to the breaking point. Carrie Lam, who had debated the students in 2014, had become chief executive in 2017. A top student at one of the city's leading Catholic schools, the hardworking Lam had risen from a poor childhood to distinguish herself as a civil servant. She earned public esteem for her leadership of the social welfare and housing departments. Yet as a political leader she proved a failure. Her stubbornness in pushing a law that would allow Hong Kongers to be sent to mainland China to face trial catalyzed the most violent wave of discontent Hong Kong had ever seen, second only to the destruction of Hong Kong during Japan's World War II occupation. An extradition bill Lam proposed in early 2019 would allow suspects to be sent from Hong Kong to the mainland and dismantle a firewall keeping Hong Kong's legal system separate from China's.

Cassian Cheung's attempts to develop new sources of revenue didn't work out quickly enough to satisfy an impatient Lai and the former Walmart executive left Next Digital in 2018. Lai came back as chairman. In 2019, he threw *Apple Daily* into the fight against the extradition bill. On Sunday, June 9, a million people took to the streets. Three days later, on June 12, police savagely beat protesters who prevented Legco from passing the bill by blockading the building. The following Saturday, June 15, a shaken Carrie Lam said she wouldn't push ahead with the legislation. Notwithstanding Lam's climbdown, a protest march the next day drew an estimated two million people, more than one-quarter of the city's population. Proportionately, it was as if ninety million Americans had marched on Washington,

DC. Hong Kongers wanted more than the withdrawal of the extradition bill—they wanted democracy.

Apple Daily played a key role in bringing the public along. This marked a pendulum change from how it had covered the 2016 Fishball protests, when it had highlighted excesses by protesters. Now it emphasized police brutality. "They reported with a lot of emphasis on police violence, how the police were just out to hurt people, that they didn't even arrest people," observes the activist who had been critical of the paper's coverage of the Fishball protests. "*Apple Daily* was not radical but very humane in their reporting. It surprised me. It also made a lot of average people sympathetic to the protesters, to more radical people. They weren't painted as rioters."

Lai took an active role in setting the editorial direction, peppering senior editors with WhatsApp messages dictating how to play specific stories. Even as the protests became more violent, Lai and *Apple Daily* remained steadfast in support. Radical activists broke into the Legco building on July 1, the anniversary of the handover to China and a public holiday—a dramatic escalation in tactics. Reflecting his new attitude, on July 2 Lai messaged *Apple Daily* associate publisher Chan Pui-man asking her to interview activist Lester Shum. He wanted to gain public support for the protesters after the controversial attack on the Legco building.

Police violence in 2019 helped obscure the generational split that had earlier weakened the democracy camp. The movement vowed not to split between radicals and moderates. Lai didn't push back when protesters adopted increasingly aggressive tactics in vandalizing property. Student protesters told Lai and his generation that thirty years of politely agitating for democracy had achieved nothing. "'So now we try our way'" is how Lai paraphrased the words of young activists at a talk at Stanford University's Hoover Institution in October 2019. "That's why they try their way, confronting the police and we see some of the violence, but even with that the younger generation and the older generation have never been as united fighting for our home, Hong Kong."

Coincidentally, *Apple Daily* in mid-2019 moved to a digital subscription strategy. The Beijing-backed advertising boycott of its publications had hurt revenues. As was occurring everywhere, print sales had slumped. Next Digital needed to climb out of a financial hole. The digital rollout occurred in three phases. In May, users had to register; in July, they were required to pay a token amount; full pricing began in September. The protests made *Apple Daily* more important than ever. By September, the site had about one million paying subscribers. No newspaper in the world had ever signed up so many paying digital subscribers so quickly. Its pitch was simple, urging readers to "resist injustice with truth. It only costs [22 cents] a day."

Lai believed the United States held the key to resolving the situation. In July 2019, he went to Washington. He received a welcome that Hong Kong officials couldn't dream of and few dissidents could achieve. He met with Vice President Mike Pence, Secretary of State Mike Pompeo, former national security advisor John Bolton, and numerous other officials and members of Congress. He wanted to communicate the message that Hong Kong's democracy movement needed and deserved U.S. support.

Pence, who agreed to the meeting at Pompeo's request, remembers him "as one of the great lions of liberty." Lai's story and his Catholic faith transformed what Pence had expected would be a routine meeting soliciting support for Hong Kong. He termed it "deeply personal" and says, "It settled my determination to be a voice for this man and freedom-loving people like him in Hong Kong and all across China." Pence remembers the forty-five-minute meeting as "one of the most profound encounters I had in my West Wing office in my four years as vice-president."

Back in Hong Kong, what united the opposition was the violence of the government crackdown. Police openly worked with gangsters. Officers stood by as thugs beat unarmed protesters and innocent passersby at a train station in July. A video of police themselves beating a train full of people at the end of August further inflamed public opinion. Massive rallies of one million, even two million people took place on many weekends. At the Hoover Institution talk, Lai lauded the willingness of young people to die, "the spirit of martyrdom" that had won support throughout the city. "We have to fight, it's the last straw."

Governments in free, open societies generally listen when most of their people take to the streets in protest. Hong Kong officials met no one from the opposition. They did not propose negotiations. Violence on both sides increased, culminating in a siege at Hong Kong Polytechnic University in November 2019 that blockaded the Cross Harbour Tunnel.

District council elections in 2019 made popular sentiment clear. At stake were hundreds of low-level positions that controlled significant municipal funds. They also played an important role in making up members of the Election Committee, the body that—something like the U.S. Electoral College—helped select the territory's chief executive. In the volatile environment of late 2019, these ward elections served as a barometer of whether the city's silent majority craved the stability and order that Beijing promised or backed the street activists' appeal for democracy.

The pro-democracy camp won a landslide victory. Beijing could have used the elections as a chance to reform its policies to bring in the democracy that Hong Kongers wanted and that China had promised. Instead, communist authorities canceled the upcoming Legco election and began arresting pro-democracy leaders. The Basic Law guaranteed freedom of the press and of assembly, alongside many other rights. Beijing paid no attention.

Lai was doing his morning exercise when the police arrived around 7 a.m. on the morning of Friday, February 28, 2020. They permitted him to take a shower before escorting him to the police station. He had enough time and the police were relaxed enough that he could send some emails. The cops didn't handcuff him. At the station, officers charged Lai with illegal assembly for taking part in a massive rally on August 31, 2019.

Authorities also dusted off an old accusation by a reporter for *Oriental Daily News*. Over a period of almost three years, the reporter had repeatedly complained to police that Lai had shouted at him during the 2017 Tiananmen vigil. For that accusation, they booked Lai on criminal intimidation charges. The arraignment process complete, they released Lai at lunchtime.

The police were back at the Kadoorie Avenue house seven weeks later. On April 18, police rounded up Lai, Martin Lee, and a dozen other prominent activists. This time authorities charged Lai with illegally taking part in rallies on August 18 and October 1, 2019. Additional charges piled up over the next several months.

One of the most egregious cases centered on Lai's part in the June 4, 2020, Tiananmen commemoration. For the first time since these remembrance vigils began in 1990, authorities refused permission for the gathering at Victoria Park, citing social distancing measures to limit Covid. On the evening of June 4, Lai nonetheless stepped out of his car at the edge of Victoria Park, said a prayer, and lit a candle in memory of those who had died in Beijing thirty-one years earlier. He remained mute in the face of questioning from reporters, silently and somberly getting back into his vehicle. He was charged with incitement for that silent, solitary act of lighting a candle and saying a prayer.

Lai remained optimistic that the challenges facing the Chinese Communist Party would lead to its downfall. In April 2020, he told the *Financial Times* that U.S. support would be the "saving grace" of Hong Kong. Lai also coordinated with activist group Stand with Hong Kong to publish advertisements in newspapers in the United States, Canada, the United Kingdom, Germany, France, Spain, Italy, Switzerland, Belgium, Japan, South Korea, Australia, and Taiwan, calling on free societies to support Hong Kong's protests.

The day after China announced that its National People's Congress would impose a National Security Law on Hong Kong in May 2020, Lai texted CEO Cheung Kim-hung with an idea to launch a campaign for support in Washington. Entitled *One Hongkonger One Letter to Save Hong Kong #TrumpSavesHK*, the petition on the White House website asked for Trump's help with regard to "public support and the diplomatic efforts of the United States to help keep our city a center of international trade and home for freedom." The campaign, which sought 100,000 signatures, eventually garnered over 113,000.

On May 25, *Apple Daily* launched an English-language version in an attempt to obtain more international support for Hong Kong's cause. Lai also started a blitz with foreign media to underscore the danger that the new security law would bring and to call for penalties on the officials involved. Lai told Fox Business host Maria Bartiromo that there should be sanctions on Chinese Communist Party apparatchiks; he repeated that message with Bloomberg, the BBC, and in a tweet directed to Trump. He also told Cheung to remind his international colleagues not to attack Trump because they would need his support.

Lai compounded the so-called "crime" of opposing the Chinese Communist Party with his call for sanctions on Chinese and Hong Kong officials. The threat of sanctions that might shut off access to foreign bank accounts or property or prevent the children of party officials from attending university in the United States especially angered Beijing.

At the end of that month, on June 30, 2020, China's National People's Congress illegally bypassed the Hong Kong legislature and imposed a sweeping National Security Law that outlawed dissent and ended the city's freedom. The bill outlawed terrorism, subversion, secession, or collusion with a foreign government. Any criticism of the government could breach the vague new rules. Maximum penalty: life imprisonment.

The law did away with jury trials, left defendants at the mercy of hand-picked judges, and would ultimately be used to deny Lai his choice of lawyer. Contact with a foreign government that called for more democracy or for sanctions against Hong Kong officials was deemed to be "collusion" with foreigners and could result in conviction. The government argued, before its secretly chosen judges, that popular slogans such as "Revolution of our times" constituted secession. The law criminalized calls for democracy.

Before the introduction of the law, authorities tried to reassure the public. Chief Executive Carrie Lam—who reportedly did not see the law until the day it was promulgated—promised that the measure would be used sparingly and only affect an "extremely small group." A spokesperson for the Hong Kong and Macau Affairs Office of Beijing's State Council said the new law "only targets those activities that attempt to split the country, subvert the state's power, organize terrorist attacks and activities of foreign and external forces to interfere" in Hong Kong. "It will not affect the rights and freedoms enjoyed by Hong Kong residents, including freedom of demonstration and assembly, as well as freedom of speech," the spokesperson added, claiming that "it will also enable Hong Kong residents to better exercise their rights in a safe environment."

Many in Hong Kong's democratic camp nonetheless took protective measures. Prominent democrat Anson Chan, who had been the first woman and the first Chinese to become the colony's chief secretary, announced in June 2020 that she would retire from politics with immediate effect. The Demosisto political party, founded in 2016 by Joshua Wong and other young activists, disbanded at the end of June 2020. Leaders including Sunny Cheung and Demosisto cofounder Nathan Law fled abroad.

The first day after the law's imposition already gave reason to worry. A motorcyclist who rode through a group of policemen on July 1 while sporting a flag reading "Liberate Hong Kong, revolution of our times" became the first person convicted under the National Security Law. Judges deemed the slogan "secessionist," claiming that the driver, Tong Ying-kit, had been "seeking to undermine national unification." This 2021 ruling made a mockery of promises that free speech would be protected under the National Security Law. Amnesty International's Yamini Mishra noted that "[t]he ruling essentially outlaws a popular slogan widely used by the pro-democracy movement." A few months later a protester, Ma Chun-man, who simply chanted slogans such as "Liberate Hong Kong, revolution of our times" and "Hong Kong independence, the only way out," received a five-year prison sentence.

On July 2, two days after the law had been imposed, *China Daily* claimed that "Hong Kong residents still enjoy the freedom to peacefully assemble and demonstrate, criticize the government, and discuss current affairs." They were empty words, at odds with a wave of arrests that continues four years later.

Lai refused to back down.

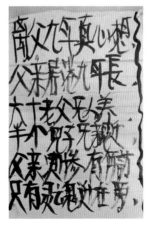

Left: Lai with his mother, twin sister Si-wai, and elder sister Huanying, early 1950s.

Middle: Picture taken shortly before Lai left for Hong Kong in 1961, age twelve.

Right: Poem written by Lai around 1960, expressing yearning for his father, who had left years earlier for Hong Kong. Lai wrote: "Who will take care of my father in his misery? / Only my soul is by his side."

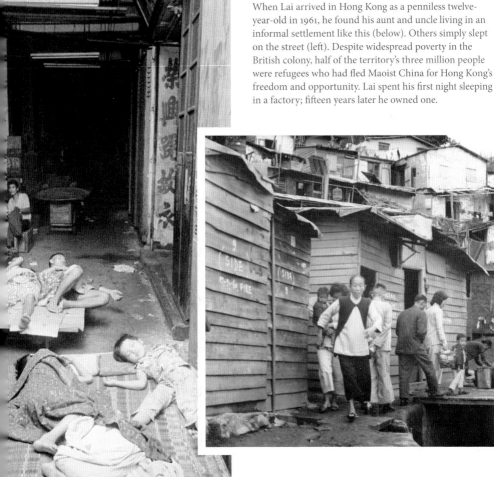

When Lai arrived in Hong Kong as a penniless twelve-year-old in 1961, he found his aunt and uncle living in an informal settlement like this (below). Others simply slept on the street (left). Despite widespread poverty in the British colony, half of the territory's three million people were refugees who had fled Maoist China for Hong Kong's freedom and opportunity. Lai spent his first night sleeping in a factory; fifteen years later he owned one.

Lai met and married Pilunya Assapimonwait (Judy), a Thai-Chinese stewardess for Cathay Pacific, in 1976. They had three children, Tim (center), Jade (left), and Ian (right). Kyoto, 1984.

Right: Judy and Lai, Bangkok, 1986.

Below: Powered by export-oriented factories like Lai's Comitex, Hong Kong's economy grew rapidly in the 1970s and 1980s and shantytowns gave way to a more prosperous city, as shown in this street scene.

Though he traveled frequently, Lai's children remember him as an involved father, whether out on the family boat in the Sai Kung area or at home in Kowloon. He often entertained friends and business associates at the family's house on Tai Po Road, high above Victoria Harbour, where the Lais moved in 1984; he gained notoriety for keeping a pet bear, among other animals (undated photo, 1980s).

Above: Lai in St. Moritz, 1986

Above: Brightly colored, inexpensive clothes at Lai's Giordano chain of retail clothing stores launched the global fast-fashion industry. He slashed delivery times for shirts and sweaters and boosted profits with new technology and innovative manufacturing techniques.

Left: Student protests in Beijing in the spring of 1989 represented the most serious threat to Chinese Communist Party rule since the country's founding forty years earlier. The protests captivated Lai and drew him into political activism for the first time. Giordano sold T-shirts featuring student leaders Chai Ling, Wu'er Kaixi, and Wang Dan (pictured, left to right) and called for the Chinese leadership to step down. Lai sent the money he raised from T-shirt sales to the students; he also dispatched tents and other supplies to Beijing. He provided financial help to the three student leaders after they left China.

Lai brought marketing savvy honed in the fashion world to *Apple Daily* with slogans including "An *Apple* a day keeps the liars away." Above, he poses in front of a colorful apple at the time of the newspaper's June 1995 launch.

Below: China took control of Hong Kong after 156 years of British colonial rule on July 1, 1997, at a ceremony attended by Prince Charles and Chinese Communist Party General Secretary Jiang Zemin.

Above: Lai's wedding to Teresa Li at Notre-Dame de Clignancourt in Paris, 1992. The wedding took place a year after the couple's civil ceremony. Because of Lai's previous marriage, the union required a letter from Pope John Paul II for the ceremony to go ahead. The photo was taken by Liu Shikun, a pianist whose fingers were broken during years of imprisonment during China's Cultural Revolution.

Above: Troops from the People's Liberation Army streamed into Hong Kong on July 1, 1997, after China took over.

Apple Daily found an audience among Hong Kongers such as leading pro-democracy campaigner Martin Lee (below) and the last governor of Hong Kong, Chris Patten (above). Hundreds of thousands of others joined them, attracted by the newspaper's bold political news and free-market economic columnists. In its early years, the paper went to the edge—and sometimes beyond—in its coverage of crime and entertainment.

A demonstration against repressive national security legislation in 2003 prompted 500,000 people to march against the government, by far the largest protest since the Chinese had taken over in 1997. The massive protest marked a turning point for Lai and his media empire. *Next* magazine and *Apple Daily* acted as cheerleaders for the pro-democracy march and helped turn out the large crowd. *Apple Daily* published a pull-out poster (visible in the window below) while *Next* reprised a cover image showing a cream pie being thrown into the face of Hong Kong chief executive Tung Chee-hwa (shown above).

A peaceful crowd, which included people of all ages, marched from Victoria Park through the streets of Causeway Bay to government offices on July 1, 2003. The protesters posed an unprecedented challenge to the Beijing-controlled government.

Left: Lai, Teresa Lai (wife), and Si-wai Lai (twin sister) celebrating their mother's birthday, late 1990s.

Above: Claire, Teresa, Lai, Sebastien, and Augustin (foreground), 2012.

Left: Sebastien, Augustin (on shoulders), and Claire, 2010.

In 2014, the seventy-nine-day occupation of three districts in Hong Kong, known as the Umbrella Movement, represented the most significant challenge to the Chinese Communist Party since the 1989 Tiananmen protests. Lai pitched a tent in the Admiralty area (below) and took part for the duration; he was teargassed as the movement began (above); he later had pig innards dumped on him.

Lai offered himself up for arrest when police cleared out demonstrators in December 2014 to end the Umbrella Movement. He was booked but not prosecuted. He resigned from his positions at Next Media in hopes of protecting the company from any punishment for his political activism, returning only in 2018.

Lion Rock towers over Kowloon; the rock outcropping symbolizes Hong Kong's can-do spirit as epitomized by people like Lai. During the 2014 Umbrella Movement activists appropriated it to hang pro-democracy slogans, as in this photo.

Left: After the Umbrella Movement, Lai cultivated ties with politicians in Washington, DC, in hopes of safeguarding Hong Kong's political freedom. He held meetings with Speaker of the House Nancy Pelosi, Secretary of State Mike Pompeo, and Vice President Mike Pence (shown here, July 2019), as well as numerous members of Congress.

Above: Hong Kong's pro-democracy protesters looked to the United States for protection against China's tightening grip on the territory, as in this 2019 prayer vigil near the U.S. consulate in Hong Kong.

Above: Teresa and Jimmy Lai in New Orleans in May 2017. Teresa met Lai when she was a summer intern at the *South China Morning Post* in 1989. He was smitten from the first meeting and wooed her when she returned to Paris for studies; they married two years later. Teresa's support and her Catholic faith have acted as important ballasts for Lai.

Left: Lai and Martin Lee met civil rights icon John Lewis at the U.S. Capitol in 2019; Lewis, in keeping with Lai's beliefs, made a video on the spot exhorting Hong Kong students to eschew violence and engage in nonviolent protests only.

Above: Lai was jailed for his part in this August 18, 2019, protest.

Authorities targeted Lai and *Apple Daily* shortly after Beijing imposed a vague and sweeping National Security Law on the territory on June 30, 2020. Police arrested Lai at home on August 10, handcuffed his hands behind his back, and perp-walked him through the newsroom. Here he is shown as he is put into a police vehicle.

Two hundred and fifty police raided the newspaper in August 2020 (above); the following June saw twice that number swarm the company headquarters. The newspaper was forced to close after authorities froze the company's bank accounts, without a court order. A supporter holds a copy of the June 24, 2021, paper, the final edition (below). An expanded print run saw one million copies sold out within hours.

Lai spends much of his time in prison drawing; this image of Christ on the cross (below) was reprinted and used for a postcard campaign by well-wishers. At left, Lai in an undated photo; in the background is a painting by his teacher and friend, the Chinese American artist Walasse Ting.

The Committee for Freedom in Hong Kong Foundation and other Lai supporters have waged an international campaign for his release; shown here are large-scale projections in New York City (Guggenheim Museum), Washington, DC (Department of Energy), and London (Tower Bridge).

Teresa and Augustin (left) and Claire (above) attending Lai's National Security Law trial, which began in 2023, in Kowloon, Hong Kong.

Right: Lai's son Sebastien campaigns for his father's release; he is no longer able to return to Hong Kong because of government threats against him for simply advocating on behalf of his father.

Left: Lai at the maximum-security Stanley Prison, in the summer of 2023, where he is held in solitary confinement; this is the most recent photo of him.

He supported a citizen's primary held in July 2020 that would allow the democrats to put together a unified slate for the Legco elections scheduled for September. As with 2014's unofficial plebiscite, Beijing protested loudly and threatened both organizers and voters; on the eve of the vote, police raided the offices of the Public Opinion Research Institute, one of the organizers, in an attempt to disrupt the poll.

Lai hoped that the citizens' primary could build on the success of the 2014 referendum and pave the way for grassroots democracy. Lai envisioned using blockchain technology to create a transparent alternate voting system. "It wasn't just about taking [Legco] seats but about setting up a parallel system that could allow people to voice what they like," says Simon Lee, who acted on Lai's behalf in the early planning for the system. (Nervousness among other program developers about working on a Lai-affiliated project prompted Lee to back out in the spring of 2019, four months before the primary.)

"The primary was more like a voter registration exercise for us," says Lee. "Jimmy was thinking much bigger. He wanted something beyond *Apple Daily*, a media platform that allowed every single individual to [speak] out in a safe way, to deliberate in real time, so that everyone has an equal voice. That was his ideal of real-time democracy using technology." Despite official threats, almost 600,000 people voted in the unofficial primary. The exercise enraged the Chinese Communist Party.

Hong Kongers' repeated booing of the Chinese national anthem at soccer games incensed Chinese officials. So, too, did defacing the national seal and the flag. In a rare news conference, officials from the Hong Kong and Macau Affairs Office decried a "horrendous" attack that saw black paint splattered on the national seal outside a government office in July 2019. They claimed that it did "serious damage to the rule of law." Former chief executive C. Y. Leung, who had held power during the 2014 Umbrella uprising, offered a reward to anyone who could find the people who tore down a Chinese flag and threw it in the harbor.

China seemed unwilling to accept that Hong Kong people genuinely wanted liberty or democracy. Beijing contends that anyone who wants the "Western" concept of freedom must be a foreign agent or a dupe of colonialism. In their news conference, officials from the Hong Kong and Macau Affairs Office fell back on familiar themes. They blamed "irresponsible figures in Western countries" who are hoping to "contain China's development."

Dictators want to be loved. Earlier, tyrannies had relied on brute force—the lash, jail, the guillotine—but today's tyrants want to preserve the fiction that their subjects have voluntarily surrendered their freedoms. China thus contended that the National Security Law actually enhanced freedom rather than undercut it.

On Human Rights Day 2020, nearly six months after the imposition of the National Security Law, state-run news agency Xinhua proclaimed that "society has returned to peace, Hong Kong residents have also regained all the rights and freedoms taken away by the social disturbances, and their human rights have been further protected and improved." The government mouthpiece claimed that people no longer had to worry about disorderly protests getting in the way of shopping or going to work or school.

The Xinhua article then veered into an attack on colonial times when "the rights and freedoms of Hong Kong residents had long been curtailed. It is an indisputable fact that the democracy, human rights, and freedoms enjoyed by Hong Kong compatriots have been established and guaranteed only after Hong Kong's return to the motherland." It concluded by contending that "the real reason" Western countries criticize the national security law is "that they try to contain China's development by playing the 'Hong Kong card.'"

Xinhua's commentary contains many tropes that China uses when discussing human rights. China is a victim—the West wants to "contain" China's economic advance. And colonialism was worse, runs the implicit argument, while life under the communist regime is better. Security matters more than anything—"society has returned to peace." The "very small number of people" arrested under the legislation can see "their human rights are protected by law, such as having to be tried in court before being convicted [*sic*], and having legal rights such as the right to counsel during proceedings and the presumption of innocence." The lack of jury trials, the loss of the ability to choose one's own counsel, and the handpicked judges who hear security trials aren't mentioned.

Yet the impact of the National Security Law has gone far beyond the number of arrests or convictions. Media organizations have been forced to close—besides *Apple Daily* and *Next* magazine, independent outlets *Stand News* and *Citizen News* were also intimidated into shutting down. The former dean of the University of Hong Kong's law school, Johannes Chan, calculates that over sixty civil society groups, among them political parties, trade and student unions, and professional and human rights groups, shut down or left Hong Kong in the first three years under the law.

Libraries have pulled books from the shelves. The Legislative Council has been refashioned: members are now almost exclusively pro-Beijing. Voters elected almost all of the 479 district councilors; now they choose only one in five. A National Security Office tips hotline has received over 400,000 reports from its launch on November 5, 2020, through April 2023—almost 450 calls a day. "In a city once known for its vibrant and diverse public square," wrote Chan, "no one feels comfortable sharing critical or even lightly satirical remarks or cartoons about the government in public, or sometimes even among friends in private."

Hong Kong officials keep extending the security law's reach. Authorities claim that the law extends globally. The government demanded that Google's YouTube and other streaming services remove the unofficial protest anthem "Glory to Hong Kong" from their sites worldwide; in 2023, authorities advertised bounties for the arrest of thirteen overseas activists living in the U.S., UK, and Australia. After a Hong Kong court ruled in the government's favor in 2024, the song was for a time removed from iTunes, Apple Music, and Spotify.

The idea that only a few people would be affected also proved illusory. After a citywide raid on the morning of January 6, 2021, forty-seven democrats were charged simply because they organized the unofficial election primary in July 2020. Prosecutors charged the group with "subverting state power" on the grounds that the legislators and activists tried to do what politicians in democratic countries do everywhere—they tried to win political power. Specifically, they wanted to use the electoral process to win a majority of the Legislative Council and force the resignation of the chief executive. Many were jailed for over three years before the completion of the trial, at which forty-five of forty-seven were found guilty.

A total of 291 people were arrested for national security offenses in the first three and a half years after the law took effect. Many of them had simply exercised free-speech rights and would not have attracted much notice, let alone an arrest, before July 2020.

Georgetown University Law School scholars Eric Yan-ho Lai and Thomas Kellogg note:

the defendants we are tracking have cumulatively served several decades in pre-trial detention, despite the fact that most were arrested for non-violent actions that would not be considered crimes in other jurisdictions. Whether intentional or not, authorities' effective elimination of bail for both NSL and other national security cases has given the authorities the power to jail anyone it chooses for months at a time.

Lai became one of the first targets under the new law, on Monday, August 10, 2020, six weeks after the imposition of the National Security Law. When he had been arrested before, he had enjoyed polite treatment—invited through his lawyers to appear at the police station for booking or, when officers came to the house, given time to take a shower before being gently escorted into a waiting vehicle. In the August arrest, Lai's hands were handcuffed behind his back, and he was manhandled by the arresting officers. Hong Kong's strict Covid restrictions on social distancing were ignored as police staged a performance for the photographers whom they had tipped off to assemble outside Lai's house.

Police bundled Lai into a police vehicle and drove him the ten miles to *Apple Daily* offices in Tseung Kwan O's industrial park. Two hundred and fifty armed police had raided the building earlier that morning. They filed through the lobby, past the busts of Lai's freedom heroes that graced the entrance—John Cowperthwaite, Milton Friedman, and Friedrich Hayek. They marched up the long curving stairs from the lobby to the third-floor newsroom.

Police escorted Lai into an elevator and perp-walked him through the maze of editorial desks and cubicles. *Apple Daily*'s journalists knew that they were witnessing a global news story. Employees livestreamed arguments between journalists and police as cops searched the office and carted away thirty boxes of material. Staff uploaded photos and videos—many of these were sent by employees hiding in the women's locker room and toilet.

Police frantically hunted for the newspaper's servers so that they could shut down the site. The year earlier the paper had moved everything to the cloud; the *Washington Post*–designed ARC content management system now hosted *Apple Daily* on Amazon servers outside of Hong Kong. ARC staff jumped in to help switch operational control to the *Apple Daily* journalists in Taiwan. "By the time they figured out how the system worked and asked us to shut it down, it was too late," remembers Mark Simon. "We said, 'We cannot—it's being run from Taiwan.'"

All of Hong Kong watched the unfolding drama in real time.

A reporter asked Lai, as police steered him to his office, "Mr. Lai, what should we do?" Lai responded with a pithy six-character Cantonese phrase: "They've cooked us a meal, we just have to eat it."

With Lai still in custody, the paper responded defiantly. On Tuesday, a front-page headline proclaimed, "Apple Will Definitely Keep Fighting." The paper increased its press run eightfold, selling 550,000 copies. The stock price hit a twelve-year high, soaring twelvefold the week of the raid as supporters rallied behind the company.

China's central government—always quick to condemn others commenting on judicial proceedings—applauded Lai's arrest, saying he "must be severely punished according to the law for colluding with external forces to endanger national security." Lai and others "have long been acting as political agents of foreign and external forces, assisting them in interfering in Hong Kong affairs, and carrying out acts of secession, subversion, infiltration, and sabotage against China," contended a spokesperson for the Hong Kong and Macau Affairs Office.

Official government newspaper *China Daily* paraphrased a government spokesperson who accused Lai of "plotting, organizing, and launching a series of illegal activities." The unnamed spokesperson from the Hong Kong and Macau Affairs Office claimed that Lai used his newspapers and magazines "to create and spread rumors, and fan and support violence." The spokesperson also said that "Lai provided financial support for anti-China elements and forces advocating 'Hong Kong independence.' Punishing Lai and other law breakers under the law is essential to uphold the rule of law."

Released in the early hours of August 12, after more than forty hours in custody, Lai's staff greeted him with sustained applause and a bouquet of flowers when he appeared in the newsroom later that day. The front page of Thursday's *Apple Daily* featured Lai sharing an emotional embrace with Cheung Kim-hung, the group's chief executive officer and the newspaper's former editor-in-chief. Cheung and Next Digital chief operating officer Royston Chow had also been arrested Monday, although they were both released later that day. Cheung appeared to shrug off the detention. Not Chow, who said later that week that the experience had shattered him. "They almost broke me," he confessed when we spoke at the end of that week at the company's annual general meeting.

Police also arrested Lai's sons from his first marriage, forty-four-year-old Tim and thirty-nine-year-old Ian, on national security and fraud charges. Neither lived with Lai and neither was involved with his business. Tim was a technology entrepreneur, and Ian ran the well-regarded Sushi Kuu Japanese restaurant. Both posted bail and were released; four years later, no charges have been filed but authorities continue to hold their passports and they must report to the police regularly.

Lai appeared unfazed. He told colleagues that his overnight stay in the police station hadn't been as bad as sleeping on a desk or chair at the factory when he first arrived in Hong Kong. In July, Lai had launched a weekly series of livestream video events, shown on Facebook and YouTube, in which he addressed the world. (I acted as the moderator.) On the day after he was released following the police raid on the *Apple Daily* newsroom, he appeared on the livestream, as defiant as ever. More than 200,000 people watched. In subsequent months, his guests would include Chris Patten, Cardinal Joseph Zen, former World Bank president Paul Wolfowitz, retired U.S. four-star general Jack Keane, *New York Times* columnist Nicholas Kristof, Ambassador Raymond Burghardt, and former *Asian Wall Street Journal* editorial page editor Michael Gonzalez. He remained unafraid. "Contrary to what they might think, I don't hate the Party," Lai had told the *New Yorker*'s Jiayang Fan in 2019. "I just don't fear them."

If Lai refused to be cowed, he understood that Hong Kong had entered a new era. In an interview in early September, he said that the newspaper would no longer advocate positions—in other words, no longer act as an antigovernment political party—but would stick to straight news reporting. He stressed that staff had to worry about their safety. If the pressure got too great, the paper would shut rather than abandon its principles. "The day we cannot operate anymore we will close it down. Compromise is not what we established this company for. . . . We just go on doing what we do, there is no balance."

For three decades, he had said he would stay in Hong Kong. He had vowed it as early as September 1994 in his *Next* column. Lai rebuffed friends who had advised him to get out while he still could. Again and again, he said that Hong Kong had given him everything and that he couldn't leave. "I only tried to talk him out of it once," says Jack Keane, who had first met Lai in 2016. "He doesn't raise his voice or get overly emotional. He is very matter-of-fact about it. He said, 'I have to stay. Leaving would be wrong and cowardly.' I was quite in awe of the strength of his response. I have never seen anyone else like that."

Prosecutors charged Lai with colluding with foreign forces when they arrested him on national security charges during the raid. Although the National Security Law is supposedly not retroactive, authorities have collected evidence of previous behavior and used it as evidence of what they claimed was a predisposition to break the law. In Lai's case, that meant his 2019 visit to Washington and meetings with U.S. officials.

Prosecutors have pointed to a WhatsApp message Lai sent Cheung Kim-hung on March 23, 2019, asking that *Apple Daily* highlight news of Anson Chan's meeting with Mike Pence. They also cite his contact with London-based human rights activist Benedict Rogers, founder of Hong Kong Watch, asking him to sound out Chris Patten for support in fighting the extradition bill, which the government introduced in early April 2019. On April 27, Lai wrote Cheung to ask him to mobilize protests against the extradition law. The next day, the first significant demonstration against the bill took place.

Lai faces a life sentence for engaging in behavior that would be regarded as normal political activity in any open society.

"When a publisher is targeted in this way it is more damaging than singling out an individual journalist," says Rebecca Vincent, the London-based director of campaigns for Reporters Without Borders. "It sends a signal to other media owners and publishers and editors about what can happen if you don't toe the line. They knew what they were doing when they raided the *Apple Daily* newsroom and led Jimmy Lai out in handcuffs."

Time ran out for Lai in December 2020. On December 3, a judge ordered that his bail be revoked. The charge concerned allegations that Lai's personal company had illegally rented part of Next Digital's headquarters in Tseung Kwan O. Technical violations of this sort—unauthorized subletting—had never been a criminal charge before. But the judge viewed a man who engaged in potentially illegal subletting too dangerous to be free. His scheduled livestream discussion with U.S. Secretary of State Mike Pompeo had to be canceled.

Lai managed to win a short reprieve over Christmas week when a judge granted bail on December 23, though Lai remained under house arrest. He spent Christmas Day and the following week with his family and friends. He knew that his days of freedom were few. On December 27, he sent a WhatsApp message to colleagues: "I'm fucked. Delete everything."

Jade had flown out from New York to be with her father over the holidays and was undergoing the mandatory two-week Covid quarantine. During her isolation period, authorities added another week to the confinement period. By the time it ended, Lai's bail had been revoked. He was put back in jail on December 31, 2020. Since then, Jade has only seen him in prison.

Herbert Chow was the only other businessman of a sizable company to speak out in favor of the protesters in 2019 and against the National Security Law in 2020. Lai, whom he had met only a few times, inspired him. "I don't know this man very well," says Chow, "but he is the most genuine, incredible person in terms of wanting what is best for Hong Kong."

As the founder and owner of the city's chain of Chickeeduck children's clothing stores, Chow was another Hong Kong success story. He had been the president of the Hong Kong Tennis Association and a supporter of ice hockey—he owned rinks in Hong Kong and the mainland. "I felt that Jimmy was doing so much and that I also have all the right ingredients to also come forward," he remembers.

In his stores, he displayed a statue known as *Lady Liberty*—a cross between the Statue of Liberty and a young Hong Kong street protester. That brought the weight of the state down on him. Authorities in China threatened his businesses there. Landlords in Hong Kong—including giant property companies Sun Hung Kai, New World, and Sino Land, which control much of the city's prime retail space—terminated his leases.

More than fifty police raided a small five-hundred-square-foot shop. They let customers leave but detained the staff—shouting, cursing, and bullying Chow and the salesclerks. They refused to let Chow call his lawyer.

"It was all white terror," he recalls from his home in England, where he moved when Hong Kong became too risky. "It was an eye-opening experience. That told me that the National Security Law was passed to create threats," like making a retail display into a danger to the nation, not to protect the country.

Chickeeduck had an annual profit of $2.6 million and Chow had a wife and three children to support. "It was never my intention to sacrifice that," he says. But sacrifice it he did. Factory owners in China that supplied Chickeeduck were told "nobody ships to Herbert Chow," he remembers. "If you ship to Herbert Chow your children will not go to school." Even friends treated him like an outcast. When a former business partner died, his family asked Chow not to send flowers because it would bring them unwanted attention. "I would have expected a lot more companies to come forward," he says. "Jimmy and I were the only two guys. We looked to the left and looked to the right and we only saw each other. That was disappointing."

Chapter Twelve

"MAKING THE LAW THE TOOL OF A RULER"

In April 2021, four days before being sentenced for taking part in the 2020 Tiananmen Square vigil, Lai managed to get one of his letters smuggled out of prison. "It is our responsibility as journalists to seek justice," he wrote in the note of encouragement to his staff published by *Apple Daily*. "As long as we . . . do not let evil get its way through us, we are fulfilling our responsibility." It is "time for us to stand tall," Lai stressed. Defending free speech was "a dangerous job now. . . . Please be extra cautious and do not take risks. Your safety is important."

Meanwhile, Lai was enduring a series of show trials. On April 16, he received his first jail sentence, a combined fourteen months for two cases of unauthorized assembly. The convictions stemmed from Lai's role in demonstrations on August 18 and August 31, 2019. Judge Amanda Woodcock also found several other longtime pro-democracy campaigners guilty. Barrister Martin Lee received an eleven-month suspended sentence, sparing the aging activist time behind bars. Among those Woodcock sent to prison were the city's most prominent trade union leader, Lee Cheuk-yan, who took money and supplies to the Tiananmen students in June 1989; longtime legislator and radical activist "Long Hair" Leung Kwok-hung; and former Democratic Party chairman Yeung Sum, Lai's brother-in-law.

Lai had been behind bars 135 days awaiting trial when, on May 14, 2021, Secretary for Security John Lee abruptly stripped him of his ownership rights in Next Digital. As a result of Lee's action, Lai could not vote or sell his shares or receive any dividends. Next Digital traded on the Hong Kong stock exchange and had a market value of around $45 million, so Lee's unilateral move denied Lai access to more than $30 million of his property.

Justifying his unprecedented action in seizing property without a court order, Lee simply stated in a letter to Lai that he believed the media owner had broken the National Security Law. He provided no justification, no examples of illegal activity. Lee also wrote Citibank, HSBC, and Singapore's OCBC bank to warn that its employees faced seven-year-prison sentences if they allowed Lai access to his accounts with those banks. Lai had nothing to do with company operations, and the company put out a formal statement saying that operations would continue as normal.

Although he had resigned as chairman and stepped down from the Next Digital board in December, two days before he went to jail, Lai closely followed events at the newspaper and magazine company he had founded. Like other media companies, and despite rapid growth in digital subscriptions with the implementation of a paywall in 2019, Next Digital had struggled to make the transition away from print to a mostly online operation. Lai applauded the decision to shut the print newspaper operations in Taiwan, where the company was losing money. Coincidentally, the company announced that decision on May 14, the same day the Hong Kong government announced that Lai would be stripped of his shareholder rights.

Five weeks after John Lee froze Lai's shares, on June 17, five hundred armed police raided *Apple Daily*. They jailed CEO Cheung Kim-hung and Editor-in-Chief Ryan Law without bail on National Security Law charges. Lee then froze bank accounts at Next Digital's key operating companies. Lee simply stated, without providing evidence to the directors to whom the letters were addressed, that the company had violated the National Security Law. The bank freeze made it impossible for the firm to pay for electricity, paper, or ink. Credit card companies wouldn't process subscription payments for *Apple Daily*'s nearly 600,000 remaining subscribers. Cash couldn't come in and it couldn't go out.

Lee had joined the police force at the age of nineteen after graduating from Wah Yan College; he served for thirty-five years, before renouncing his British citizenship and joining the security bureau in 2012. He had been sanctioned by the United States in late 2020 for his role in pushing the 2019 extradition bill.

After the June 17 police raid, Lee advised journalists to "cut ties with these criminals," presumably referring to Jimmy Lai as well as Cheung Kim-hung and Ryan Law. Everyone on the board of directors was either in jail or outside of Hong Kong. Worried staff quit. Spooked by rumors of yet another police raid, one day in the middle of a board meeting, members of the IT department could be seen outside fleeing the building en masse. The arrests understandably exacted a high psychological price. One senior executive confided to the board of directors that he had considered suicide.

The National Security Law had flipped Hong Kong's legal system on its head. When China took over Hong Kong in 1997, it had promised that defendants would be presumed innocent until found guilty, in keeping with the common-law practice introduced during the British colonial period. That promise would no longer be honored. Mere suspicion by the secretary for security guaranteed a presumption of guilt. China had also promised jury trials. No national security law defendant to date has enjoyed the protection of a jury trial. Instead, handpicked judges from a secret list oversee cases. Any criticism of the government, any act of resistance, can be construed as a National Security Law violation. Defendants have no chance of a fair trial. Three years after the introduction of the law, the police chief boasted of a 100 percent conviction rate. (Two people were acquitted the following year.)

In letters written at the time of the second police occupation of the building, Lai tried to minimize the emotional impact of the raid on *Apple Daily*. Other prisoners—who "look sad and speechless"—asked him if Hong Kong would ever see the newspaper again. "Since I am here I cannot do anything about it," Lai wrote in his entry on Monday, June 21. "As for me and my staff, we have no regrets in Hong Kong—[we will] fight to its last day." The end came three days later. The final edition appeared on Thursday, June 24.

Lai delivered a tribute to the newspaper and its crusading journalists in an English-language missive:

Oh Lord, help my staff. Give them peace and consolation, may they live in hope of your promise in love. They had kept their promise of 25 years ago that we would be Hong Kong people's newspaper. Giving in to no power, and corrupted by none, they have not shirked from the promise and its responsibility. Despite constant ridicule, calumnies, blemishes and ostracism, [and being] banned from covering news in China, government functions, and [press] conferences. They fight until the last day, at the fall of Hong Kong. Bearing the pain of the cross standing tall. Salute to them.

They had never allowed their comfort [and] safety to rise above truth and justice nor allowed their lives to become lies at all cost. They have laid down a standard of integrity for Hong Kong's future journalists to follow when freedom of speech resumes again, as one day it will. Dictatorship is a dangerous business in today's online world, [where] intelligence is prevailing and information is making truth transparent. Dictatorship lives in lies [and] has become an emperor without clothes. Will people, knowing the truth, still succumb to fear of a liar?

Lai was well-informed about what was going on in Hong Kong. In jail, he subscribed to the *Ming Pao* newspaper, a publication that retained a degree of independence. Until his initial conviction in April 2021, his status was that of someone simply being held without bail; at that time he could receive almost unlimited visitors. He saw his lawyers regularly. Cardinal Zen celebrated Mass for him. CEO Cheung Kim-hung and barrister Martin Lee also counted as regular visitors in early 2021. After the guilty verdict that April, authorities allowed the newly convicted prisoner only two to four visits each month. In 2022, Teresa moved out of the Kadoorie Avenue house to the south side of Hong Kong Island in order to be closer to Stanley Prison and visited him as much as prison regulations allowed. Tightened Covid restrictions in 2022 curtailed visits for much of the year and stopped even visits by Lai's doctor. Lai himself contracted Covid that year. He subsequently underwent cataract surgery at a prison hospital.

The *Apple Daily* closure hit Lai hard. He wrote that "pain started to creep into my heart and soul with wrenching commotion." Although he tried to convey an air of serenity, he couldn't sustain the charade. "[I]t was my willpower suppressing my emotion underneath." Lai, a diabetic, wrote of his alarm at seeing his blood sugar shoot up to a dangerous 9.8 millimoles per liter from his normal level of 6.5 despite receiving insulin from prison authorities. His blood pressure hit a dangerous 165, elevated from the usual 130. At night, he continuously recited the rosary, but found sleep elusive.

Lai compared the experience to the loss he felt at his mother's death.

The shutdown is not as serious as that blow but the pain and sorrow weigh me down. I just don't want to talk to anyone about it. Someone comes to my cell to ask me about it and I just smile. I couldn't say a word.

The chief psychiatrist came this morning to the meeting room. Asked me whether I wanted to see her. I said no. I thought it was just her routine consultations. Later I found out she came especially for me. I felt really sorry. I wrote a letter to explain and apologize. Repentance in this case is charity. I felt better afterward.

Martin Lee and a pair of colleagues had visited him immediately after the June raid. "Martin looked troubled and compassionate about what happened to *Apple Daily* yesterday" and commiserated on "the loss of my work, my life, my vocation." Lai initially feigned indifference ("knowing that sooner or later it would happen anyway"), saying that his only concern was for his colleagues, though he conceded that "emotion swelled up from my heart [is] making me speechless." Although the shock of the raid had prompted many staff to resign, Lai clung to the hope that operations would go on.

His visitors brought questions from his staff—should they shut the newspaper now, work until the last day and shut it, or make most staff outsourced contributors and keep a skeleton crew to put the paper out and keep the online site alive? "I said the only consideration they should have is to consider their safety. And they should make the decision themselves. I should not make decisions for them here knowing so little of their real situation. They will have the full support of me and I think the board, too, whatever is their decision." Lai noted that "the [prison] guard never hurried us, seemed very sympathetic."

Lai's grief continued in writings that week. Here is an extract from his diary of Tuesday, June 22, two days before the final edition.

The forced closure of *Apple Daily* Hong Kong showed clearly what a shipwreck life in Hong Kong has become. The damage done by the Hong Kong government to Beijing's long-term legitimacy is much greater than the temporary benefit of quieting down the voice of freedom of speech. Yes, this barbaric suppression and intimidation works. Hong Kong people are all quieted down. But the muted anger they have is not going away. . . . The *Apple Daily* shutdown only aggravates it, making it [clear] to people that the hopelessness of Hong Kong is irreversible. . . . It is a vicious circle of suppression, anger, and distrust that eventually will turn Hong Kong into [one large] prison—like Xinjiang.

As journalists readied *Apple Daily*'s final edition early on the morning of Thursday, June 24, thousands of supporters swarmed around the company headquarters in Tseung Kwan O. They waved illuminated cell phones in a demonstration of support, cheering the newspaper staff who gathered on the building roof and applauding the trucks filled with newspapers as they left the compound one final time in the predawn hours. Elsewhere in the city, long lines formed at stores throughout the night. The editors who weren't in jail and who stayed to the end decided to go out with a bang. They printed one million copies, twelve times the normal print run. The newspapers quickly sold out. The era of media freedom in Hong Kong had ended.

Hong Kong has no concept of U.S.-style bankruptcy protection, where existing assets are preserved while the capital structure—loans and shares—are reshuffled. Next Digital's only realistic option was to sell everything and distribute the assets. The board did not have this power, so the four of us who remained as directors resigned together in early September, recommending that the company be liquidated. (Authorities subsequently subjected the board to four official investigations, trying to blame it for the company's failure, in an attempt to divert attention from their actions in freezing bank accounts and arresting staff.)

By the end of July, authorities had jailed six Next Digital and *Apple Daily* staffers in addition to Lai. Authorities charged CEO Cheung Kim-hung, previously *Apple Daily*'s editor-in-chief, along with current editor-in-chief Ryan Law, both of whom had been detained in the June 17 raid, with "conspiracy to commit collusion with a foreign country or with external elements" as well as "conspiracy to publish a seditious publication." The first charge is a National Security Law violation and carries a minimum penalty of ten years and a maximum penalty of life in prison. The second charge, a colonial-era offense rarely used until recent years, is currently being treated as if it were a national security offense. As in the national security trials, sedition defendants appear before national security judges, are rarely granted bail, and are denied jury trials.

Executive editor Lam Man-chung remained free after the June 17 police raid on the newsroom and put the final edition of the newspaper to bed. His freedom lasted only a few more weeks. Authorities took him into custody on July 21, 2021. He faces the same charges of collusion with foreign forces and seditious conspiracy.

Police arrested three others that same day.

Associate publisher Chan Pui-man, who from 2015 to 2017 had served as the paper's first and only female editor-in-chief, had been detained in the June 17 raid and then released on bail. On July 21, authorities rearrested her. That same day they picked up editorial writer Fung Wai-kong as well as Yeung Ching-kee, who oversaw the paper's new English-language website. All faced the same foreign collusion and seditious conspiracy charges. (Chief Operating Officer Royston Chow and the head of the web page, Cheung Chi-wai, also were arrested but released on bail.)

Authorities insisted that the arrests had nothing to do with the suppression of press freedom. The Chinese communist press, Beijing officials, and the Hong Kong government all solemnly claimed that the prosecutions were not political but were meant to ensure that everyone was punished "according to law."

In May, Lai had received another sentence. On May 17, three days after his Next Digital shares had been frozen, Lai pled guilty to organizing a demonstration on China's National Day, October 1, in 2019. Lai's nine codefendants also admitted guilt. Among them again were Lee Cheuk-yan, Yeung Sum, and "Long Hair" Leung Kwok-hung. Albert Ho, another former head of the Democratic Party, also pled guilty and went to prison. Judge Amanda Woodcock sentenced Lai to fourteen months in prison for his actions. She noted that Lai, a firm believer in nonviolent protest, and the other defendants "did call for a peaceful, rational, and nonviolent procession" but she dismissed the calls as "naïve and unrealistic" given the political tensions at the time.

Lai's writing for that day tells a different story: "I was given fourteen months sentence of imprisonment [for an offense] which, just a few months ago would be a fine of a couple thousand Hong Kong dollars. How much the law has changed!"

Lai expanded on this theme a few months later in his writing. These disproportionate sentences, he wrote, are "legal injustice—this injustice makes the case ridiculous and a tool for political expediency. Yes, it is blatant dishonesty, making the law the tool of a ruler. It sterilizes the law and in the process makes the legal system a fraud."

As recently as September 2020, Lai had received what he regarded as a fair trial after he had been prosecuted for purported criminal intimidation after the episode in which he lost his temper with a photojournalist from the rival *Oriental Daily News*. Lai shouted at the photographer during a 2017 Tiananmen vigil in Victoria Park, threating to "mess [him] up." Lai's outburst wasn't judged sufficiently serious to merit punishment. His 2020 criminal intimidation trial resulted in an acquittal, Lai's last by a Hong Kong court.

Oriental Daily News staff regularly staked out Lai's house and photographed his visitors, often following them when they left Kadoorie Avenue. They intruded into private occasions, once publishing a photograph of a dinner Lai hosted to celebrate *Asian Wall Street Journal* editorial page editor Hugo Restall's wedding. (The paper claimed the event proved Lai's CIA connections.)

The newspaper even ran a fake obituary of Lai in 2014, a stunt that the *New York Times* termed "the journalistic equivalent of putting a horse's head in your rival's bed." The full-page fake obituary claimed that Lai, whom the paper nicknamed "Fatty," had died of cancer and AIDS, prompting Lai to produce a video in which he proclaimed that he remained alive and well.

In June 2021, Lai was overjoyed to run into his brother-in-law Yeung Sum in the prison's washing-up area. Soon, however, authorities separated the two. Lai reflected:

It was such a joy to see Yeung Sum every day when I had to go to bathe. Even just exchange a few words. Now this joy is no more. They moved him to another cell because of our contact, for security reasons. Before, when we were outside [the prison], if I didn't see him for a month, I did not miss him. Now cut off [from] contact, I feel sad and miss him.

Lai, ever inquisitive, often engaged guards.

A young prison guard asked me, when no one was around: "Why didn't you leave before they arrested you, for surely everybody knew that it was coming to you?" "No, I could not leave, otherwise I could not raise my head and walk tall again. I must face the consequences of my actions, just or unjust. It is also a way to uphold the dignity of Hong Kong people, as one of the leaders for the fight of freedom. Also, if I shirk my responsibility and run away, I would be setting a very bad example for my children, [encouraging them to] run away from trouble and their responsibilities—indirectly I would destroy them. Besides while my colleagues and *Apple Daily* are holding the fort of press freedom and I run away from my responsibility, what kind of captain of the ship am I? No, there was no option for me but to face it.

Lai's trial for fraud, which centered on a minor lease violation, showed just how far the government would twist the law in order to keep him in jail. Next Digital owned two buildings in the Tseung Kwan O Science and Technology Park, built on land it had leased from the government. In a holdover from the British colonial practice of leasing rather than selling land, the government keeps title to all the territory's land. Freehold ownership, the practice in the United States, doesn't generally exist (a notable exception is St. John's Cathedral). The government remains the ultimate landlord, typically renting property to tenants for fifty years, imposing whatever conditions it chooses.

Following *Apple Daily*'s successful launch, the company needed more space. The Hong Kong Science and Technology Parks Corporation wooed the company with land in a new industrial park it was building. Next Digital signed on. Its lease specified that the company would use the property for newspaper and related businesses and would secure permission from Hong Kong Science and Technology Parks to sublease space to unrelated companies. Next Digital had received such permission to sublet space to more than two dozen companies. It did not ask for or receive permission to sublet to one company, Dico Consultants.

Dico functioned as Lai's family office. Lai owned Dico, and the company in turn managed Lai's private affairs. Dico had title to his yacht and arranged the insurance on his Kadoorie Avenue house. It also employed some of the people who worked for his private ventures, such as Thomas Crampton and Mark Simon.

Dico paid rent. Prosecutors noted that rent payments totaled $140,000 from April 2011 to March 2020. There was nothing exceptional about the use of a private company to manage a wealthy owner's personal affairs. That Lai paid rent to Next Digital, rather than have the publicly listed company subsidize his private one with free office space or staffing, showed his concern for proper governance. Even Judge Stanley Chan appeared puzzled about the case, given that Dico paid for the use of its tiny space.

Dico rented space almost continuously from the time Next Digital moved into the Tseung Kwan O facility in April 1998 until May 2020. The sublet totaled 646 square feet—an area less than half of one side of a tennis court (less than two-tenths of 1 percent of the total area Next Digital occupied).

Prosecutors termed Dico's use of the office "fraud." Yet it wasn't clear who was getting defrauded. Hong Kong Science and Technology Parks got the large up-front payment for the land lease. Next Digital shareholders benefited from Dico's rent payments.

The verdict came at the end of October 2022. Lai recorded it in his writings: "So I was found guilty of fraud on the charge of my violation of my company's land lease. So they don't care [about] the negative implications of this verdict to the commercial community." Lai continued: "I was disappointed too but took it as it came. Believing that I am in the hands of God, not theirs. Claire was so sad and despondent. Poor girl. I grieve for her." Lai's main worry concerned the guilty verdict meted out to his longtime manager, Wong Wai-keung. "He was just the head of general administration, not a decision-maker. His sin is only that he was a loyal colleague of mine." Lai comforted himself with the hope that Wong, who was in poor health, would be able to avoid jail time.

To Lai's dismay, Wong Wai-keung received a twenty-one-month sentence. Chan sentenced Lai to five years and nine months. Charges were dropped against former chief operating officer Royston Chow after he testified for the prosecution.

Until he received the guilty verdict, Lai had continued to believe that Hong Kong's court would rule fairly. After all, the belief that everyone would get a proper hearing in court, no matter who they were, set the city apart from the rest of China. Undercutting that sense of impartiality would destroy its reputation as an international business center.

Following the fraud conviction, Lai received yet another sentence, of thirteen months, for his role in the 2020 Tiananmen vigil.

Lai wrote a statement that his lawyers read in court. "I did not join the June 4th vigil in Victoria Park. I lit a candle in front of reporters to remind the world to commemorate and remember those brave young men and women who thirty-one years ago in Tiananmen Square put truth, justice, and goodness above their lives and died."

The statement continued: "If commemorating those who died because of injustice is a crime, then . . . let me suffer the punishment . . . so I may share the burden and glory of those young men and women who shed their blood on 4 June [1989]." In sentencing Lai, Judge Woodcock wrote that Lai and other protesters must be punished because they had taken part in "an act of defiance and protest against the police."

Hong Kong had always prided itself on rule of law. The British didn't institute democracy but they had seemed to have left a strong legal system behind. Protection of property rights lay at the heart of that system. Seizing company shares and freezing bank accounts without a court order—all while jailing key executives—didn't look good in a place that called itself a global financial center. So Hong Kong authorities set out to prove that Next Digital hadn't collapsed because of what *they* did. Instead they tried to weave a false narrative alleging that Lai and his team had wrecked the company.

Financial secretary Paul Chan appointed Clement Chan, managing director at international accounting firm BDO (and no apparent relation), as a special inspector, purportedly to figure out why Next Digital collapsed. Clement Chan's investigation seemed superfluous, given that the Securities and Futures Commission, the Stock Exchange of Hong Kong, and the Financial Reporting Council all announced separate investigations. Corporate governance expert David Webb noted that it had been more than two decades since an inspector had been appointed to examine a company in Hong Kong. The Securities and Futures Commission had been granted expanded investigative powers in the meantime. Why did the financial secretary need another investigator? Webb judged that the appointment was a political move.

Paul Chan claimed that possible fraud and misconduct required a special investigator. He cited the company's collapse shortly after the board stated that the company's financial health remained robust. Chan professed himself concerned with "upholding the integrity and reputation" of Hong Kong's corporate governance system, "which is the hard-earned result of the continuous efforts of the government, regulators, and the business community over the years." Ensuring that publicly traded companies adhere to governance standards "is vital to Hong Kong in maintaining the quality, fairness, and effectiveness of its market." Chan underscored the importance "in line with international practice," of ensuring "that any suspected serious wrongdoings of a company, in particular a company that is publicly listed, should be investigated if the circumstances so warrant."

Chan professed particular concern that audited financial statements weren't filed on time. But Next Digital's board of directors had been due to finalize the accounts on June 21, the Monday after police raided the offices, detained senior executives, and froze bank accounts. These events made those statements meaningless, and it would have been misleading at best to release them. Chan also expressed concern that Lai had been charged with fraud and that he and other executives had been arrested under National Security Law violations (though no convictions had been secured). That caused him to ask if Next Digital's major shareholder and senior staff had been looking after their "personal interests" and expressed his "grave concerns" about "serious mismanagement" and "alleged criminal offenses."

Inspector Clement Chan took a similar approach in his investigation. The shock of a raid by five hundred police, the jailing of senior executives, and the cutoff of bank accounts didn't seem to concern him. Instead he focused on the early repayment of part of a series of interest-free shareholder loans totaling $83.3 million that Lai had extended to the company in 2019–20 to tide it over while it rolled out its digital subscription strategy. Directors saw this early repayment as a sign of financial health. Paul Chan and Clement Chan professed to see sinister self-dealing.

Clement Chan was due to wrap up his investigation in six months, by the end of January 2022. His appointment has, as of 2024, been repeatedly extended. An unreleased interim report Chan produced, dated September 14, 2021, provided ammunition for the government to get a court order to seize the company and sell its assets even as the Hong Kong Science and Technology Parks took back Next Digital's two buildings. In an example of the circular logic of a twisted legal system, the Science and Technology Parks justified its seizure by citing Secretary for Security John Lee's contention that Jimmy Lai had broken the National Security Law. One sentence from Lee set in motion a legal process that destroyed a company and a newspaper.

The Hong Kong government killed *Apple Daily*. It used lawfare—weaponizing the legal system to achieve predetermined state aims—to give a veneer of respectability to property theft. Journalism as practiced by Lai and his staff for a quarter century now meant jail.

Chapter Thirteen

PRISON

On December 31, 2020, as the world marked the end of the first pandemic year, Jimmy Lai reported back to the Lai Chi Kok Reception Centre, where all Hong Kong prisoners begin their journey. He had been jailed on December 3 but released on bail for the Christmas holiday. He hasn't been free since returning to jail on that New Year's Eve.

He is currently held at Stanley Prison, Hong Kong's oldest, a maximum-security facility that opened in 1937. An internment camp during Japan's World War II occupation of the colony and the city's execution site until the colonial government banned capital punishment, Stanley Prison occupies a beautiful setting on a peninsula that juts into the South China Sea. The prison is at the edge of the town of the same name and about a thirty-minute drive from the city's Central business district.

The town of Stanley is named for the colonial secretary at the time the British occupied Hong Kong in 1841 and it was the first administrative headquarters of the new government. The Hong Kong Tourism Board invites visitors to "recall Hong Kong's past and unwind in [this] charming seaside town." The Chinese People's Liberation Army's main facilities in Hong Kong occupy the southern portion of the peninsula—immediately next door to the prison. The PLA troops mostly keep to their barracks, but it's a tangible reminder of who is in charge.

Lai cannot communicate freely. He sees his family between two and four times a month for thirty-minute monitored visits. When preparing for a trial, his lawyers can visit. His friends and supporters can only see him during his court appearances. Cameras are not allowed in the courtroom and so few photos of Lai have been seen since the end of 2020. His mail is censored and limited. Authorities arbitrarily decided that he could not receive postcards, thus short-circuiting a postcard campaign from Catholic schoolchildren. Because he is a symbol of Hong Kong resistance, authorities want to erase him. That means limiting contact with and pictures of him.

Samuel Bickett, a former corporate lawyer who worked for Bank of America in Hong Kong and was jailed on political charges in 2019, describes the disorientation most prisoners feel on arrival at the Lai Chi Kok Reception Centre: "The first several days are really, really tough. You are sitting in a crowded room on benches for hours on end, with no information on what is going to happen. You're called up. Then they sit you back down. There is just a lot of sitting around and waiting."

Bickett describes the disorienting experience. "One of the most difficult things in Hong Kong prison is that there are no clocks. You don't know what time it is. You can't see much outside." Guards prohibit even talking to other prisoners. "You have no books, no writing instruments. No visits. Literally the only thing you can do is just sit there."

Prisoners are supposed to receive an orientation shortly after entering. Officials are meant to explain prison rules, prisoner rights, and prisoner services. "None of this ever happens—at least to me or anyone I was in prison with," says Bickett. "In Stanley, the 'orientation' consists of watching a documentary series made by commercial broadcaster TVB for two days straight, eight hours a day, profiling various prisoners. No explanation or orientation whatsoever beyond that. I got more helpful orientation from the triad members who run the 'unofficial' services in Stanley than I ever got from prison officials."

Most prisoners are in group cells. These are supposed to hold eight people but are often stuffed with sixteen. One of Bickett's cellmates died during Covid. Although the inmate hadn't died of Covid, staff feared picking the cadaver up. Prisoners huddled for hours on the other side of the cell, as far from the corpse as possible.

Lai, by contrast, is in solitary confinement. This isolation can prompt mental health issues such as anxiety, depression, suicidal thoughts, and psychosis. Despite four years, mostly in solitary confinement, Lai exhibits little but optimism. "He doesn't feel the injustice" of his captivity, marvels Teresa. "He is so free. It is incredible."

In preparation for court appearances, Lai is first strip-searched, then restrained with cuffs and chains. He is locked inside a metal cage that in turn rests inside an armored car flanked by additional security vehicles. Hong Kong's rulers dictate this treatment for an elderly man who hews to a creed of nonviolence, a man who had every chance to flee Hong Kong to live comfortably in his apartments in Paris or London.

Bickett describes what's involved in court appearances for prisoners: "They do everything they can to make it very difficult. They wake you up very early, you have to eat quickly standing up, they scream at you to hurry up."

Prisoners are chained for transport. "When they finally put the chains on, you say 'thank goodness,'" says Bickett. "Putting the chains on you means they're about to take you out to the bus and get you moving to court."

Prison buses are air-conditioned, unlike prisons: "They were the nicest place I sat in for months," remembers Bickett. After the bus ride, prisoners are taken to a holding cell in the court. "You are in chains from when you leave the prison until they take the chains off in the holding cell." Lai received harsh treatment. "They had Jimmy in ridiculously over-the-top hand and leg chains."

The Chinese Communist Party usually gets its way in Hong Kong through quiet intimidation, often by threatening someone's job or their parents. By refusing to back down, Lai knocked his opponents off their stride. From the harassment of Giordano to the ad boycotts of *Apple Daily,* Lai had refused to put his business interests above his belief in freedom, even at a high financial cost. That alone made him unusual. Now he was refusing to quietly submit to the new National Security Law regime. Lai was going to force the Chinese Communist Party to reveal its ruthlessness to the world.

Lai chose the path of resistance. His willingness to suffer for speaking out for freedom reveals the truth about China's rule. Lai has documented his time as a political prisoner in hundreds of pages of daily letters. He writes in English with a pencil. Though he usually writes at the end of a day, he sometimes writes of the previous day's events early the following morning.

Some of the entries written during his first two years in prison have made their way out of Stanley. The prison writings paint a vivid portrait of life behind bars. The inevitable frustrations of captivity—not knowing what time it is or even being able to turn his cell light on or off—fade into the background of the spiritual and personal struggle Lai wages behind bars. His writings show a man who rises above the physical prison to find himself mentally freer than ever. They portray a man at peace. He has chosen jail as a way of showing his commitment to freedom. His clarity and focus have been sharpened by prison.

Lai understands that his task is very simple: He must survive with dignity. He must remain mentally and spiritually free, and remain true to his principles. His days have the structure and simplicity of a Benedictine monk. He wakes early; he spends his day reading, meditating, and drawing, in addition to performing mandatory prison labor. "The way I think of prison for him is that he is living a monastic life," says Bill McGurn, now a *Wall Street Journal* editorial board member, who regularly corresponds with him.

Prison is designed explicitly to humiliate and to dehumanize prisoners. From the moment he wakes, Lai is reminded that his jailers are in charge. Prison regulations prohibit clocks and watches. Waking in the predawn dark on June 28, 2022, a guard told Lai it was 4:30 a.m.

I asked him to turn the light on for me he said "no, maybe a couple of turns [of his patrol route] later." So I started my morning stretching exercise and ate my morning orange [saved from dinner the night before]. . . . While I was cleaning up, the guard came and switched the light on for me, as if his conscience revoked his earlier decision not to help me. He was not biased against me but extra strict with rules. I was touched by his sympathetic help. When he passed by again, I gave him a picture of Christ on the cross. He was very pleased.

One of Lai's chief occupations in prison is drawing. His two main themes during his first four years in prison were Christ on the cross and the Virgin Mary.

Lai had long harbored artistic ambitions. He has a good eye for color, honed during his years at Comitex and Giordano and on frequent museum visits with Teresa wherever they traveled. He and Teresa met Chinese American painter Walasse Ting in 1994. Lai and Teresa formed a close friendship with Ting; they traveled together to India in 1995. Ting had been part of the New York pop art scene in the 1960s and counted Andy Warhol as a friend and Roy Lichtenstein as a neighbor. Coincidentally, Ting's signature style featured bright acrylics reminiscent of Lai's clothing colors at Giordano. In the mid-1990s, Lai spent several months studying painting with Ting in Amsterdam, where the artist had a studio. A pair of pictures from 1996 shows Jimmy and two-year-old Sebastien with Ting in his New York studio. Until Ting suffered a stroke in 2002, Lai and Teresa visited him frequently.

Lai works on improving his artistic skills in prison, producing hundreds of finely drawn colored pencil drawings of religious figures. He often draws for hours each day. One Monday at the end of June 2022, Lai noted that he had finished his weekly quota of making six hundred envelopes. This mandatory labor earned him wages of $25.64 for the month, about one penny per envelope. "The work was strenuous. So I canceled my exercise to have more time to do my other works." He drew two pictures of Christ on the cross and read a chapter from a theology book. He went to bed at 8 p.m., amongst "rampant" cockroaches.

Art in the service of faith preoccupies him. Much as he tries to keep his ego in check, Lai takes pride in his work. In mid-June 2022, he professed himself "really pleased" with a "beautiful portrait of the Holy Mother." Although the drawing took the entire day, Lai noted his rapid improvement. "This gives me hope that I may accomplish my dreams to become a religious painter to serve the Lord." He planned to send that drawing along with three others to Teresa. "She would appreciate how good it is and give it to the right person." Lai closed his entry for the day with a quote from theologian Thomas Merton. "The turning of our whole self to God can be achieved by a deep and sincere faith in life and by hope, which knows that something is possible, and love, which desires above all things to do His will."

Prison conditions magnify the discomfort of even minor illnesses. Lai contracted a cold in late October 2022. He noted: "had little sleep . . . but went to piss about 20 times. My bones are aching. I still have to sleep during the day today. I shall ask officer for permission later." The aside reveals how prison strips away individual autonomy—an ailing Lai must ask for permission simply to take a nap during the day. He's not complaining, just stating the fact.

Prison food caused constipation. A prison doctor authorized him to receive an extra 15 grams of fiber a day. The recommended daily allowance for men is 38 grams a day, equivalent to what is found in about two-thirds of a pound of broccoli, so Lai's doctor had prescribed the equivalent of an extra one-quarter pound of broccoli a day. Instead, the prison chef simply gave him a portion that was 15 grams larger than normal, or about half an ounce of extra vegetables. The guard agreed with Lai's complaint, so he phoned the kitchen superintendent who responded that, "yes, fifteen grams is only four tiny pieces of vegetable—you should not be able to see the difference." Lai kept a sense of humor at the error, but just barely.

It is a joke: How can any doctor with any sense think that four tiny pieces, each the size of a fingernail, can ease someone's constipation! The doctor must be a miracle doctor, and this must be a miracle cure. If it is a miracle, I don't need a doctor, I need only God. Things as ridiculous as this can happen in the correctional service bureaucracy because of its strict rules.

Constipation in turn led to Lai obtaining laxative pills. He was subsequently charged for possession of three unauthorized pills. "I'll have to go to the prison court for the sentence tomorrow for this three-pill charge. They had me make a statement, just like in the police station. Then they came back later to give me a statement to ask whether I plead guilty or not. I pleaded guilty." Lai had to go to a prison court (a "port"), with no lawyer to defend him, a guard as a prosecutor and a superintendent trying to look like a judge ("with a wooden face and a judge's solemnity—quite comical"). Lai received a five-day sentence mandating no snacks or soft drinks, no newspapers, radio, or books, except for religious ones. Authorities confiscated five days' wages (the government website notes that prison wages are $4.87 to $20.90 a week; Lai's earnings were toward the bottom of that range).

With temperatures that top 90 degrees and humidity levels occasionally registering 100 percent, the lack of air-conditioning takes a toll on inmates. Lai noted how hard the heat makes it to sleep. He applied for an extra tin of baby powder each month to make sleep more comfortable. "Living in an air-conditioned world outside I never knew about baby powder. Now in a non-air-con environment I found it a saving grace to have. In hot weather, without air con your body sticks to the cloth and at night when you turn your body the straw mattress sticks and turns with your body. Baby powder is indispensable in hot weather without air con," Lai wrote in late May 2021, the beginning of his first hot season in jail.

A few days later Lai celebrated recent rains for breaking the heat wave and cooling the cell ("made life so much easier"). "But the guard warned me, after the rain the mosquitoes would have a field day and 'feast on you.' That, luckily, has not happened yet. Maybe the fan that blows directly on me really helps. Or I just got used to mosquito bites and don't feel the itches anymore?" A month later Lai still worried about mosquitoes, relieved that he was only bothered by cockroaches. "Cockroaches are a nuisance but don't bite. All I care is that mosquitoes—which bite bitterly—have been reduced greatly. A summer without mosquito bites in prison is a miracle."

After a judge found Lai guilty of civil disobedience charges in April 2021, he traded the gray uniform of a prisoner held without bail for the brown uniform of a convict. Conviction also brought with it a work requirement, thus the envelope-making assignment. He spent a good deal of time trying to do this task quickly so that he would have more time for his drawing and meditation and reading. Lai's embrace of efficiency even when it came to prison labor reflected an approach he first adopted at Comitex. His thoughts on the best way to make envelopes in turn became a meditation on hope.

While I was doing my envelope folding and sticking, a guard who is friendly with me passed by my cell, looked at what I was doing, stopped and said, "Why try so hard? Take it easy." I smiled and said unapologetically "no this is the only way I know. Yes, it is lowly work. Still, I want to give myself all to it. It is about me, not the job. It is my nature." He laughed and moved on. When I first started doing the envelope folding and sticking job, I was fumbling, trying to figure out the best way to do it. Soon I was doing 89 per hour, I thought that was good. No, the guard said, the good ones are doing 100 per hour. Two days later I was doing 105. I told the guard who came with a cellmate helper delivering mail. The cellmate helper said, "Well, there are a few doing 120 per hour." So a week later I did 120 per hour. Then another cellmate helper came and said, "The fastest one is doing 140 per hour." Oh my God, that is challenging. Now my goal is 150 per hour, so I can finish my working quota in two days each working for two hours. But now after a few more days I'm still stuck at 120—140 per hour may be beyond my reach.

It is good to have a goal so I'm always alert and trying. It is not just about reaching the goal. It is keeping hope. You hope for what you do not have. Each act of hope is one's free act, yet it is also a gift from God.

Lai thinks about food a lot. He looks forward to Sundays and the curry gravy on offer, which "makes the whole meal so much more enjoyable. Meals here are of tepid taste. So hot sauce makes a great difference." In mid-2021 he indulged in an extended reverie about the joys of simple home-cooked food, eaten in the freedom of his home and shared with his wife Teresa. "When I am really hungry, I can't resist thinking about food. When I come out of here, I'm going to eat a simple breakfast—just toast, butter, jam, honey, and coffee; lunch just a bowl of soup with rice." Lai indulged in an extended reverie:

> I can teach the Indonesian maid to chop up 10 pieces of chicken or pork or beef. She will fire up the pot with some oil, a few small slices of ginger, fry for 20 seconds, put the meat in and fry for a minute then put three bowls of water and boil with medium fire for 20 minutes or so till it becomes one bowl of soup, put vegetables in for a few minutes, then sauce with some salt. This would be a delicious soup for lunch. Dinner would be cooked by Teresa. She is an excellent cook. To cook [and eat] her simple steamed fish or her chicken western style with mushrooms would be wonderful!

Lai's prison writings are filled with wonder, along with compassion and empathy for visitors and even the prison's guards. He embraces the physical restrictions of prison as a way of nurturing mental and spiritual freedom. During the long midsummer days, Lai wakes up with the birds. A June 19,

2021, entry, from his first summer in jail, notes "what a changed perspective prison life" makes. "The morning choir of birds singing at around 3:00 is such a joy—it makes me look forward to the day." At 5:30 Lai rises to begin his morning meditation prayer and exercise.

One day, to reward the birds for their singing, Lai threw them some bread. A cockroach got to the food first. "When the cockroach finished eating, it dropped a dung on top of the bread to preserve it for itself. The birds, repulsed by its dung on the bread, passed by it without even glancing at it. The cockroach dung smell must be very strong if the bird avoided passing that way. Would I have the curiosity to watch this if I were not in prison? No. Prison life is a new pattern."

A cockroach or cockroaches entered his cell at night. "It crawls over my face while I'm asleep. I just wipe it off. But now, as I was praying, they crawl across over my legs, I interrupt my prayer and kill them. That may offend the Lord and I ask for forgiveness for I just cannot tolerate them around. So eerie. I kill at least one, mostly more, every morning."

Lai seizes any opportunities prison presents to improve himself. On the outside Lai was impatient, a hard-charging entrepreneur who didn't let niceties stand in the way of what he wanted. Previously always quick to act, quick to speak, he cultivates patience in prison. Once a guard hurries Lai, urging him to stop what he was doing in order to meet a visitor.

I lost my temper at the guard. "I'm a prisoner—that doesn't mean I'm not a human being!" I ignored him until I finished my business. He kept quiet and seemed to be intimidated by my tantrum. On the way to the visiting room, he kept his head down and seemed to be ashamed of himself. I was sorry. I should not let off my temper. I turned to him and in a contrite manner held my hand out to shake his hand and apologize. He was surprised and smiled. From then on, he was friendly to me. Repentance with a contrite heart solves person-to-person problems so easily. I wonder why I have not done it more often.

Lai knows that the guards are victims of the same system that imprisons him. "We are prisoners from seven a.m. to seven p.m.," guards joke to inmates. Reporting to work, they must surrender their cell phones and subject themselves to searches. They enter the cell blocks with only their uniforms. One guard helps Lai by giving him two cups of cold water after exercise. Mentioning this to another guard, the second guard immediately cautions Lai: "If any of us do anything extra nice to you, never say it to anyone or you would get him into trouble."

He worries for a guard who was friendly to him. The man has "a strange disease" that prevents him from perspiring. Lai details the man's symptoms: in hot weather, his heart races and he suffers from headaches and dizziness. Because he doesn't perspire much, he goes to the toilet often. He should drink water but is afraid that will force him to use the bathroom even more often. One of the other prisoners, a nurse, told him that he should drink much more water. He's been drinking more water for the past eight months and has some improvement, with perspiration from his nose and the side of his forehead. "I started praying for him today. I don't know whether he would be receptive if I give him a picture of Christ on his cross and on the back, I write down the Lord's Prayer and ask him to pray for God's help. Since this isn't an incurable disease the Lord may help him. Let me try to talk to him more."

Another guard wanted one of Lai's many drawings of Christ on the cross that he has done in prison. He was afraid of being caught by the prison's surveillance system. "Finally, he said, better give it to him in the exercise court where there is no surveillance camera. And I did two days later, when he escorted me there. He was happy to have it and said sorry for the trouble. I hope the picture of Pietà brings him and his family God's blessing and peace."

Teresa has remained in Hong Kong despite harassment and the potential that she, too, could be arrested. She often visits with their daughter Claire. Lai saw his teenage son Augustin for the first time in three years after Covid restrictions ended. (Augustin's elder brother Sebastien lives in Taiwan and would almost certainly be arrested if he returned to Hong Kong—simply for speaking out for his father.) His sons Tim and Ian from his first marriage still live in Hong Kong and are frequent visitors. His daughter Jade still lives in New York but visited her father in prison frequently when she came to Hong Kong in 2020–21 and again in 2023. The family visits take place in a large reception room and prisoners speak through a telephone, separated by thick Plexiglas. The restrictions notwithstanding, the weekends when his family cannot visit found Lai despondent.

"Sunday my family members visit, and it usually is a day of joy. Not today, for I used up my monthly three visits. I felt lost, so I prayed and regained my peace and went back to my daily routine feeling okay. [As I wrote earlier,] Sunday breakfast is my favorite because of the curry gravy." Curry gravy is no substitute for family, but small pleasures loom large in prison.

The democracy activist Martin Lee was for a time a frequent visitor and source of information about the outside world. In July 2021, Lee brought news of fellow activist Albert Ho, also in jail.

Martin and Janet [Pang, a fellow lawyer] visited me and told me that they had just visited Albert Ho in the nearby prison. He didn't look so good. Seemed to have slight depression. It is easy to suffer depression in prison when you feel sorry for yourself. And angry for the injustice, for what he has done was to fight for Hong Kong people's freedom. This injustice weighs heavy on his heart and mind. That depresses him. I will pray for him. But if you have done nothing wrong—and did not allow your safety, comfort, and well-being to take precedence over justice, truth, and goodness and your life to become a lie—but instead became a beacon for human dignity and honor? What a great and honorable position God has put you into. Yes, you suffer but God suffers with you and shares his glory with you. Have peace and pride. You should consider yourself chosen. I'm going to write to Albert to this effect.

With the shutdown of Next Digital and *Apple Daily* in June 2021 and continuing pressure on civil society organizations, Lai pondered the future of the movement and the most effective way to resist government oppression. Forty-seven opposition figures had been arrested at the beginning of 2021; most were denied bail and being held awaiting trial.

Lee and Pang visited on August 14 with news that the activist group that honors Tiananmen victims would also close. One of the group's leaders, Chow Hang-tung ("a brilliant lawyer," noted Lai), did not want to close it down but instead force the authorities to shut it in order to demonstrate the government's ruthlessness. Lai wondered whether Chow—who was openly courting arrest—could fight more effectively behind bars or outside. "It's logical thinking in normal times [to risk arrest] but now a big political storm is raging. If they decide to face up to the risk, nobody has a right to gainsay them, but [we must] respect their courage and heroism. Are they more effective upholding the resistance movement outside or in jail? For they are sure to be arrested. So many of us are already in jail they won't boost the spirit much. Rather, being outside they could make and reinforce relationships locally and overseas, especially since Hung is such an effective leader."

Martin Lee was perhaps as close as anyone to Lai outside of his family, except Cardinal Zen. Lai provided most of the funding for Lee's Democratic Party and sometimes joined Lee on his Washington, DC, lobbying trips. Lai, Lee, and Janet Pang had met Speaker of the House Nancy Pelosi in October 2019 as part of the campaign for Hong Kong democracy. In April 2021, as noted, Lee was sentenced to eleven months in prison, but the sentence was suspended on account of his age. Lee could stay out jail, provided he avoided further legal trouble. With the threat of prison hanging over his head, Lee's visits dwindled as the space for political activity shrunk. That prompted Lai to wonder how far the crackdown would go and how long it would continue.

> Martin Lee became afraid to visit. Coming so regularly, Martin is afraid
> of being implicated and censured by the authority. Now the authority
> wants to cleanse any sign of resistance and opposition. Anyone who

helps those persecuted may be persecuted himself or herself. They have banned crowdfunding to help pay for lawyers for those persecuted and for organizations to spend on necessities like soap, towels, pens, notebooks, and snacks for political prisoners. Next will come [pressure on] lawyers who visit political prisoners and remanded defendants [those held without bail] too frequently.

We don't know how far this cleanup operation goes. Hong Kong becomes a city of quiet and calm—but is dead. But Hong Kong people's hearts are shouting and the spirit of resistance is soaring. How long they can keep people's instinct for freedom down?

Flashes of anger give way to contemplation. When the ward's head of security failed to come talk to him to explain why supporters' postcards to Lai had been blocked by his jailers, Lai reflected on his anger over the denial. The delay in the visit by the security head "gives me more time to contemplate the incident and learn from it. I certainly let my ego go ahead." Even though a decision not to allow him to receive postcards from supporters abroad was "unreasonable and arbitrary," his strong reaction "shows that I'm not humble enough. I should treat everyone I deal with as God hidden behind him, especially with cases so humiliating. It would be God's way of training me to be humble. I rejected it, now to my regret. Humility is to be humble where it is too insulting to be humble."

Lai's success in surviving prison stems from this relentless self-examination, this determination that he can be mentally free even when he is physically imprisoned. "I should repent of [being angry with] even someone who deserves not just no respect but reproach. That is what humility is in serving God."

Lai monitors international events. In October 2022, he followed news of the Party Congress, a meeting held once every five years that is the country's most important political event. The 2022 gathering held special significance because supreme leader Xi Jinping sought a precedent-breaking third five-year term as the Communist Party's general secretary. As the Congress continued, Lai confided his belief Xi would not get the third term. (He was one of the few who doubted Xi's reelection.) Then came the disappointment. Xi not only won, but his day was capped when senior staff members escorted his bewildered predecessor away.

> Finally the news came. Xi Jinping is definitely continuing his reign. Not only in the grip of power but more powerful than before. In the last day of the Congressional meeting, in the middle of it, he had guards take Hu Jintao away from the meeting, with a smile on his [Xi's] face. A display of his unquestionable supreme power. Something like when North Korea's supreme leader Kim [Jong Un] arrested his uncle in the middle of a meeting of national leaders. Now Xi wants to show he has absolute and supreme power just like Kim. . . . The regime never had a leader so exalted in his ruthless power like this, not even Mao. It is so out of bounds. It must have unintended consequences. Let's wait and see. I was greatly disappointed but soon recovered my peace and hope because of my trust in, my faith in, God. He must have the best plan for me, though it is beyond my comprehension. God, I believe, please help my unbelief.

Lai continues to take an active role in managing his business affairs. In 2021, he worked to keep $69 million in a Singapore bank out of the Hong Kong government's clutches following the May 2021 asset freeze in which his shares in *Apple Daily* were seized. These moves followed John Lee's warnings to the banks not to let Lai access his accounts. A summer 2021 letter from a financial advisor noted that money from accounts at Citibank and OCBC had been moved from Singapore to Taiwan because of concerns that Hong Kong authorities could seize the funds ("various concerns about the security of Singapore custodial accounts").

From Taiwan, the money was moved again ("We are unable to stay in Taiwan, again due to custodial concerns"). These moves betray an audacity on the part of Hong Kong and China authorities in trying to seize assets being held at banks in Singapore and potentially Taiwan absent any legal basis other than a sweeping assertion under Hong Kong's widely derided National Security Law. These moves to take Lai's money were made before any trial, let alone conviction.

This same letter seeks approval for the "SaaS equity campaign." Lai had for several years favored SaaS (Software as a Service) companies for his stock investments. The financial advisor wrote that the list of proposed investments was much the same as before with the addition of an exchange-traded fund that invested in SaaS companies and Google, which he noted was becoming a company that had many of the same characteristics of SaaS companies. Lai wrote: "Okay, but make sure they are SaaS. I don't want anything else mixed with them."

Other companies on the list included Shopify, Intuit, Trade Desk, Salesforce, Adobe, Paylocity, Splunk, Zendesk, Microsoft, and Nvidia. The total investment would be $57 million out of the $69 million brought out of Singapore, with the remaining $12 million reserved for legal bills "paid over the last year," an indication of the expense Lai was incurring in his fight against communist China.

A note asked Mark Simon to safeguard the animation unit's avatar technology, which "was developed with my own money, and belongs to me, not to Apple." As liquidators dismembered the company, Lai wanted to make sure that his personal assets would be protected as much as possible.

Friends and strangers alike continue to write to him. The postcard campaign mentioned above featured Lai's drawing of Christ on the cross. Hundreds of students, mostly from Catholic schools and universities, wrote to Lai using the cards. Separately, a stranger named Ting sent a newsletter written by a twenty-six-year-old Hong Kong writer who lives in New York and writes under the name Parachute. "What a wonderful letter. She writes so simply and beautifully. A born writer indeed. She really knows Hong Kong and her strong love for Hong Kong and her unflinching determination to fight for her home is so admirable it moved me to tears. Bravo! Hong Kong has such young and talented people determined to fight for us. We have hope."

Chapter Fourteen

"LIVING IN COMPLETE FREEDOM"

Jimmy Lai's visitors say that he is as free in prison as he has ever been. "He doesn't see it as punishment," says Teresa. "He is living in complete freedom." Although he is held in solitary confinement and shackled during transport to court appearances, he has a clear goal: maintain his innocence and continue to resist his captors with dignity and honor. He knows what he is doing. Behind bars since the last day of 2020, now with his prison cell window boarded up, he has been purified by the experience, approaching it as a spiritual quest and a test of his faith.

His moral and physical courage coupled with financial resources and a willingness to publicize his plight command attention. Perhaps not since Nobel Peace Prize laureate Liu Xiaobo died in Chinese custody in 2017 has the cruelty and barbarity of the Chinese communist system been so nakedly and publicly displayed.

For a quarter century, Lai steeled himself for the possibility of prison. By speaking out against the Chinese Communist Party, he knew he was putting himself at risk. As legal maneuvers against him increased, he did what he often did—read and talked to others, studying how to be a model political prisoner. In a discussion in mid-November 2020, just weeks before he was jailed, Lai talked about the charges he faced and his expected imprisonment.

"The more danger I am in," said Lai, "the more effectively I can bring the attention of the outside world to Hong Kong," he said in a livestream discussion with longtime Soviet dissident Natan Sharansky, whom authorities held in the gulag for nine years.

Sharansky cited Galileo's moment of weakness four hundred years earlier, when the scientist recanted his assertion that the earth revolved around the sun. Four centuries later, said Sharansky, those actions still reverberated in the form of talking points for Soviet inquisitors. "The KGB was trying to use Galileo, to say 'follow his example,' in return for leniency." Sharansky refused immediate freedom rather than surrender his beliefs.

I later spoke with Sharansky about Lai. The pair talked three times in the two months before Lai's jailing. "He was not yet in prison, but he had this deep feeling—maybe it was his fate to go to prison and continue to be a free person," Sharansky tells me. "It was very inspiring and very unusual." Lai wanted to translate Sharansky's prison memoir, *Fear No Evil*, into Chinese. Lai even had a Chinese publisher, Sharansky says, "but they wanted to take a few phrases out that referred to China—I refused. Not that it was that important. But a book about freedom of speech cannot be censored." Lai intended to press ahead, remembers Sharansky, "but he didn't have time."

More than 1,400 days in confinement, every day that Jimmy Lai resists constitutes a triumph of freedom over totalitarianism. He served his fourteen-month sentence for the convictions stemming from peaceful protests in 2019 and 2020 and is now in the midst of serving a sentence of five years and nine months for the office lease violation. He is enduring a National Security Law trial that will result in a conviction and a lengthy sentence. The outcome isn't in doubt, given the almost unbroken string of convictions for national security trials. Lai is the most symbolically important prisoner and it's improbable that he will be found innocent, whatever the evidence.

As a Class A prisoner—a category usually reserved for murderers and other particularly dangerous inmates—Lai has been held in solitary confinement for most of the time since the end of 2020. Solitary confinement for a nonviolent prisoner flouts international convention. In 2015, the UN General Assembly adopted the Nelson Mandela Rules, named in honor of one of the world's most famous political prisoners. The Mandela Rules restrict solitary confinement to "a measure of last resort, to be used only in exceptional circumstances." Mandela himself, who spent twenty-seven years in prison as part of his successful struggle against South Africa's apartheid system, called solitary confinement "the most forbidding aspect of prison life. There was no end and no beginning; there's only one's own mind, which can begin to play tricks." Yet China keeps Lai in solitary confinement even as it claims to believe in a rules-based international order.

Unusually for a dissident, Lai doesn't crave political power. He's simply idealistic, perhaps even romantic, about the virtues of democracy. Despite providing tens of millions of dollars in financial support to Hong Kong's pro-democracy movement, he never sought to push any agenda other than free markets and freedom for people.

"He's not attracted to power and money," says James Cunningham, who met Lai when he served as U.S. consul general in Hong Kong. The two men developed a friendship based on their shared interest in politics. "He is attracted to people who do good things, not people who are flamboyant and politically powerful. The people he felt most comfortable with were those like Cardinal Zen and Audrey Donnithorne, modest normal people who did good. He isn't like the normal Hong Kong rich—thinking about political power, business, and building a political base. Jimmy likes living well, eating well, and being good to his friends."

His many friends and acquaintances notwithstanding, Lai has walked a solitary path—yet he embodies the universal aspiration for freedom. He can travel this road because he is stubborn, determined, and confident. The sort of hardships he endured as a child shattered many people in China. Mao's three-decade reign left in its wake a nation of brutalized and mostly numbed survivors. Lai survived and thrived, exemplifying Friedrich Nietzsche's notion that "out of life's school of war—what doesn't kill me makes me stronger."

Many people who counted Lai as a friend when times were good have gone quiet. People fear China's retaliation. Notwithstanding the Hong Kong government's claims that the city is safe for business, they fear that their bank and brokerage accounts in Hong Kong could be frozen, just as they have been for many activists. They fear that they might be prevented from coming to Hong Kong or, worse, arrested while there, as was a Hong Kong student in Japan whose Facebook posts earned her time in prison when she returned. They have seen the bullying and harassment endured by relatives of those overseas activists subject to bounties for their arrest. They fear for the safety of their children and parents and brothers and sisters in Hong Kong and China.

"He was always taking enormous risks," says Matt Pottinger, who first met Lai more than twenty years ago as a *Wall Street Journal* reporter and last saw him when he was serving as Donald Trump's deputy national security advisor. Pottinger keeps a picture of Christ on the Cross that Lai drew and sent to him from Stanley Prison in 2022. "This is someone who has, maybe late in life, deeply contemplated the intersection between democracy, fundamental rights, and the role of God and protecting those rights as an expression of his religious faith."

Pottinger went on to ridicule the National Security Law charges that Lai faces of colluding with a foreign government. "How is he an agent of a foreign power if he comes to tell us he is worried about the deterioration of the rule of law in Hong Kong, something that was guaranteed in an international treaty registered at the United Nations?" He notes that "there have been a parade of Hong Kong officials who came and visited the State Department and the White House and elsewhere to exchange views. [Former Hong Kong chief executive] Tung Chee-hwa spent a lot more time in the White House talking about Hong Kong than Jimmy Lai ever did. It strains credulity to talk about Jimmy Lai as an agent of anybody."

In the midst of his own troubles, Lai conveys a spirit of generosity. He sent a present to an inmate whose daughter was getting married; he helped another inmate get a job as a security guard after his release and looked into how another soon-to-be-released convict could apprentice in the building trades. He wanted to help a jail guard, until his advisors pointed out that it could look like attempted bribery. It seemingly hadn't occurred to him that it could be anything other than an unselfish gesture.

This fondness for helping others was obvious long before his imprisonment. He bought his brother Choi-ying a noodle shop in Hong Kong's Tsuen Wan district; when Choi-ying sold the property for triple the original sale price, Lai congratulated his brother on his business acumen. He often let his old friends Bob and his wife Penny Aschkenasy use his Paris apartment; when the Lais' apartment there was under renovation, he paid for the family to stay at the Hotel Meurice. When one of the Aschkenasy sons got married, Lai bought the newlyweds everything on the gift registry that hadn't already been purchased by others.

A twenty-eight-year-old journalist found herself similarly bedazzled by Lai's generosity. But for Mary Kissel, the sharing centered on ideas. Meeting Lai after moving to Hong Kong to run the *Asian Wall Street Journal*'s editorial page in 2004, "I was a know-nothing from Jupiter, Florida, and he was this billionaire tycoon and we enjoyed an exchange of ideas." Over the six years she spent in Hong Kong, Lai hosted her at home and on his boat with guests ranging from the economist Gary Becker to the Acton Institute's Robert Sirico. "It was this great banquet of thought leaders, of leading-edge iconoclastic thinkers—it was amazing," says Kissel, who later, as the senior advisor in the State Department, arranged Lai's 2019 meeting with Secretary Pompeo.

Brad Hamm met Lai for the first time in Kyoto. The two started a conversation one evening at dinner and picked up at lunch the next day. The meeting took place in March 2015, three months after Lai had been arrested at the close of the Umbrella Movement. He had recently stepped down as chairman of Next Media, though neither Hong Kong politics nor Lai's legal troubles featured in their conversation. Nor did the communist-led advertising boycott of the company. Instead, they touched on topics ranging from technology to the future of journalism. Hamm is also a twin, and the coincidence sparked a discussion about siblings and parents.

Lai volunteered that he had not been as good a husband in his first marriage as he would have wished. "I asked about his mother," remembers Hamm. "He really wanted his mother to be proud of him. You could tell how much she meant to him. He cried. I had a sense of Jimmy as a person. He had this booming voice, and he could seem forceful and he might have intimidated people. It didn't matter whether or not he had millions of dollars, whether he was famous, whether he had achieved all these things—all she wanted him to be was a good man." Certainly, Lai told colleagues, his mother wouldn't hold it against him that he was in prison. After all, she had been unjustly sent to a labor camp by the communists.

Lai counts as a special kind of hero in the eyes of Jack Keane, a retired four-star U.S. general. "I have lived a life among heroes," says Keane. The military heroism he saw was impulsive. "You react instinctively to something where you can save a life or stop something bad from happening." Lai's courage, by contrast, "is not impulsive. It is well thought out and it is deliberate and he knows how horrible the ending could be for him. . . . It is an extraordinary display of courage—in what he is doing, he redefines heroism for me."

Lai had the enthusiasm of a recent convert when Father Robert Sirico first met him. That zeal has come to include a "defense of human dignity, human rights, and a deeper focus on prayer and meditation," says Sirico. "The more Lai studies, the more religion becomes his sustaining core. This is the threat to the [communist] regime. You cannot break a man who is not concerned about money or about freedom. He is deepening this mystical sense. It moves mountains. It is what Mandela had in a secular way. That is the trajectory of his spirituality and his faith. Remember he converted under John Paul, who was a great image of a freedom fighter."

Lai and Cardinal Zen once agreed that it would be "wonderful" to die in prison for their beliefs. Of course, neither his family nor his friends, nor perhaps even the Chinese Communist Party, wants Lai to make that ultimate sacrifice. But "there is no meaningless suffering," says Julie McGurn. "It's all worth it." Along the way, Lai hopes that his incarceration raises the cost to the Communist Party for its destruction of Hong Kong.

Lai knows what he wants to do. The Chinese Communist Party will decide whether he dies in prison or enjoys his last years with his family. Lai has no say in that decision. But whether in prison or outside it, Jimmy Lai Chee-ying has chosen a life of freedom.

EPILOGUE

On February 7, 2024, Wong Wai-keung was released after serving fourteen months for a fraud conviction relating to the purportedly illegal sublet of the Next Digital headquarters. Wong had paid a heavy price for refusing to testify against his longtime boss.

Wong's freedom was welcome news to Lai and his family and a good start to a year that would be dominated for them by his lengthy National Security Law trial. Wong remained loyal to Lai's ideal of freedom. Shortly after his release, he made a pilgrimmage to Scotland to visit the grave of Lai's hero, Hong Kong's laissez-faire financial secretary John Cowperthwaite.

The trial started in December 2023, a year behind schedule and forty months after Lai was first arrested on the security charges. Procedural wrangling and a prolonged dispute over Lai's legal representation caused delays. In a dubious first for Hong Kong, Lai had been denied his choice of lawyer.

Lai wanted Tim Owen, a well-known London-based barrister, to represent him. Although Owen had represented clients in Hong Kong, authorities revoked Owen's visa and hastily rewrote the rules regarding foreign lawyers to deny him the ability to defend Lai. Apparently the Hong Kong government feared Owen's performance might be so compelling that it would spoil their show.

Authorities certainly made a spectacle of the trial. After his motorcade snarled traffic during the initial transfer from Stanley Prison, security forces moved him to the nearby Lai Chi Kok detention facility. Although designed to minimize traffic disruption, Lai's transfers from Lai Chi Kok to the West Kowloon Courts continued to take place under the sort of security associated with a terrorist. He rode shackled in a cage in a huge armored vehicle surrounded by a phalanx of accompanying security vehicles. At the court, hundreds of police and their dogs kept watch.

Teresa and Claire attended every day of the trial. Authorities seated them in the back of the courtroom with a policeman nearby. Augustin came during the early weeks, while he was in Hong Kong over his school holiday. Sebastien remained in Taiwan, unwilling to risk arrest by returning to Hong Kong. He married in October 2022; his father was unable to attend the wedding and hasn't seen Sebastien's daughter, born in February 2024.

Father Robert Sirico made an unannounced visit to Hong Kong to attend the trial; although they weren't allowed to talk, tears ran down Lai's cheeks when he saw his old friend in the courtroom.

Lai seemed energized when prosecutors showed photos of the 2019 demonstrations. Five years on, the photos reminded him what he did.

Jade visited Hong Kong shortly before the trial began and saw her father in prison. Although Ian and Tim had been arrested in the original August 2020 national security raid, they have not been formally charged. The charges remain pending and they must report periodically to the police, and their travel outside of Hong Kong remains restricted. Their mother, Judy, acts as their personal guarantor when they apply for permission to leave Hong Kong.

Despite promises that the National Security Law would not be applied retroactively, much of the testimony against Lai centered on events that occurred in 2019 and the first half of 2020, before the law took effect. Prosecutors have focused on Lai's active participation in so-called lunchbox meetings in 2019 and 2020, where he periodically met with top editors to discuss the paper's coverage. The court proceedings detailed the minutiae of daily newspaper operations, from the meetings called by Lai to discuss broad guidelines, to editorial decisions about where to place a story, what the headline should say, and even a prosecutorial catalog of revisions that occurred from the first edition to the second edition of the paper.

Prosecutors asserted that Lai was masterminding illegal behavior. Instead, they only succeeded in showing Lai and the *Apple Daily* editors at work making some of the hundreds of decisions necessary to put out each day's newspaper. Lai often looked more like a hands-on editor than a modern executive chairman, jumping into the editorial fray like an old-time press baron, a contemporary incarnation of Joseph Pulitzer or William Randolph Hearst.

Prosecutors showed excerpts from former CEO Cheung Kim-hung's Slack chat detailing some of the decisions that came out of these meetings. The catalog of issues raised at one meeting range from protest-related graphics to internal competitions to finding content for a special Sunday section on parents and pets:

> For the interviews in Apple Pictorial and Entertainment People, we should spend more time with the interviewees to dig out their life stories. The same requirements should be made for outsourcing.
>
> For the weekend editorial section, we can try to invite authors from [local online news sites] *The Initium* or *Stand News* who write well.
>
> After the graphic layout design competition, we should continue to hold weekly voting, provide rewards, and even have a monthly or quarterly award.
>
> For the Sunday supplement on parenting and pets, we can try to see what's suitable from the content on the parenting and pet mini-sites.
>
> We can compile the three major protest graphics of the extradition bill movement for publication.

Despite the mountains of evidence prosecutors provided over the monthslong trial, it proved difficult to understand what was illegal. Lai and *Apple Daily* practiced advocacy journalism. They always had. This approach hadn't been a problem for the previous thirty years. Now authorities outlawed even banal statements. Prosecutors attempted to tie Lai to a subscription advertisement, stating, "Hong Kong and Taiwan share [a] common destiny / Watch the fate of Hong Kong and Taiwan together." (Former editor-in-chief Chan Pui-man said this represented Lai's view.) It's hard to see what was objectionable—let alone illegal—about contending Taiwan's and Hong Kong's fates are interrelated.

Chan Pui-man testified about Lai's stance toward Covid-19. *Apple Daily*, apparently at Lai's suggestion, called the disease the "Wuhan plague" or "Wuhan pneumonia," referring to the city where the disease broke out. He wrote a column entitled "Wuhan Plague, the CCP's Funeral Bell." Prosecutors worked to establish that Lai's use of "plague" was more pejorative than "pneumonia." Plague or pneumonia, Chan said that Lai wanted to sound the alarm that the Chinese government wasn't being transparent about the disease.

In early 2003, *Next* had won plaudits for breaking news about SARS. Now Lai was being prosecuted for performing a clear public health service to the community by calling for openness about the disease. China had also said it wanted transparency. But it thwarted a visiting World Health Organization investigation team that came to the country; when Australia called for a thorough investigation of Covid's origins, China cut off imports of Australian beef, barley, wine, and other goods.

Testimony showed that Lai often took a direct hand in the newspaper after 2014, even though he had stepped aside for a time, particularly after Cassian Cheung left the company and Lai returned. Prosecutors worked hard to prove the obvious. Lai owned 71 percent of the company and reassumed the post of executive chairman in May 2018. As the owner of a newspaper business, it would be odd if his views weren't reflected in the newspaper.

And they were. Lai gave directions to make a big deal of former Hong Kong chief secretary Anson Chan's meeting with Mike Pence in

2019. A few months later, Lai, with no time to write a piece on his own, ordered up a question-and-answer story of his trip to the United States in July 2019.

As evidence of Lai's purported wrongdoing, prosecutors showed pictures from his phone from October 2019, when he posed with House Speaker Nancy Pelosi and, separately, with Senator Ted Cruz, former chief secretary Anson Chan, and Legco members Dennis Kwok and Charles Mok. Given that Washington and Hong Kong were not enemies, it represented a dramatic shift in the law to criminalize meetings of this sort seeking support for Hong Kong's democracy movement.

Prosecutors tried to establish an element of collusion between Lai and a London-based human rights activist because both used the common English-language phrase "moral high ground." They quoted an open letter from Benedict Rogers, founder and head of the UK-based pro-democracy group Hong Kong Watch, advocating that protesters remain nonviolent in order to occupy the "moral high ground." Prosecutors then prompted Chan Pui-man to confirm that Lai often used the phrase "moral high ground" in interviews with foreign media.

Prosecutors alleged that Lai engaged with conspirators abroad. As well as Benedict Rogers, these included former Hong Kong governor Chris Patten, human rights activist Bill Browder, and James Cunningham. Browder, who says that he has never met or spoken to Lai, appears to have been targeted because he met Sebastien Lai. Rogers, Patten, and Cunningham all speak out on Hong Kong issues. Targeting these high-profile advocates for Hong Kong isn't an accident. "[F]oreigners are frequently portrayed as seeking to undermine the authority of the CCP," notes the Harvard political scientist Tony Saich. "As the 2019 Hong Kong demonstrations expanded, it was inevitable that the party would 'discover' that Britons and Americans had been stirring up trouble. . . . This tendency to see conspiracy everywhere is a legacy of the prerevolutionary struggle."

Prosecutors make much of Lai's personal involvement with the newspaper; his contacts with foreigners, especially democratically elected officials in the U.S.; and his opposition to antidemocratic policies and legislation in Hong Kong. Unless journalism is a crime, Lai is innocent.

Even before the 1989 Tiananmen killings—and years before he met Milton Friedman—Lai endorsed the idea that moving to a more market-oriented economy would threaten the power of the Chinese Communist Party. He believed that trade and economic liberalization would change China, just as globalization and economic growth had laid the foundations for political liberalization in South Korea and Taiwan. That was also the strategy for successive American administrations from George H. W. Bush to Barack Obama.

If Lai is guilty of anything, it is excessive optimism about China. He has conceded that he was wrong about economic openness and widespread access to technology leading to political liberalization. Far from being a crime, Lai's actions are those of a Chinese patriot.

On April 26, 2020, as the pandemic intensified and Beijing secretly prepared the National Security Law, Lai wrote a column titled "Defying Tyranny's Suppression, Our Courage Persists." "What keeps us going now is our [love for] the rule of law and our love for freedom. We have no illusions about the tyranny of the CCP. What we can persist in . . . is our courage to do what we know is impossible."

China's Communist Party cannot fathom Jimmy Lai. He is a man who lives by his principles. He knows his life is at stake. "He has made it clear that if that's what it takes, the fight is worth it," says Rebecca Vincent. "I think they fundamentally misunderstand people like Jimmy Lai and what they misunderstand threatens them. Perhaps they miscalculated. He is courageous, he stayed, he is fighting, and his presence in jail will tarnish what is left of the reputation of Hong Kong and Beijing."

Lai often speaks of faith and of his belief in miracles, of the optimism and hope he always carries with him. From his childhood he dreamed of freedom and of the city that embodied it, Hong Kong. He fought to make those dreams come true. From a childhood scrapping with other traders when he cut prices on the streets of Guangzhou to the Hong Kong newspaper wars of his middle age, he has never shied from conflict.

Now he is in the fight of his life. Speaking at the memorial for his friend Glynn Manson in 2015, Lai might as well have been speaking about himself—his zest for life, the idea of breaking the rules and then doing everything better. The vow to "fuck the quota" could stand as Lai's credo. This wasn't nihilistic anti-authoritarianism, but working around government regulations in a way that led to the invention of hot-selling new fabrics. It was about having fun, making money, and working for freedom.

"He has such a love for life," a tearful Lai said of the man he had known for thirty-nine years. "He never gave up—he was so optimistic," Lai remembered of the dozen visits he made at the end of Manson's life to visit his friend. "He still believed in hope," concluded Lai. "What an inspiration this guy is."

Lai wants out. Make no mistake about that. The decision to let him leave prison will be made by the Chinese Communist Party. Until then, he is content simply to live in prison as a free man.

ACKNOWLEDGMENTS

Although he hasn't been able to help with this book, my thanks go to Jimmy Lai, whom I met more than thirty years ago and whose life inspired me to write this biography.

Until Jimmy, as almost everyone in Hong Kong calls Lai, went to prison, I never thought of writing a book about him. I don't know if he is aware of this book; mine is a sympathetic biography but not an authorized one. No one from the Lai family has read the manuscript or tried to influence the editorial content in any way.

One disheartening aspect of this project was the fear I encountered even on the part of those who only knew Lai decades ago; a good number of the roughly one hundred people who helped with this book requested anonymity, afraid that the Chinese Communist Party could punish them, their family, or their business if they are seen as partial to Lai. My thanks go to the following people, whom I spoke with about Jimmy or who helped in other ways.

Bob Aschkenasy; Judy Pilunya Assapimonwait; Carolyn Bartholomew; Ellen Bork; Raymond Burghardt; Sandrina Caruso; Chai Ling; Chan Kin-man; Chen Hao; Mai-wah Cheung; Sunny Cheung; Ching Cheong; Antonio Chiang; Ed Chin; Herbert Chow; Tom Crampton;

Acknowledgments

Gordon Crovitz; James Cunningham; Michael Davis; David Feith; Tim Ferguson; Mike Gonzalez; Odette Heung; Frances Hui; Ted Hui; Victoria Tin-bor Hui; Ip Yut-kin; Jin Zhong; Tara Joseph; Elic Lam; Jack Keane; Mary Kissel; Eric Kohn; Anna Kwok; Dennis Kwok; Jade Lai; Finn Lau; Shirley Leung; Michael Logan; Bill McGurn; Ben Miller; Stacy Mosher; Jay Nordlinger; Kazuko Ouchi; Chris Patten; Mike Pence; Matt Pottinger; Sheridan Prasso; Hugo Restall; Benedict Rogers; Robert Sirico; Andrew Tanzer; Steve Vines; Rebecca Vincent; Wang Dan; Paul Wolfowitz; Cori Wong; Minky Worden; Wu'er Kaixi; Zhou Fengsuo; and Seth Zucker.

Thanks to Robert Messenger at Simon & Schuster, whose immediate and unflagging enthusiasm for the book was matched by his deep knowledge of what's at stake when one man stands against a totalitarian regime. I benefited from a wonderful team at Simon & Schuster. My profound thanks go to production editor Rachael DeShano, who patiently and somehow cheerfully shepherded this book through several iterations on the way to publication. Martha Kennedy oversaw the cover and Wendy Blum designed the book itself. Thanks to Elizabeth Venere for marketing and Omesha Edwards and Elizabeth Herman for publicity. Last but certainly not least, thanks to Simon & Schuster editor-in-chief Priscilla Painton who, on the strength of a note of introduction from Bill Browder, immediately saw the value of this book.

My warmest thanks go to my agent Leah Nathans Spiro at Riverside Creative Management, not only for representing me for a third book but for her unflagging enthusiasm for my work. Ellen Kadin went above and beyond as we worked on the initial proposal and unearthed an enormous amount of material about Lai.

Thanks to Grace Young for quick, thorough, and reliable research, photo searches, and fact-checking. Kelly Sandefer at Beehive Mapping once again provided excellent maps.

Sam Bickett, Ted Clifford, Brad Hamm, Simon Lee, Perry Link, Mark Simon, and Larry Zuckerman are among those who have read part or all of the manuscript in various incarnations. Their comments helped make this

Acknowledgments

an immeasurably better book. My deepest gratitude goes to Pamela Mensch, who has patiently and repeatedly read all of the manuscript through every draft and strengthened it in thousands of places. Special thanks to Carroll Bogert, who helped me find new paths both in this manuscript and beyond.

A final thanks goes to Natan Sharansky, whom I first encountered when I moderated an extraordinary livestream discussion with Jimmy and Natan; after Jimmy's arrest, Natan shared insights into their other conversations and kindly wrote the foreword, writing for which his nine years in a Soviet gulag made him uniquely qualified.

NOTES

A note on sources: Lai's life following the 1989 Tiananmen killings and his entry into media is well documented in his own writing as well as in hundreds of interviews and articles. Testimony and documents introduced at the 2023–24 National Security Law added yet more details to a very public record chronicling Lai's media and political activities, especially over the past decade.

The story of Lai's first four decades relies on his writings, interviews by me and others, and secondhand accounts. In researching these first forty years, the approximately 1,600 weekly columns that Lai wrote for *Next* magazine from its founding in March 1990 until he went to prison in December 2020 proved particularly useful in revealing details of his childhood and early years in Hong Kong.

I have also benefited from numerous video interviews filmed over more than a decade by Robert Sirico; in addition to material used in *The Hong Konger*, a documentary about Lai, Father Robert Sirico and his team at the Acton Institute kindly made many additional hours of footage available to me. I have sourced all of these as Sirico interviews.

I also benefited from access to previously unpublished letters Lai has written from prison. They provide intimate insight into his incarceration.

Lai's video interviews and prison letters are in English. The columns have been translated from Chinese; I am particularly grateful to Simon Lee for his translation work. Key Lai columns and writings are available at www

.jimmylai.subbstack.com. I do also want to acknowledge unnamed others who assisted in translating hundreds of additional columns. Lai's writings and comments have been lightly edited for clarity.

All local Hong Kong currency amounts have been converted to U.S. dollars at the prevailing rate; for most of this period US$1 was equivalent to HK$7.80.

ix   *"Do not get lost in a sea of despair"*: Katherine Q. Seelye, "John Lewis, Towering Figure of Civil Rights Era, Dies at 80," *New York Times*, July 17, 2020, updated August 4, 2020, https://www.nytimes.com/2020/07/17/us/john-lewis-dead.html. Coincidentally, Lai briefly met Lewis in October 2019 while in the U.S. Capitol with Martin Lee; with Representative Tom Suozzi, civil rights icon Lewis made a short video in support of Hong Kong's democracy protesters and underscored the importance of nonviolence. "Jimmy had earlier met with Suozzi and had expressed his strong concern about damage caused by the violent tactics which involved a small number of the demonstrators but which were nonetheless featured in all the news reports," remembers Ambassador James Cunningham, who was present. "Suozzi, Jimmy, and Lewis met in the Capitol corridors by chance, and Suozzi introduced the two. Suozzi asked Jimmy if it would be helpful if Lewis, famous for his advocacy of nonviolent protest, sent a message to the people of Hong Kong about the necessity for non-violent demonstrations. 'Absolutely,' said Jimmy, and Lewis filmed a short message to the protesters."

Prologue: The Troublemaker

3   *He had money—a fortune estimated at $1.2 billion*: Russell Flannery, "Hong Kong's 40 Richest 2008," *Forbes*, January 28, 2008.

6   *China reacted with fury*: "China Objects to Mike Pompeo Meeting Jimmy Lai," *The Standard*, July 9, 2019.

Chapter One: "Food Is Freedom"

12   *He had a brother*: The Lais were Cantonese but some members of the family, especially those who remained longer in China, used Mandarin Chinese spellings for their names. (The languages are distinct but use similar written characters.) Hyphenated names denote Cantonese spellings; names with no hyphens are in Mandarin Chinese. Jimmy Lai's Mandarin

name is Li Zhiying (the family name is Li). Biying and Huanying kept the Mandarin spelling, so they are Li Biying and Li Huanying.

12   *She was periodically sent*: Lai has consistently said his mother was sent to a labor camp, but labor camps are a sort of prison; inmates aren't released on weekends. It seems that she was subjected to some sort of forced labor but not incarcerated in a labor camp.

12   *"Adults were very busy being cursed"*: Sirico interview.

14   *"I don't know if they were tired or sad"*: "Angel," *Next*, December 28, 2008 (the column is dated Christmas Day).

17   *His mother worried that "going to Hong Kong is like going to the moon"*: Michael Barbaro with Austin Ramzy, "*The Daily*: Jimmy Lai vs. China," *New York Times*, September 3, 2020.

21   *"It was the first time I saw so much food"*: Barbaro with Ramzy, "*The Daily*: Jimmy Lai vs. China."

22   *Lai lived in the factory*: Yasuo Awai and Jennifer Lo, "Jimmy Lai Still Dashing to Freedom in Hong Kong," *Nikkei Asia*, March 25, 2016.

22   *"I knew I had a future"*: "Hong Kong Useless" column, March 20, 2014, and Sirico interviews.

24   *"Since I was conscious"*: From a piece dated to 2004 by Lai's statement that he would be fifty-six years old "this year."

Chapter Two: "What's Your Magic?"

25   *"I was able to perform"*: Michael Barbaro with Austin Ramzy, "*The Daily*: Jimmy Lai vs. China," *New York Times*, September 3, 2020.

27   *The market more than doubled*: In a column dated November 27, 2003, Lai says that he set up the margin account to "buy and sell short." He notes that the market soared in 1972 and plummeted in 1973 so he may have played the downturn precipitated by the October 1973 war adroitly. Whether he was long or short in stocks, the use of borrowed money amplified his gains.

27   *"Before I knew it"*: Lai repeatedly said in English-language interviews that he turned his HK$10,000 into HK$250,000, but in a 2003 Chinese-language column he says it was "nearly HK$200,000." I have converted the amounts at the prevailing exchange rate of $1 = HK$5.085.

27   *"When I made money"*: Sirico interview.

27   *A 4,000-square-foot sweater factory*: *Next* column.

30   *Lai named the company Comitex*: Sirico interview and *Next* column. Corporate records state the company was officially founded June 10, 1975.

33 *"We are really lucky"*: Next column.

38 *"Hey, it's really great"*: Next column.

41 *"Why don't we fuck the quota?"*: Jimmy Lai's eulogy at Glynn Manson memorial service, March 20, 2015 (private video).

43 *So Lai plunged*: In 1994, *Wall Street Journal* columnist Tim Ferguson asked Lai who his hero was. Ferguson expected that Lai "would say Milton Friedman or Ronald Reagan," especially given that he worked for the *Wall Street Journal*. "His answer threw me because he said Karl Popper," remembers Ferguson. "In retrospect that informs his struggles since then and his role as someone speaking truth to power—that kind of guy and the social philosophy of Popper fits with his struggle and his willingness to incur the wrath of Beijing authorities in pursuit of his philosophical beliefs. . . . It better captures the full Jimmy Lai than a Milton Friedman answer would have. It suggested to me that there was lot of depth to this seemingly rough self-taught guy." See also Tim W. Ferguson, "From Street Hawking to Karl Popper," *Wall Street Journal*, July 19, 1994.

Chapter Three: The Father of Fast Fashion

45 *A napkin stuffed*: Sirico interview.

46 *They slashed delivery times for retailers*: Jimmy Lai's eulogy at Glynn Manson's memorial service, March 20, 2015 (private video).

50 *His success attracted*: Hideki Yoshimura, "From Hiroshima to the World: Tadashi Yanai on the Secrets of UNIQLO's Success," *Japan Forward*, January 20, 2020.

51 *He now has a net worth*: Naazneen Karmali, ed., "Japan's 50 Richest 2024," *Forbes*, May 28, 2024.

52 *That return is almost double*: Preceding financial information is found in Giordano Holdings Ltd., *Annual Report 1993*, 2. Return on equity is found in NYU Stern School, "Return on Equity by Sector (US)," data as of January 2023, https://pages.stern.nyu.edu/~adamodar/New_Home_Page/datafile/roe.html.

54 *The faster pace allowed Lai*: Andrew Tanzer, "Picking the Eyes from Retail's Gods," *Forbes*, June 18, 1993.

Chapter Four: "Like My Mother Calling"

57 *By 1997, they and other*: https://eh.net/encyclopedia/economic-history-of-hong-kong/.

57 *Comitex partnered with a state-owned*: Laurence Zuckerman, "China Buying Deeper into Hong Kong," *International Herald Tribune*, July 13, 1991.

61 *One Giordano shirt*: Geremie Barmé, "Culture at Large: Consuming T-Shirts in Beijing," *China Information* 8, nos. 1/2 (1993): 4, esp. n. 15.

63 *"It was very exciting"*: Sirico interview.

64 *"An entrepreneur is more motivated"*: Sirico interview.

Chapter Five: "Turtle Egg"

69 *"I was involved in it"*: Sirico interview.

70 *Lai named the magazine* Next: Sirico interview.

71 *Lai put $6 million*: Monica Gwee, "Lai Enjoys Platform of Media Politics," *South China Morning Post*, April 8, 1990.

72 *By 1994, it was selling 180,000 copies*: Tim W. Ferguson, "From Street Hawking to Karl Popper," *Wall Street Journal*, July 19, 1994.

77 *In August, Chinese authorities*: Mark Clifford and Lincoln Kaye, "Lai Low," *Far Eastern Economic Review*, August 25, 1994.

78 *"Yes, I am anti-communist"*: *Next*, "An Open Letter to the Bastard Li Peng," July 1994, and "I Will Stay," September 9, 1994.

Chapter Six: The Bulldozer

81 *But Lai didn't give way*: Giordano Holdings Ltd., *Annual Report 1994*, 27 ("Report of the Directors"); Giordano International Ltd., *1995 Annual Report*, 14 ("Chairman's letter," dated March 21, 1996); Adela Ma, "Sale of Lai Holding in Giordano Scrutinized," *South China Morning Post*, March 1, 1996.

82 *Lai dubbed his newspaper* Apple Daily: Note that Lai's prayers took place in the early to mid-1990s, before he converted to Catholicism.

83 News *and pro-Taiwan* United Daily News: Clifford Lo and Kim Black, "Two Newspapers Close as Price War Bites," *South China Morning Post*, December 17, 1995.

85 *The newspaper had been founded in 1969*: Wikipedia, s.v. "Ma Sik-chun," last modified July 13, 2022, 16:58, https://en.wikipedia.org/wiki/Ma_Sik-chun.

86 *"I always thought of* Next*"*: Simon's positions in the media businesses included assistant general manager (2002–2004); general manager (2004–2006); CEO, Digital (2006–2007); chief revenue officer (2008–10); general manager, Next Animation (2010–12); group director (2012–20). He has

been chairman of Lais Hotels since 2003 as well as managing director of the family office since 2003.

88 *"I have the advantage"*: Tim W. Ferguson, "From Street Hawking to Karl Popper," *Wall Street Journal*, July 19, 1994.

88 *The most notorious feature*: Craig S. Smith, "Elusive 'Fat Dragon' Supplies and Rates a Red-Light District," *Wall Street Journal*, May 16, 1997; Jane Li, "Where Hong Kong Got Its Thing for Crowning People King—of Shops, Props, Toilets, Toys . . . and Kowloon," *South China Morning Post*, April 11, 2017.

89 *He also had to apologize*: Stephen Vines, "Media: Hong Kong's Gore Wars," *Independent*, November 17, 1998; Albert Chen and Albert Cheng, "The Taipan with a Conscience," *South China Morning Post*, January 14, 1996.

90 *In their memoirs, Friedman*: Milton Friedman and Rose D. Friedman, *Two Lucky People: Memoirs* (Chicago: University of Chicago Press, 1998), 550–51.

91 *Friedman also noted Lai's adventurous eating habits*: Friedman and Friedman, *Two Lucky People*, 557.

91 *The Friedman children*: Cato Institute, "Jimmy Lai: Winner of the 2023 Milton Friedman Prize for Advancing Liberty," 2023, https://www.cato.org/friedman-prize-2023.

92 *When longtime staff member Simon Lee*: Lai's management style became a source of contention in his National Security Law trial. Former CEO Cheung Kim-hung insisted that he only carried out Lai's orders. Testifying on January 29, 2024, against Lai in his national security trial, Cheung said that "I had no choice" but to follow Lai's direction in specific editorial matters. Cheung's testimony should be viewed in light of his role as a witness for the prosecution, in hopes of winning leniency, after pleading guilty and being held without bail for three years. (Nothing in Cheung's or Chan's testimony seemed out of the ordinary in my experience of working directly for two newspaper proprietors in Hong Kong as the editor-in-chief and publisher of *The Standard* and editor-in-chief of the *South China Morning Post*.) Trial, Day 18, January 29, 2024, www.supportjimmylai.com/trial-updates.

93 *In March 2003*: Keith Bradsher, "Hong Kong: Budget Official Avoided New Tax," *New York Times*, March 11, 2003.

95 *The government's flawed estimate*: Philip P. Pan, "Hong Kong's Summer of Discontent," *Washington Post*, July 14, 2003.

96 *In Lai's case, dissent*: It's worth noting that a handful of businessmen on the mainland have also spoken up and paid a price. Property tycoon Ren Zhiqiang, an acerbic critic of the Chinese Communist Party, was sentenced

to eighteen years in prison after he called Xi Jinping a "clown" in 2020 over his handling of the Covid pandemic.

97   *In 2023,* Condé Nast Traveler: Caitlin Morton, "The 50 Most Beautiful Small Towns in the World," *Condé Nast Traveler*, May 5, 2023.

Chapter Seven: "God Suffers with Me"

109   *Lai donated generously to the church*: Paul Hong, "I Received Millions and Spent Them for the Church and the Poor, Card Zen Says," PIME Asia News, October 20, 2011.

110   *New York City*: Catholic Schools in the Archdiocese of New York, "2023–2024 New York Catholic Schools at a Glance," https://catholic schoolsny.org/about-us/.

110   *The Catholic Church took*: Beatrice Leung, "The Hong Kong Catholic Church: A Framing Role in Social Movement," in *Social Movements in China and Hong Kong: The Expansion of Protest Space*, ed. Khun Eng Khuah-Pearce and Gilles Guiheux (Amsterdam: Amsterdam University Press, 2009), 246.

111   *As the handover approached*: Leung, "The Hong Kong Catholic Church," 247.

111   *Hong Kong's Catholics aren't all democrats*: Leung, "The Hong Kong Catholic Church," 248.

113   *Donnithorne enjoyed close ties*: George Weigel, "Audrey Donnithorne, Woman of Valor," *Catholic World Report*, June 12, 2020; Michel Chambon, "Audrey G. Donnithorne, a Great Lady of China," *UCA News*, June 12, 2020.

116   *"We inherited Western culture and values"*: Sirico interview.

Chapter Eight: "Crazy Hype and Arrogance"

120   *"I was so rich"*: Thomas Crampton, "Deconstructing Dot-Com Death in Hong Kong," *International Herald Tribune*, December 18, 2000.

122   *"I was blinded by crazy hype"*: Crampton, "Deconstructing Dot-Com Death in Hong Kong."

123   *"After building a base here in Hong Kong"*: Crampton, "Deconstructing Dot-Com Death in Hong Kong."

125   *"Welcome to the new world of Maybe Journalism"*: Noam Cohen, "In Animated Videos, News and Guesswork Mix," *New York Times*, December 5, 2009, https://www.nytimes.com/2009/12/06/business/media/06animate.html.

Chapter Nine: "I Want to Be Taiwanese"

134 *In 2003, Lai wrote shareholders*: Next Media, *Annual Report 2003*, 7. Lai specifically refers here to the so-called Three Links (a proposal to open postal, transportation, and trade ties), but he made it clear in conversations as early as the first half of 2000, immediately after Chen's election, that he viewed Taiwan as a jumping-off point for Next Digital to enter the mainland market.

134 *In just thirteen years*: Next Media, *Annual Report 2003*.

134 *By way of comparison*: Jacques Steinberg, "Report Has Mixed News for Papers," *New York Times*, November 4, 2003.

136 *In the Taiwan media*: East-West Center, Bangkok Media Conference, 2008.

137 *"[W]e believe that the island's fundamentals"*: Next Media, *2007 Annual Report*, 13.

139 *A 1993 speech by Murdoch*: Stephen Kotkin, "How Murdoch Got Lost in China," *New York Times*, May 4, 2008.

139 *"When I first went into the Taiwanese market"*: East-West Center, Bangkok Media Conference, 2008.

139 *"Such a bad government is a test"*: East-West Center, Bangkok Media Conference, 2008.

142 *"Why would a Chinese hire an American"*: East-West Center, Bangkok Media Conference, 2008.

143 *Pro-Beijing businessman Tsai Eng-meng*: Lisa Wang, "China Times Group Is Sold to Want Want," *Taipei Times*, November 5, 2008.

143 *Lai confidently set about shaking*: Next Media, *Annual Report 2012*, 7.

146 *He put his Taiwan operations up for sale*: Aries Poon, "Next Media Secures Sale of Taiwan Media," *Wall Street Journal*, November 28, 2012.

Chapter Ten: Umbrellas and Tear Gas

147 *An iconic* Time *cover photo*: Hannah Beech, "Hong Kong Stands Up," *Time*, October 13, 2014.

148 *Chinese officials vowed*: The phrase was also invoked post-1997, as in Xi Jinping's speech marking the twentieth anniversary of the handover. Xi Jinping, "Full Text: Xi's Speech at Meeting Marking HK's 20th Return Anniversary, Inaugural Ceremony of 5th-Term HKSAR Gov't," Xinhua, July 1, 2017.

149 *China's State Council*: Information Office of the State Council, *The Practice*

of the "One Country, Two Systems" Policy in the Hong Kong Special Administrative Region, 2014, Conclusion.

149 *Two days before voting began*: Jonathan Kaiman, "Hong Kong's Unofficial Pro-Democracy Referendum Irks Beijing," *Guardian*, June 25, 2014.

149 *"We're seeing over 250 million"*: Parmy Olson, "The Largest Cyber Attack in History Has Been Hitting Hong Kong Sites," *Forbes*, November 20, 2014.

150 *Said Lai: "Whoever is behind"*: Alan Wong, "Pro-Democracy Media Company's Websites Attacked," *New York Times*, June 18, 2014.

153 *"The aim of the counter-revolutionary rebellion"*: Quoted in Rush Doshi, *The Long Game: China's Grand Strategy to Displace American Order* (New York: Oxford University Press, 2021), 50, 52.

154 *"Horses will still run"*: For a recent reiteration of this statement, see Ministry of Foreign Affairs, "Foreign Ministry Spokesperson Zhao Lijian's Regular Press Conference on July 7, 2020."

157 Time *wrote that the students*: "TV Face-Off Dramatizes Gulf Between Hong Kong Protesters and Officials," *Time*, October 21, 2014.

157 *The area includes eighty-five residences*: Venus Feng and Frederik Balfour, "How a Family Turned a Barren Hillside into a $4.4 Billion Property Empire," Bloomberg, August 27, 2018.

158 *Police had foiled a murder plot*: Joyce Man, "Suspected Hit Man Tells Court He Had Never Heard of Alleged Target," *South China Morning Post*, June 30, 2009.

158 *A car had rammed the gate*: Michael Forsythe and Neil Gough, "Hong Kong Media Worries Over China's Reach as Ads Disappear," *New York Times*, June 11, 2014.

159 *A Beijing-orchestrated advertising boycott*: Forsythe and Gough, "Hong Kong Media Worries."

159 *"I am fine"*: "Firebombing Hong Kong's Democrats," *Wall Street Journal*, January 12, 2015.

160 *Lai was among several people*: Four years later, organizers Benny Tai, Reverend Chu Yiu-ming, and Chan Kin-man were prosecuted on public nuisance charges and sentenced to sixteen months in jail each (Chu's sentence was suspended on account of his age).

160 *Lai was despondent*: Personal communication, January 2015.

160 *Now he was putting his body*: Former editor-in-chief Chan Pui-man made this point while testifying, for the prosecution, as a so-called accomplice witness. See testimony of February 2, 2024, www.supportjimmylai.com /trial-updates/.

Chapter Eleven: "We Just Have to Eat Their Meal"

162 *Authorities arrested sixty-one protesters*: "The Fire-Monkey Stirs: Street Violence and Politics," *Economist*, February 13, 2016; Chris Lau, Danny Lee, Joyce Ng, Clifford Lo, Nikki Sun, and Stuart Lau, "Shots Fired and Bricks Thrown: Hong Kong Tense After Mong Kok Mob Violence on First Day of Lunar New Year," *South China Morning Post*, February 9, 2016.

163 *After 2008, Hong Kong people*: Syaru Shirley Lin, "Analyzing the Relationship Between Identity and Democratization in Taiwan and Hong Kong in the Shadow of China," *Asan Forum*, December 20, 2018.

163 *In 2012,* Apple Daily *ran*: Jason Chow, "'Locust' Ad Breaks in Apple Daily," *Wall Street Journal*, February 1, 2012.

165 *"So now we try our way"*: Hoover Institution, "Jimmy Lai and the Fight for Freedom in Hong Kong," special edition of *Uncommon Knowledge* with Peter Robinson, October 20, 2019.

166 *At the Hoover Institution talk*: Hoover Institution, "Jimmy Lai and the Fight for Freedom in Hong Kong."

167 *Violence on both sides increased*: SCMP Reporters, "As It Happened: Hong Kong Protesters Set Cross-Harbour Tunnel Tollbooth Alight Again as Tear Gas Fired in Kwai Chung and Yuen Long," *South China Morning Post*, November 13, 2019.

167 *Authorities also dusted off*: Rachel Wong and Tom Grundy, "Hong Kong Police Arrest Pro-Democracy Newspaper Tycoon Jimmy Lai and Labour Party Vice-Chair Lee Cheuk-yan," *Hong Kong Free Press*, February 28, 2020.

168 *On the evening of June 4*: Brian Wong, "Jimmy Lai Trial: Timeline of Hong Kong Media Mogul's Arrests, Charges and Court Appearances," *South China Morning Post*, December 18, 2023; Committee to Protect Journalists, "Hong Kong Police Arrest Next Digital Founder Jimmy Lai," April 18, 2020.

168 *In April 2020*: "Arrest of Outspoken Media Boss Renews Fear of Hong Kong Clampdown," *Financial Times*, August 12, 2020 [video featuring April 24, 2020, interview].

168 *Entitled* One Hongkonger One Letter: *One Hongkonger One Letter to Save Hong Kong #TrumpSavesHK*, created May 23, 2020.

168 *The campaign, which sought 100,000 signatures*: Ironically, given the trouble his ties with Washington have caused him, Lai had not always welcomed U.S. intervention. He vehemently opposed the first U.S. invasion of Iraq, 1991's Operation Desert Storm, and ordered *Next* magazine to retract a pro-invasion editorial. This counted as the only time in three decades that

he attempted to interfere in the magazine's editorial stance. Editors disregarded Lai's instruction.

169 *He also told Cheung*: Simon became ensnared in controversy at the time of the 2020 U.S. presidential election when he spent $10,000 of Lai's money funding secret research into Hunter Biden's activities in China; Lai said he knew nothing about the expenditure. Ben Collins and Brandy Zadrozny, "How a Fake Persona Laid the Groundwork for a Hunter Biden Conspiracy Deluge," NBC News, October 29, 2020; "Hong Kong Media Boss Distances Himself from Contentious Hunter Biden-China Report," Reuters, October 31, 2020; Chris Lauin, Kinling Lo, and Sarah Zheng, "Hong Kong Media Mogul Jimmy Lai 'Unknowingly Funded' False Persona Report Discrediting Joe Biden," *South China Morning Post*, October 31, 2020.

169 *Before the introduction of the law*: Kelly Ho, "Freedoms Assured Under Security Law; Hongkongers Can Say What They Like 'for Time Being,' Says Leader Carrie Lam," *Hong Kong Free Press*, May 26, 2020.

169 *A spokesperson*: Zhang Yangfei, "National Security Law 'Timely,' Spokesperson Says," *China Daily*, May 22, 2020.

170 *This 2021 ruling made a mockery*: Kelly Ho, "Activist Tong Ying-kit Jailed for 9 Years in Hong Kong's First National Security Case," *Hong Kong Free Press*, July 30, 2021.

170 *A few months later a protester*: "Hong Kong's 'Captain America' Protester Jailed Under National Security Law," BBC, November 11, 2021; Kelly Ho, "Hong Kong Protester 'Captain America 2.0' Wins Appeal Against National Security Sentence, Jail Time Reduced to 5 Years," *Hong Kong Free Press*, August 3, 2022.

170 *On July 2, two days*: "National Security Law for HK: A Constitutional Perspective," *China Daily* (video), July 2, 2020.

171 *As with 2014's unofficial plebiscite*: Helen Davidson, "Hong Kong Primaries: China Declares Pro-Democracy Polls 'Illegal,'" *Guardian*, July 14, 2020; James Griffiths, "600,000 Vote in Hong Kong Opposition Primary Despite Fears of New Security Law," CNN, July 13, 2020; Tiffany May and Austin Ramzy, "Hong Kong Police Raid Pollster on Eve of Pro-Democracy Camp Primary," *New York Times*, July 10, 2020.

171 *In a rare news conference*: "Hong Kong Protests: China Condemns 'Horrendous Incidents,'" BBC, July 29, 2019.

171 *Former chief executive C. Y. Leung*: Kris Cheng, "New Hong Kong Website Promises Cash Bounties for Information on 'Wanted' Anti-Gov't Protesters," *Hong Kong Free Press*, August 27, 2019.

172 *They blamed "irresponsible figures"*: "Hong Kong Protests," BBC.

172 *On Human Rights Day 2020*: "Experts Say National Security Law Returns 'Freedom from Fear' to Hong Kong Residents," Xinhua, December 11, 2020.

173 *The former dean of the University of Hong Kong's law school*: Johannes Chan, "Hong Kong's National Security Law Turns Three," *U.S.-Asia Law Institute* 3, no. 25 (June 21, 2023).

174 *Many of them had simply*: "Explainer: Hong Kong's National Security Crackdown—Month 44," *Hong Kong Free Press*, March 2, 2024.

174 *Georgetown University Law School scholars*: Eric Yan-ho Lai and Thomas Kellogg, "Arrest Data Show National Security Law Has Dealt a Hard Blow to Free Expression in Hong Kong," *ChinaFile*, April 5, 2022.

175 *With Lai still in custody*: Jiayang Fan, "China's Arrest of a Free-Speech Icon Backfires in Hong Kong," *New Yorker*, August 14, 2020.

175 *China's central government*: "Central Government Firmly Supports Arrest of Jimmy Lai," Xinhua, August 11, 2020.

176 *Official government newspaper* China Daily: "Central Government Firmly Supports Arrest of Jimmy Lai," Xinhua.

177 *"Contrary to what they might think"*: Fan, "China's Arrest of a Free-Speech Icon Backfires in Hong Kong."

177 *"The day we cannot operate anymore"*: Tom Grundy, "Interview: Pro-Democracy Media Mogul Jimmy Lai Says Apple Daily Won't Change, but No More Protest Activism," *Hong Kong Free Press*, September 8, 2020.

Chapter Twelve: "Making the Law the Tool of a Ruler"

181 *In April 2021*: Agence France-Presse, "'Be Extra Cautious': Hong Kong Media Tycoon Jimmy Lai Writes Letter to Staff from Jail," *Hong Kong Free Press*, April 13, 2021.

181 *On April 16, he received*: Jessie Pang and James Pomfret, "Hong Kong Tycoon Jimmy Lai Gets 14 Months in Prison for Unauthorised Assembly," Reuters, April 15 [*sic*], 2021.

182 *Lai had been behind bars 135 days*: Jessie Pang and Twinnie Siu, "Hong Kong Freezes Listed Shares of Media Tycoon Lai Under Security Law," Reuters, May 14, 2021.

182 *Lee also wrote Citibank*: Greg Torode, James Pomfret, and Sumeet Chatterjee, "Hong Kong Threatens Lai's Bankers with Jail If They Deal in His Accounts," Reuters, May 27, 2021.

183 *After the June 17 police raid*: Candice Chau, "'Cut Ties with These Criminals': Hong Kong Security Chief Warns Reporters to Shun Apple Daily Detainees After Raid," *Hong Kong Free Press*, June 17, 2021.

183 *Three years after the introduction*: Kelly Ho, "Hong Kong Security Chief Hails 100% Conviction Rate in National Security Cases," *Hong Kong Free Press*, April 14, 2023.

186 *As journalists readied* Apple Daily's *final edition*: Jesse Pang, "Hong Kong's Pro-Democracy Apple Daily Signs Off in 'Painful Farewell,'" Reuters, June 24, 2021.

188 *Associate publisher Chan Pui-man*: Chan Pui-man had taken a seven-month medical leave after she was diagnosed with stage 3 cancer in 2016; on her return she took up the less demanding associate publisher role. See her testimony on February 2, 2024.

188 *She noted that Lai*: Kelly Ho, "Hong Kong Media Mogul Jimmy Lai and 9 Other Democrats Plead Guilty over 2019 National Day Protest," *Hong Kong Free Press*, May 17, 2021.

189 *Lai shouted at the photographer*: Jennifer Creery, "Hong Kong Pro-Democracy Media Mogul Jimmy Lai Cleared of Criminal Intimidation Against Reporter," *Hong Kong Free Press*, September 3, 2020.

189 *The newspaper even ran a fake obituary*: Michael Forsythe and Alan Wong, "Hong Kong Newspaper Prints Fake Obituary of Rival's Owner," *New York Times*, August 14, 2014.

192 *Lai wrote a statement*: The first part of the statement comes from Lai's original. The second part was quoted by the BBC: "Hong Kong: Media Tycoon Jimmy Lai Gets 13 Months Jail for Tiananmen Vigil," BBC, December 13, 2021.

193 *Corporate governance expert David Webb*: David Webb, "Observations on Next Digital (0282)," webb-site.com, July 28, 2021.

193 *Paul Chan claimed that possible fraud*: Hong Kong Government, "Inspector Appointed by Financial Secretary Under Section 841(2) of Companies Ordinance (Cap. 622) to Investigate into Affairs of Next Digital Limited," July 28, 2021.

Chapter Thirteen: Prison

195 *On December 31, 2020*: "Explainer: Hong Kong's New Legal Precedents After 3 Years of the National Security Law—Part I," *Hong Kong Free Press*, July 8, 2023.

195 *He is currently held*: During his lengthy national security trial that began in 2023 and took place in the West Kowloon Magistrates' Court (acting as the High Court), authorities often placed him a nearby jail, the Lai Chi Kok Reception Centre.

195　*The Hong Kong Tourism Board*: "Stanley: Recall Hong Kong's Past and Unwind in Charming Seaside Town," Hong Kong Tourism Board, https://www.discoverhongkong.com/us/explore/great-outdoor/wellness/stanley.html#:~:text=The%20picturesque%20seaside%20town%2C%20with,of%20the%20territory's%201841%20cession (retrieved February 28, 2024).

Chapter Fourteen: "Living in Complete Freedom"

213　*In 2015, the UN General Assembly*: Andrew Gilmour, "The Nelson Mandela Rules: Protecting the Rights of Persons Deprived of Liberty," United Nations, https://www.un.org/en/un-chronicle/nelson-mandela-rules-protecting-rights-persons-deprived-liberty (retrieved February 28, 2024).

213　*Mandela himself*: Gilmour, "The Nelson Mandela Rules."

213　*"He's not attracted to power and money"*: Cunningham currently serves as chairman of the Committee for Freedom in Hong Kong Foundation, of which I am president.

Epilogue

221　*Prosecutors showed excerpts*: Trial, Day 26, February 8, 2024. For detailed trial coverage, see various press articles posted on www.supportjimmylai.com/trial-updates/ as well as coverage by the *Hong Kong Free Press* (www.hongkongfp.com).

222　*Prosecutors attempted to tie Lai*: Trial, Day 25, February 7, 2024.

222　*In early 2003, Next*: Trial, Day 27, February 9, 2024, Chan Pui-man testimony.

223　*Prosecutors tried to establish an element of collusion*: Trial, Day 26, February 8, 2024, Chan Pui-man testimony.

223　*"[F]oreigners are frequently portrayed"*: Tony Saich, *From Rebel to Ruler* (Cambridge, MA: Belknap Press of the Harvard University Press, 2021), 14–15.

224　*"What keeps us going now"*: Trial, Day 26, February 8, 2024, Chan Pui-man testimony. Lai credits Chan Pui-man for the statement that people should have the "courage to do what we know is impossible." Chan said in court that she "admired the perseverance" of people who continued to protest even though they knew that their demands for democracy would not be realized.

PHOTO CREDITS

Endpapers

Hong Kong: Beehive Mapping
China: Beehive Mapping

Insert

Page 1
Top left: Private collection
Top middle: Private collection
Top right: Private collection
Bottom left: Popperfoto/Getty Images
Bottom right: Universal Images Group/Getty Images

Page 2
Top: Private collection
Middle: Private collection
Bottom left: Pierre Barbier/Getty Images
Bottom right: Private collection

Page 3
Top: LightRocket/Getty Images
Top inset: Private collection
Middle: Archive Photos/Getty Images
Bottom: Archive Photos/Getty Images

Page 4
Top: AFP/Getty Images
Top inset: Private collection
Bottom: *Apple Daily*

Page 5
Top left: *Apple Daily*
Top right: *Apple Daily*
Bottom: *Apple Daily*

Photo Credits

Page 6
Top: *Apple Daily*
Bottom: *Apple Daily*

Page 7
Top: *Apple Daily*
Bottom: *Apple Daily*

Page 8
Top: Private collection
Middle: Private collection
Bottom: Private collection

Page 9
Top: *Apple Daily*
Bottom: *Apple Daily*

Page 10
Top: *Apple Daily*
Bottom: *Apple Daily*

Page 11
Top: Private collection
Middle left: *Apple Daily*
Middle right: Julie McGurn
Bottom: *Apple Daily*

Page 12
Top: Bloomberg/Getty Images
Bottom: *Apple Daily*

Page 13
Top: Private collection
Bottom: LightRocket/Getty Images

Page 14
Top: Private collection
Bottom: Private collection

Page 15
Top: Committee for Freedom in Hong Kong Foundation
Middle: Committee for Freedom in Hong Kong Foundation
Bottom: Committee for Freedom in Hong Kong Foundation

Page 16
Top left: Bloomberg/Getty Images
Top right: AFP/Getty Images
Middle: Private collection
Bottom: AP Photo/Louise Delmotte

INDEX

Index

Index

China, People's Republic of (*cont.*)
  refugees as fleeing to Hong Kong colony
    from, 9, 20, 23, 109
  State Council of (*see* State Council)
  Taiwan's relations with, 130–31
  Tiananmen Square protests and
    massacre in (*see* Tiananmen Square
    protests and massacre)
  2003 SARS outbreak in, 73, 93, 222
  2019 extradition bill proposed by, 164,
    178, 183
  U.S. and other Western countries
    villainized by, 153, 172, 223
  WTO joined by, 133–34, 142
  See also Chinese Communist Party
China Daily, 170, 176
China Resources, 58
China's Economic System (Donnithorne),
  113
China Times, 143
Chinese Communist Party (CCP), 3–4, 6,
  9, 11, 23, 52, 60, 62, 64, 87, 104, 109,
  112, 130, 131, 132, 136, 140, 141–42,
  144, 152, 154, 160, 168, 169, 171,
  197–98, 208, 211, 217, 223, 224, 225
  Hong Kong's democracy movements
    against (*see* Hong Kong democracy
    movements)
  KMT's conflict with, 10
  Lai perceived as threat by, 3, 5, 8, 77–78,
    92, 95, 96, 198
  Lai's mother punished by, 12, 16, 69, 216
  Lai's 1994 column as critical of, 76–79,
    81
  media as controlled or cowed by, 82, 84,
    96, 139, 141, 155, 162, 172, 173, 178
  Party Congress, 208–9
  propaganda of, 3, 13, 16, 69, 172–73
  See also China, People's Republic of

Ching Cheong, 3
Chipotle, 65
Chow Hang-tung, 207
Chow, Herbert, 179–80
Chow, Royston, 176, 188, 192
Chu Yiu-ming, 148, 151, 160, 239n
CIA, 99, 142, 151, 189
Citibank, 182, 209
Citizen News, 173
Civic Party (Hong Kong), 155
"Civil Disobedience, the Most Lethal
  Weapon" (Tai), 148
Cloudflare, 149
CNN, 66
The Collected Works of St. John of the Cross
  (John of the Cross), 114
Columbia University, 38
Comitex, 30–34, 38, 40, 43, 45–47, 48, 54,
  57–58, 64, 67, 102, 199
  acquisition of San Po Kong factory for,
    27–30
  first JCPenney order of, 32–34
  Lai's fashion industry innovations at, 31,
    41, 46–47, 128
  The Limited contract with, 46–47
Committee for Freedom in Hong Kong
  Foundation, 8, 244n
Committee to Protect Journalists, 6
Condé Nast Traveler, 97
Congress, U.S., 166
The Cost of Discipleship (Bonhoeffer),
  114
Council on Foreign Relations, 5
Covid-19 pandemic, 2, 168, 174, 179, 185,
  195, 197, 205, 222, 224
Cowperthwaite, John, 175, 219
Crampton, Thomas, 101, 120, 122, 124–25,
  127, 128, 191
Cross Harbour Tunnel, 167

Index

Index

Index

Index

Index

Index

Index

Index

Index

ABOUT THE AUTHOR

MARK L. CLIFFORD lived in Hong Kong from 1992 to 2020. An award-winning journalist and PhD historian of Hong Kong, he was the editor-in-chief of the *South China Morning Post* and publisher and editor-in-chief of *The Standard*. He first met Jimmy Lai in 1993 and was serving on the board of directors of Lai's media company, Next Digital, at the time of Lai's jailing in 2020 and the Hong Kong government's shutdown of the group's pro-democracy newspaper, *Apple Daily*, in 2021. He is president of the Committee for Freedom in Hong Kong Foundation.

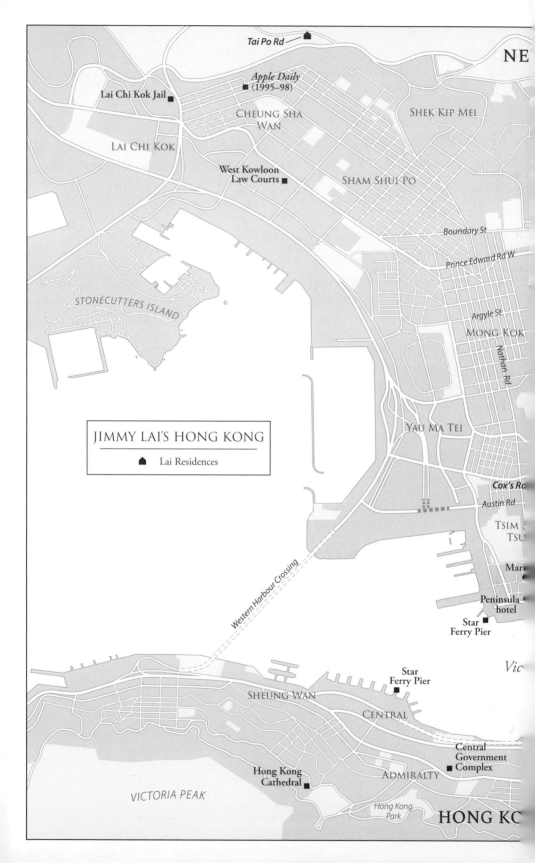